MAX WEBER'S SOCIOLOGY

This volume outlines Max Weber's comparative-historical sociology of "interpretive understanding" (*verstehen*) in a manner that clarifies his complex mode of analysis and multi-causal focus. Presenting the central features of his methodology, it demonstrates the strengths of his research strategies through discussions of his major works and overarching concerns. Among other themes, this study addresses the origins of the American political culture, the longevity of its civic sphere, and the multiple causes behind the unique historical pathways followed by several civilizations. Indeed, through summaries of Weber's procedures and their application in his own empirical studies, *Max Weber's Sociology* sustains a simultaneous orientation to his "big picture" themes and his rigorous manner of analysis. It demonstrates in so doing the capacity of Weber's sociology to ground firmly both "ideal-type" theorizing and empirically oriented investigations. This volume will appeal to scholars throughout the social sciences with interests in the American civic sphere, the West's uniqueness, "the Protestant ethic thesis," the multiple ways that civilizations develop, and the diverse twists and turns of Weber's comparative-historical sociology.

Stephen Kalberg is Professor of Sociology Emeritus at Boston University and a Local Affiliate of the Center for European Studies at Harvard University. He is the author of *Max Weber's Sociology of Civilizations: A Reconstruction, Max Weber's Comparative-Historical Sociology, The Social Thought of Max Weber, Searching for the Spirit of American Democracy: Max Weber's Analysis of a Unique Political Culture,* and *Max Weber's Comparative-Historical Sociology Today.* He is also the editor of *Max Weber: Readings and Commentary on Modernity* and the translator of Weber's *The Protestant Ethic and the Spirit of Capitalism.*

Routledge Studies in Social and Political Thought

For a full list of titles in this series, please visit www.routledge.com/series/RSSPT

MAX WEBER'S SOCIOLOGY

From "the Protestant Ethic Thesis" and the American Political Culture to a Sociology of Civilizations

Stephen Kalberg

Routledge
Taylor & Francis Group

LONDON AND NEW YORK

Cover image: Artist Edgar Ruiz in Mexico City

First published 2024
by Routledge
4 Park Square, Milton Park, Abingdon, Oxon OX14 4RN

and by Routledge
605 Third Avenue, New York, NY 10158

Routledge is an imprint of the Taylor & Francis Group, an informa business

© 2024 Stephen Kalberg

British Library Cataloguing-in-Publication Data
A catalogue record for this book is available from the British Library

ISBN: 9781032631769 (hbk)
ISBN: 9781032631806 (pbk)
ISBN: 9781032631813 (ebk)

DOI: 10.4324/9781032631813

Typeset in Sabon
by codeMantra

To my students, with gratitude, from whom I have learned so much.

The fate of a cultural epoch that has eaten from the tree of knowledge is that it must realize that we cannot read off the meaning of events in this world from the results – however complex they may be – of our scrutiny of those events, but that we ourselves must be able to create that meaning. We have to realize that the advance of empirical knowledge can never produce "world view," and that consequently, the most lofty ideals, those that move us profoundly, will forever only be realized in a struggle against other [ideals] that are just as holy for others as ours are for us. Only an optimistic syncretism – which sometimes results from the relativism of developmental history – will be able to ignore the theoretical implications of this immensely serious state of affairs, or to elude its consequences in practice. ("Obj" pp. 104–05)

The strata typical of…brotherhoods in the Occident and in Islam were identical: petty bourgeois and especially artisans. Viewed externally, numerous Hinduist religious communities appear to be "sects" just as do those of the Occident. The sacred value, however, and the manner in which values were mediated point to radically different directions. ("I," p. 292)

Not ideas, abut material and ideal interests, directly govern men's conduct. Yet very frequently the "world views" that have been created by "ideas" have, like switchmen, determined the tracks along which action has been pushed by the dynamic of interests. "From what" and "for what" one wished to be redeemed and, let us not forget, "could be" redeemed, depended upon one's image of the world. ("I," p. 280)

CONTENTS

ACKNOWLEDGMENTS

This collection of essays on Max Weber has been published over a 25-year period. All have benefitted from the comments by a variety of colleagues and friends scattered widely across the globe. Although I am highly indebted to all for assistance and support, I am most grateful to Michael Kaern, Ulrich Nanko, Robert Antonio, and the late Guenther Roth for their sustained suggestions.

I am also obligated to the numerous publishing houses that have generously permitted the reprinting of this volume's chapters: Oxford University Press, Sage Publications, Blackwell, SUNY Press, Routledge, and Max Weber Studies. The American Sociological Association provided permission for the publication of this book's two Appendices.

ABBREVIATIONS

AG   1976 [1909]. *The Agrarian Sociology of Ancient Civilizations*. Translated by R. I. Frank. London: New Left Books.

AJ   1952 [1920]. *Ancient Judaism*. Translated and edited by Hans H. Gerth and Don Martindale. New York: The Free Press.

EEWR   *The Economic Ethics of the World Religion*. The title of the series of studies that include volumes on China (*RofC*), India (*RofI*), and ancient Judaism (*AJ*).

"EK"   2012 [1913]. "On Some Categories of Interpretive Sociology." Pp. 273–301 in *Max Weber: Collected Methodological Writings*. Edited by Hans Henrik Bruun and Sam Whimster; translated by Hans Henrik Bruun. London: Routledge.

E&S   1968 [1921]. *Economy and Society*. Edited by Guenther Roth and Claus Wittich and translated by Roth, Wittich, et al. Berkeley: The University of California Press.

GEH   1927 [1923]. *General Economic History*. Translated by Frank H. Knight. Glencoe, Ill.: Free Press.

"I"   1946 [1920]. "Introduction." Pp. 267–301 in *From Max Weber* (as "The Social Psychology of the World Religions"), edited and translated by H. H. Gerth and C. Wright Mills. New York: Oxford University Press.

"IR"   1946 [1920]. "Religious Rejections of the World."
          Pp. 323–359 in *From Max Weber*, edited and translated
          by H. H. Gerth and C. Wright Mills. New York: Oxford
          University Press.

"Obj"   2012 [1904]. "The 'Objectivity' of Knowledge in Social
          Science and Social Policy." Pp. 100–38 in *Max Weber:
          Collected Methodological Writings*. Edited by Hans
          Henrik Bruun and Sam Whimster; translated by Bruun.
          London: Routledge.

PE   2011 [1920]. *The Protestant Ethic and the Spirit of Capi-
          talism*. Translated and introduced by Stephen Kalberg.
          New York: Oxford University Press.

PE II   1968 [1910]. "Antikritisches zum 'Geist' des Kapital-
          ismus." Pp. 149–87 in *Max Weber: Die protestantische
          Ethik II, Kritiken und Antikritiken*, edited by Johannes
          Winckelmann. Hamburg: Siebenstern Verlag.

PED   2001 [1907–1910]. *The Protestant Ethic Debate: Max
          Weber's Replies to His Critics, 1907–1910*. Edited by
          David Chalcraft and Austin Harrington and translated
          by Harrington and Mary Shields. Liverpool: Liverpool
          University Press.

"PR"   2011 [1920]. "Prefatory Remarks" to *Collected Essays in
          the Sociology of* Religion. Pp. 233–50 in *The Protestant
          Ethic and the Spirit of Capitalism*. Translated by Stephen
          Kalberg. New York: Oxford.

"PV"   1946 [1919]. "Politics as a Vocation." Pp. 77–128 in *From
          Max Weber*, edited and translated by H. H. Gerth and C.
          Wright Mills. New York: Oxford University Press.

RCM   2005. *Max Weber: Readings and Commentary on Modernity*.
          Edited by Stephen Kalberg. New York: Wiley-Blackwell
          Publishers.

RofC   1951 [1920]. *The Religion of China*. Translated and ed-
          ited by Hans H. Gerth. New York: The Free Press.

RofI   1958 [1920]. *The Religion of India*. Translated and edited
          by Hans H. Gerth and Don Martindale. New York: The
          Free Press.

"SV"   2005 [1917/1919]. "Science as a Vocation." Pp. 139–41,
          321–34, 337–40 in *Max Weber: Reading and Commentary*

on Modernity. Edited by Stephen Kalberg. New York: Wiley-Blackwell Publishers.

"Sects I"   2011 [1906]. "'Churches' and 'Sects' in North America: An Ecclesiastical Socio-political Sketch." Pp. 227–32 in *PE*. Translated by Colin Loader and revised by Stephen Kalberg. New York: Oxford University Press.

"Sects II"   2011 [1907/1920]. "The Protestant Sects and the Spirit of Capitalism." Pp. 209–26 in *PE*. Translated by H.H. Gerth and C. Wright Mills; revised by Stephen Kalberg. New York: Oxford University Press.

"VF"   2012 [1917]. "The Meaning of 'Value Freedom' in the Sociological and Economic Sciences." Pp. 304–34 in *Max Weber; Collected Methodological Writings*. Edited by Hans Henrik Bruun and Sam Whimster; translated by Bruun. London: Routledge.

[Further, less frequently used sources are noted in the References section]

INTRODUCTION

Max Weber (1864–1920) was born in Erfurt, Germany, into a distinguished and cosmopolitan family of entrepreneurs, scholars, and politicians. The excellent schools he attended in Berlin demanded strenuous engagement in philosophy, literature, languages, and ancient and medieval history. He studied economic history, law, and philosophy at universities in Heidelberg, Berlin, Strassbourg, and Goettingen.

Weber is widely acknowledged to be the most significant social scientist of the twentieth century. The founder of Sociology in Germany and a giant of interdisciplinary scholarship, Weber addressed the dynamics of modern and premodern societies alike. His highly detailed investigations ranged across 2,600-year developments in the East and the West. They included various studies on Old Testament prophecy, the medieval origins of Western music, the possibilities for democracy in Russia, the rise of the caste system in India, and the expansion of Confucianism in China.

Many of Weber's questions resonate widely today. In what diverse ways have each of the world's great religions influenced the behavior of believers? How does a civilization's "track" of development remain firm over millennia in some cases yet fragile and short-lived in others? Do status-based inequalities congeal even in highly egalitarian societies? Under what circumstances do authority-based relationships become "routinized" back to ones anchored in power-based and

DOI: 10.4324/9781032631813-1

utilitarian motives? Are stagnant, closed, and highly bureaucratized societies likely on the horizon in the West? When do charismatic leaders arise? Under what circumstances do their attempts to transform their societies succeed?

Weber was impressed by the capacity of Western industrial and democratic societies to sustain high standards of living across large populations. Nevertheless, their fundamental features opposed ideals he held dear: the autonomy of the individual and the personality oriented to – and unified by – a constellation of values. Will a range of ethical values endure broadly despite the expansion of utilitarian patterns of action under developed capitalism? The modern epoch, Weber worried, might call forth the hegemony of instrumental action incapable of nourishing a series of ideals, including a strong ethos of compassion. "Where are we headed," he queried, and "how shall we live in this new era?" Will relationships, political cultures, and economic cultures devoid of binding values prevail (see Löwith, 1970; Mommsen, 1974; Kalberg, 2017, pp. 10–14)?

Two overarching goals linked tightly his concerns. He wished to define the singularity of the modern West and its developmental route, in particular in reference to the singular features and historical pathways followed by China and India. He desired also to demarcate, through systematic comparisons, the major causes behind the West's contours and trajectory.

These themes are evident even in his early volume, *The Protestant Ethic and the Spirit of Capitalism* (PE). In this famous study, Weber sought to comprehend how the goal of seventeenth-century "Puritan Divines" – to acquire a "certainty of salvation" (*certitudo salutis*) – led to the placing of "psychological premiums" upon methodical work and the systematic accumulation of profit and wealth. Did Puritanism play a significant *causal* role, he then questioned, as a source for the eighteenth century's secular *spirit of capitalism*?

Did this group of believers create a set of values and goals conducive in some regions to a particular, deep cultural infrastructure, namely, one that eventually sustained in the nineteenth century the growth of a highly organized and bureaucratized version of capitalism? Weber viewed his investigations of the major "world religions" – Islam, Hinduism, Buddhism, Confucianism, ancient and medieval Christianity, and ancient Judaism – as indispensable case studies, each of which cast a sharp beam of light upon Puritanism's singularity (see *PERW*, pp. 238–40; *AJ, RofC, RofI*).

However, his two overarching goals soon pushed Weber's research beyond the world religions and America's early Puritanism. His cross-civilizational goals required a *broadly* multi-causal methodology, he recognized. Moreover, he came to view clear models – or "ideal types" (see below) – and comparative procedures as necessary: they assisted identification of both the long- and short-range influence of the past upon the present. Why did industrial capitalism in the nineteenth century, he queried, expand more vigorously in Western Europe and Northern America than in China or India? Prominent in the West's nineteenth century, why was this *modern* form of capitalism largely lacking in the West's ancient and medieval epochs?

These inter-civilizational questions stood at the foundation of Weber's wide-ranging scholarship on the varying impact of Eastern and Western religions. They also grounded the complex interweaving of each world religion's "economic ethic" with multiple types of law, rulership (*Herrschaft*), and economies. He sought to understand, for example, how capitalists in the West in the seventeenth and eighteenth centuries constructed a stable legal framework supportive of modern capitalism's expansion, yet capitalists in China and India failed to do so (see "PR," p. 245).

Furthermore, Weber's two overarching goals failed in another manner to guide his expanding comparative-historical agenda. In *PE* and later writings, he pursued an additional central goal: he wished to "interpretively understand" (*verstehen*) how people in different civilizations and epochs – and in reference to unique juxtapositions across multiple groups – attribute *meaning* to *certain* activities on a regular basis. His queries are clear: how does "subjective meaning" become manifest in singular ways in various groups, in clusters of groups, and in influential groups? Why, for example, was scholarship meaningful to the Confucian literati, meditation meaningful to Buddhist monks, and disciplined labor meaningful to Puritans?

Once again, Weber saw the indispensability of additional research procedures and conceptual tools. However, he opposed vehemently all approaches that addressed causality by reference exclusively to "structures," linear research designs, and presentist and mono-causal presuppositions. He also rejected all theorizing anchored in holistic premises.

Comparative-historical studies must instead take cognizance, Weber held, of the *various* ways in which the patterned, meaningful activities of people in groups permeate – or don't – arrays of groups and even *societal domains*: the economy, religion, rulership, social status (*Staende*), family, clan, and law spheres. Even groups with sources in the distant past should be investigated, he argues, through research procedures and hypothesis-forming models that acknowledge the influence of numerous groups and their particular "meaning clusters," Weber maintains, including their tensions and alliances. Multi-causal and contextual presuppositions must be given high priority, as well as the past and present juxtapositions of groups. Finally, careful empirical observation must anchor all constructs and research procedures utilized by comparative-historical investigators, he argues (see Kalberg, 1994, 2021).[1]

In sum, this volume discusses many of Weber's themes, concerns, procedures, and goals. In addition, it employs his main research strategies and conceptual tools in order to convey how Weber's procedures and concepts are rooted in an overall aim, namely, to define, through interpretive understanding, the meaningful action patterns of persons in delineated groups.[2] Throughout, comparisons between Weber's research strategies and those at the foundation of major schools in Sociology will be illustrated. The uniqueness of his procedures and presuppositions will be illuminated in this manner.

How shall we proceed? An investigation of central aspects of his singular methodology remains indispensable if this volume's multiple aims are to be conveyed. This discussion will instruct the reader in respect to the ways in which a *Weberian* comparative-historical analysis must proceed. Hence, we must first turn to brief explorations of the major goals, concepts, and research procedures indigenous to Weber's sociology.

The remainder of this Introduction addresses this necessary preliminary task. It then offers a chapter-by-chapter summary of this volume's main themes. Here, we examine Weber's "Protestant ethic thesis" (Part I, Chapters 1–4), the development of his sociology of religion after *The Protestant Ethic* volume (Part II, Chapters 5–6), his analysis of the origins and uniqueness of the American political culture (Part III, Chapters 7–9), and central elements of his sociology of civilizations (Part IV, Chapters 10–15). Two appendices conclude this volume. The first offers an interview with the author on the overarching civilization's theme in Weber's work and the second examines critically the original translation of *The Protestant Ethic* by Talcott Parsons.

0.1 Weber's Sociology: Main Concepts, Goals, and Research Procedures

This section explores Weber's interpretive understanding, or subjective meaning, approach. His multi-causal presuppositions, "four types of social action," and notion of "social carriers" are first defined. The "ideal type" – his central heuristic construct – will then be explained, as will his definition of "value-freedom." The overarching goal of his sociology will also be investigated. Weber's perpetual intertwining of past and present groups, as well as his elevation of hypothesis-forming models to centrality, will become apparent.

In combination, these features define the conceptual and procedural foundation for his comparative-historical sociology. They guide the reader through this volume's chapters and its various attempts to demarcate Weber's research strategies.

His concepts and procedures stand sharply in opposition to those approaches that view societies as composed of "parts" fully integrated into a "system" of "objective structures." These "organic" schools comprehend the collectivity as a demarcated structure and the individual's activity as subordinated to – and expressions of – this "whole." Comte and Durkheim ground this tradition.

Weber questions the high societal integration presupposed by organic theories. Fragmentation is frequent, he holds, as are open conflicts and the regular exercise of domination and power. Moreover, organic theories run the risk of "reifying" society and of comprehending individuals as simply the socialized products of bundles of external social forces. Persons, Weber argues, are capable of interpreting their social realities and of bestowing subjective meaning upon selected aspects of it: "[We are] cultural beings endowed with the capacity and the will to adopt a deliberate position with respect to the world and to bestow meaning (*Sinn*) upon it" ("Obj," p. 119; original emphasis).

Thus, he rejected positivism's goals: to follow the experimental procedures offered by the natural sciences, to define sets of general laws in history, and to explain all specific developments by deduction. Furthermore, Weber opposed firmly the position that the social sciences should aim "to construct a closed conceptual system, in which reality would be configured and structured in a way that was somehow definitive, and from which [reality] could then in its turn be deduced" ("Obj," p. 121).

To Weber, laws themselves never comprise causal explanations. Individual cases, developments, and the subjective meaning of persons in groups cannot be deduced from laws. Thus, they fail to provide the *empirical* knowledge Weber sees at the foundation of causal explanations, he maintains. Particular cases and developments can be explained causally only by other "equally individual configurations" ("Obj," p. 116; see Kalberg, 1994, pp. 81–84).

Hence, he orients his research to the causal analysis of specific cases and developments. His goal is stated clearly: "We wish to understand on the one hand its context (*Zusammenhang*) and the cultural significance of its particular manifestations in their contemporary form, and on the other the causes of it becoming historically so, not otherwise" ("Obj," p. 114; translation altered, original emphasis; see also *E&S*, p. 10).

Weber's major foundational concepts and procedures must be further examined in this Introduction.

The Embrace of Multi-Causality and Social Carriers. Weber abjured all hopes of discovering a single "guiding hand" or "engine of history." His rejection of all such overarching "forces" and "stages of historical development" enabled his focus upon empirical reality and the individual's subjective meaning. It also turned his sociology toward multi-causal modes of explanation. Innumerable values, traditions, emotions, and pragmatic interests rose to the fore as causes, he holds.

Weber's empirical research also led him to conclude that change and stability both required "carriers." Values, ideas, interests, traditions, and currents of thought of every imaginable variety have arisen in every epoch and civilization, he insists. However, whether regularities of action acquire cohesive proponents remains a separate question. As Weber notes: "Unless the concept 'autonomy' is to lack all precision, its definition presupposes the existence of a bounded group of persons which, though membership may fluctuate, is determinable" (*E&S*, p. 699; translation altered). Sometimes, political, civic, and rulership groups constituted carriers; at other times, status, religious, and economic groups have served as carriers. Empirical reality very often constitutes a perpetually moving terrain, Weber asserts.

Thus, if to become causally significant, patterned action must acquire a carrier group. A group may then successfully oppose patterned action carried by a competing – though weaker – group. Regularities of social action in some groups can be recognized as firm, and carriers can be seen to be powerful in some cases; others fail to carry action forcefully and prove fleeting. Patterned action may fade and then later, owing to an alteration of *contextual* regularities of action, acquire carriers and become reinvigorated and influential. Weber's wide-ranging investigations led in this respect to a clear conclusion: no causal "resting point" can be found (see Kalberg, 1994, pp. 58–62; 2021, pp. 135–43).

Nonetheless, the internal cohesiveness of groups does not alone account for their influence as social carriers, Weber maintains; pivotal also is their possession of a certain minimum of power or acknowledged legitimacy. Indeed, in his many discussions of influential carriers, power and legitimacy play important roles. Whenever strong carriers appear and endure, a group may even extend its influence beyond the epoch of its creation. Weber's "Protestant ethic thesis," for example, rather than exclusively focusing on ideas and values, explores ideas and values *in reference to* the churches, sects, and strata that carried these ideas and values (see below, pp. 97–120). He defines a wide variety of carrier groups in *E&S*, *GEH*, and EEWR (Economic Ethics of the World Religions).

Weber's Multicausality: The Broad Spectrum.[3] Power and the search to legitimate action as "valid" have been omnipresent causes of new patterned action throughout history, Weber argues (see *E&S*, pp. 30–38). Also pivotal for him at times are, for example, technological innovation, significant historical events, economic interests, and status honor. And, by the sheer force of their personalities, as noted, great charismatic leaders can mobilize large populations on behalf of their missions. Religious and secular value constellations may also, even if never enunciated by an extraordinary figure, erect the amenable foundation for influential patterned action and groups (see Kalberg, 1994, pp. 50–78).

Values may be powerful enough to deflect or even curtail regular social action placed into motion by political and economic interests, Weber contends, especially if a cohesive stratum or organization or class congeals as their carrier. However, the reverse occurs regularly, he sees: the content and shape of a value configuration may be strongly influenced by political and economic interests ("I," pp. 267–69; *E&S*,

p. 341). At other times, the sheer weight of immovable tradition effectively confronts all innovative patterns of action, regardless of their sources. Even the capacity of charismatic personalities to introduce dramatic transformations, as mentioned, depends upon a facilitating context of groups.

As discussed, innumerable clusters of regular action develop into groups in Weber's sociology. These groups may then become strong carriers of this patterned action and, on this basis, pursue independent pathways. Moreover, the sources of regular action are extremely pluralistic, he insists; all attempts to locate a "resting point" – a single causal force – must be seen as a futile endeavor ("I," p. 268; E&S, p. 341; 1988, p. 456). Even structurally identical organizations – even sects – do not carry the same sets of values by virtue of this similarity, according to Weber ("I," p. 292). And a causal analysis that focuses alone on economic interests will remain blind to the manner in which, for example, the authority of tradition in China – once strengthened by widespread magic – thwarted for centuries the pursuit of economic interests (see RofC, pp. 227–29). The "development of an organized life oriented systematically," Weber maintains, "toward *economic* activity has confronted broad-ranging internal resistance" wherever "magical and religious forces have inhibited the unfolding of this organized life" ("PR," p. 246).

Thus, interests, whether political, social, or economic, always motivate people, Weber contends; nonetheless, a broad spectrum of causes outside the inexhaustible sway of interests also always exists. Furthermore, he repeatedly discovers tensions and conflicts across patterns of action and across and within groups, as well as fissions and fusions, which then cause further shifts and realignments. "Ideas and interests" merge and diverge in the most complex ways. New regularities of social action are placed into motion with newfound coalitions. New carrier groups crystallize, yet they often remain unstable and fragile. Completely unforeseen consequences appear frequently; Weber sees paradoxical events and developments regularly.

As he repeats on various occasions, "no significant generalizations can be made" and no "general formula" will establish a "prior" or "dominant" pattern of social action (E&S, pp. 341, 577, 1179; PE, pp. 178–79). "We would lose ourselves...in these discussions if we tried to demonstrate these dependencies in all their singularities" ("I," p. 268; see below pp. 97–120).

Interpretive Understanding and Subjective Meaning. Sociologists must attempt to understand interpretively the ways in which persons view their own "social action," Weber maintains. Rather than "reactive" or "imitative" behavior (as occurs, e.g., when persons in a crowd expect rain and simultaneously open their umbrellas), this *subjectively meaningful* action comprises the social scientist's concern. Social action involves both a "meaningful orientation of behavior to that of others" and an interpretive, or reflective, aspect by the individual (*E&S*, pp. 22–24). Persons are social, but not only social. They possess the capacity to actively interpret situations, interactions, and relationships by reference to values, beliefs, interests, emotions, power, authority, law, traditions, ideas, and so forth:

> Sociology ... is a science that offers an interpretive understanding of social action and, in doing so, provides a causal explanation of its course and effects. We shall speak of "action" insofar as the acting individual attaches a subjective meaning to his behavior – be it overt or covert, omission or acquiescence. Action is "social" insofar as its subjective meaning takes account of the behavior of others and is thereby oriented in its course. (*E&S*, p. 4; translation altered, original emphasis)

Behaviorist and structuralist approaches, because they attend alone to external activity, neglect considerations of importance to Weber: the diverse motives behind observable activity and the manner in which the subjective meaningfulness of activity varies accordingly. This capacity of the human species to lend meaning to conduct implies that, Weber asserts emphatically, the social sciences should never seek to adopt natural science methodologies.

The Four Types of Social Action and Subjective Meaning. Social action can be best conceptualized as involving one of four "types of meaningful action," Weber contends. Each analytically distinct type refers to the motivational orientations of actors. He defines action as *means-end rational (zweckrational)*:

> ...when the end, the means, and the secondary results are all rationally taken into account and weighed. This involves a rational consideration of alternative means to the end, of the relations of the end to the secondary consequences, and finally of the relative importance of different possible ends. (*E&S*, p. 26)

Persons also possess the capacity to act *value-rationally*. This occurs when social action is:

> ...determined by a conscious belief in the value for its own sake of some ethical, aesthetic, religious, or other form of behavior, independently of its prospects of success ... Value-rational action always involves 'commands' or 'demands' which, in the actor's opinion, are binding (*verbindlich*) on him. (*E&S*, pp. 24–25)

In addition, *affectual* action, "determined by the actor's specific affects and feeling states," involves an emotional attachment. Finally, *traditional* action, "determined by ingrained habituation" and age-old customs, often approaches merely a routine reaction to common stimuli. It lacks a highly self-conscious aspect and stands on the borderline of subjectively meaningful action (*E&S*, pp. 24–26).

Each type of meaningful action can be found in all epochs and all civilizations. The social action of even "primitive" peoples may be means-end rational (see, e.g., *E&S*, pp. 400, 422–26), and modern persons are not endowed with a greater inherent capacity for a certain type of action than their ancestors. However, as a result of identifiable social configurations, some epochs may tend predominantly to call forth a particular type of action.

Weber is convinced that by utilizing the types of social action typology as a heuristic tool and by undertaking detailed research, sociologists can understand – and hence explain causally – even the ways in which the social action of persons living in radically different cultures and epochs is *subjectively* meaningful. His interpretive sociology in this manner empowers the sociologist to comprehend action in terms of the actor's own intentions (see *PERW*, pp. 248–50; Kalberg, 2014; Albrow, 1990).

His foundational emphasis upon a pluralism of motives distinguishes Weber's sociology unequivocally from all approaches that endow norms, roles, and rules with a determining power over persons. He stresses that even social action seemingly tightly bonded to a social structure must be recognized as implying a heterogeneity of motives. A great array of motives within a single "external form" is both analytically and empirically possible – and sociologically significant. The subjective meaningfulness of action varies, Weber argues, even within the firm organizational structure of the political or religious sect. Hindu and Calvinist sects, for example, did not vary in respect to external forms, yet the devout endowed radically different action with meaning (*PERW*, p. 250; "Obj"; "I," p. 292).

Far from formal methodological postulates only, these foundational concepts, procedures, and distinctions directly anchor Weber's empirical studies. The investigation of the subjective meaning of action stood at the very center, for example, of his "Protestant ethic thesis." Here, Weber wished to understand the diverse ways in which persons far and wide can subjectively "make sense" of their activities. He argues that sociologists must attempt to do so even when the subjective "meaning-complexes" they discover seem strange or odd to them (see "PR," pp. 248–50).

Value-Freedom and Value-Relevance. Hence, Weber's research does not seek to discover "an objectively 'correct' meaning or one which is 'true' in some metaphysical sense" (*E&S*, p. 4; "PR," pp. 249–50). Moreover, neither empathy toward nor hostility against the actors under investigation is permitted. With respect to the research process, researchers are obligated to set aside – on behalf of impartiality – their likes and dislikes (of Puritans, e.g., or the bureaucracy's functionaries) as much as humanly possible. Professional standards of inquiry are binding, Weber maintains, upon researchers even if the habits, values, and practices of the groups under investigation appear repulsive.

Social scientists must also strive to exclude all value-judgments that pronounce, in the name of science, a particular activity or way of life as noble or base, ultimately rational or irrational, provincial or cosmopolitan. Those values from the Sermon on the Mount cannot be proven scientifically to be "better" than those of the Rig Vedas (*RCM*, p. 331). Weber pronounced this ethos of "value-neutrality" as indispensable to the definition of sociology – if it wished to be a social science "[practiced as] a 'vocation' [and] organized in special disciplines in the service of self-clarification and knowledge of interrelated facts" (*RCM*, p. 334) rather than a political endeavor: "It is not the gift of grace of seers and prophets dispensing sacred values and revelations, nor does it partake of the contemplation of sages and philosophers about the meaning of the world" *(RCM*, pp. 334–35).

Accordingly, Weber insists that, as noted, professors must not offer value judgments, personal views, and political opinions in university classrooms (*RCM*, pp. 333–34). In turn, students should not expect leadership and guidance from their professors. Unlike politics, science excludes the activity – the clash of values – on the basis of which leaders arise (see *RCM*, pp. 332–36). How do sociologists ascertain – in an unbiased fashion – subjective meaning in the groups they investigate? This query requires a brief discussion of Weber's *ideal types*. As noted, they stand at the center of his mode of analysis.

Ideal Types. Weber focuses his attention also upon the diverse ways in which persons act in concert in groups rather than upon the social action of the isolated individual. Indeed, to him sociological investigation is oriented to the subjective meaning of persons in delimited groups and to their regularities of action within these groups: "There can be observed, within the realm of social action, actual empirical regularities; that is, courses of action that are repeated by the actor or (possibly also: simultaneously) occur among numerous actors because the subjective meaning is typically meant to be the same" (*E&S*, p. 29; translation altered, original emphasis).

These patterns of action constitute the concern of sociological research. An orientation to values, the emotions, traditions, and even means-end rational calculations, Weber contends, grounds such regularities action.

His major heuristic concept – the ideal type – "documents" patterns of meaningful action as they occur among people in groups. The construct Puritan, for example, identifies the regular action of these believers (e.g., an orientation toward methodical work and the reinvestment of profit). Here, the focus of Weber's sociology is evident, namely, away from the social action of isolated individuals, detailed historical narrative, and diffuse, nonempirical concepts (such as "society," "social differentiation," and "the question of social order"). His numerous studies are oriented instead to the patterned action of persons in groups as captured by ideal types. How are ideal types formed?

A typology of social action tells the story only partially. Rather, and although construction of the ideal type is rooted thoroughly in empirical reality, it is formulated (a) through a conscious exaggeration of the essential features of a pattern of action of interest to the sociologist in light of his chosen theme and (b) through a synthesis of these characteristic action regularities into an internally unified and logically rigorous concept:

> [An ideal type] is obtained by means of a one-sided accentuation of one or a number of viewpoints and through the synthesis of a great many diffuse and discrete individual phenomena (more present in one place, fewer in another, and occasionally completely absent), which are in conformity with those one-sided, accentuated viewpoints, into an internally consistent analytical construct. In its conceptual purity, this construct cannot be found empirically anywhere in reality. ("Obj," p. 125; translation altered; emphasis in original)

Inductive procedures from empirical observations are first followed; deductive procedures then guide the logical ordering of the identified patterns of action into a unified and precise construct that captures an essence. Nonetheless, the anchoring of ideal types empirically precludes their comprehension as "abstract" or "reified" concepts ("Obj," pp. 124–34).

Above all, according to Weber, ideal types serve *to assist* empirical, cause-oriented inquiry rather than to "replicate" the external world (an impossible task, he holds) or to articulate an ideal development. Thus, the "Puritan" portrays accurately the subjective meaning of neither a particular Puritan nor all Puritans (*E&S*, pp. 19–22). The same holds for ideal types of, for example, intellectuals, charismatic leaders, and functionaries in bureaucracies. As Weber notes: "...concepts are, and can only be, theoretical means for the purpose of intellectual mastery of the empirically given" ("Obj," p. 135).

Once formed as clear constructs that capture, from particular vantage points, the regular action of persons in groups, ideal types ground Weber's causal sociology in a fundamental fashion: they enable the precise definition of empirical patterned action. As a logical concept that documents regular social action, the ideal type establishes clear points of reference – or guidelines – against which patterns of subjective meaning *in a particular case* can be compared and identified precisely. Hence, the uniqueness of a case can be defined through an assessment of approximation to – or deviation from – the theoretically constructed type: "Ideal types ... are of great value for research and of high systematic value for expository purposes when they are used as conceptual instruments for comparison and the measurement of reality. They are indispensable for this purpose" ("Obj," pp. 128–29; see also pp. 125–26).

This central methodological tool separates Weber's level of analysis distinctly from the emphasis of organic holism schools upon social structures on the one hand and from all narrative and phenomenal approaches that focus upon the isolated individual on the other hand (see Kalberg, 2017, pp. 31–130).

What Can Arise: The Importance of Context. Social action is embedded deeply in social contexts, according to Weber. He queries: "What patterns of action *can* arise in a specific milieu?" "What action regularities and groups *can* become sociologically significant?"

Comprised exclusively from arrays of patterned social action, contexts influence new regular action – indeed its substance as well as its impact. New continuities of action arise and attain significance amid facilitating contexts of patterned action. Carrier groups play important parts in this process, yet Weber now moves a step farther. For him: "...the 'singular occurrence' is inserted as a link and as a *'real* cause' in a real, concrete context" (2012, p. 152; translation altered; emphasis original). Only a few illustrations can be offered.

Even the rise of charismatic leaders depends upon a milieu of conducive action and groups, he maintains. Ethical prophecy, which Weber sees as an extraordinary force capable of shattering sacred norms and of revolutionizing daily life, is normally dependent for its development upon the existence of a "certain minimum of intellectual culture" (*E&S*, p. 486; see pp. 577, 1116–17). A fertile ground in the period of the First Exile (586 BCE) in ancient Israel facilitated the impact of this prophecy far and wide, yet it confronted suffocating barriers in ancient India, China, and Egypt (see *E&S*, pp. 418–19, 447–50).

Weber's examination of markets, the legal education, and the social status of entrepreneurs, for example, also focuses upon social contexts. The expansion of the market economy depends in part upon whether a legal context – in the form of a substantial degree of guaranteed contractual freedom and a broad legal authorization of transactions – exists (*E&S*, p. 668). And what array of patterned action and groups, he queries, allowed for a type of legal education to arise?

> The effects of legal training are bound to be different where it is in the hands of *honoratiores* whose relations with legal practice are professional .... The existence of such a special class of honoratiores is, generally speaking, possible only where legal practice is not sacredly dominated and legal practice has not yet become too involved with the needs of urban commerce. (*E&S*, p. 793)

Finally, while the status of the entrepreneur and businessman in Antiquity and the Middle Ages was alike quite low, Weber stresses that the reasons for this evaluation varied according to social milieu: it resulted in the ancient world from the contempt of a leisure class of rentiers for traders and tradesmen, while it originated in the Middle Ages from criticism of commercial relations by the Catholic Church – for these interactions could not be regulated by ethical norms (*AG*, pp. 66–67; *E&S*, pp. 583–88).[4]

New patterns of action, even if powerful classes, organizations, or status groups are their carriers, never spread across constellations of groups in a uniform manner, Weber insists. They confront at every step configurations of groups. The multiple ways in which, depending upon whether a facilitating milieu exists, arrays of patterned action juxtapose and crystallize into groups and unique configurations of groups and organizations captures his attention (*AG*, pp. 39–40, 341; Kalberg, 1994, p. 83).

In general, the emphasis Weber's sociology places upon ideal types, social carriers, societal domains, and the broad and multi-causal origins of regular action leads him to conclude that patterned action must be viewed as situated within contexts of further patterned action. Utilizing this armament of concepts, he can assess whether regular action is located significantly within a milieu of *many* amenable groups and organizations. And does a particular *type of social action* reign "across" several ideal types and even several societal domains (see below, pp. 27–41, 97–153, 197–206)?

Just as patterned action can be conceptualized as becoming located in contexts of regular action and in groups that erect boundaries, societies as well – because comprised exclusively of *multiple* configurations of patterned action as located in multiple groups – can be best conceptualized as constituted from arrays of group-based dynamics, Weber insists. Furthermore, some patterns of action regularly place thrusts into motion and other patterns of action regularly resist these impulses, he contends; some thrusts remain weak and marginal while other constellations of regular action become widespread – indeed, when powerful carriers appear, they may become cohesive and bounded groups.

However, even these groups seldom call forth significant social transformations if further facilitating groups fail to congeal. And every development calls forth a reaction, according to Weber. Social groups that start out strong as carriers of new ideas, interests, and values may fade quickly, smothered by heretofore latent groups now crystallized into a solid opposition against the new.

Weber's concepts and procedures allow him also to see that *some* milieu – where traditional action prevails widely, for example – can be understood as closed and resistant to new patterns of action. In this case, even the message of a great charismatic figure will likely go unheard, as noted. Even technological innovations and massive power may fail to introduce new regularities of action and groups.

In sum, to Weber, every constellation of groups delineates a singular context that influences the formation of new action patterns and groups. "What *can* arise" relates directly to a social milieu – a web of existing regular action and bounded groups. Consequently, Weber's sociology rejects "universal laws," for they imply to him a level of analysis inadequately rooted in complex empirical realities and hence inadequately cognizant of the influence of unique contexts. Similarly, sweeping generalizations (bureaucratization, rationalization, evolution, value-generalization, adaptive upgrading) remain blind to the level of analysis – patterns of action and constellations of groups – demarcated by his ideal types and broad-ranging multi-causality.

The Perpetual and Tight Interweaving of Past and Present. Weber's emphasis upon the multi-causal origins of the regular action that constitutes groups anchors the close interweaving in his sociology of the past with the present. Further foundational features of his sociology also do so: ideal types, social carriers, and societal domains.

In addition, acknowledgment of the important role of social contexts, he stresses, proves indispensable: it allows identification of the milieu in reference to which patterns of action become firm and – manifest as groups – acquire powerful carriers. These groups may then, given the facilitating configurations of further groups, develop autonomously and even penetrate deeply into a subsequent epoch. To Weber, "that which has been handed down from the past becomes everywhere the immediate precursor of that taken in the present as valid" (*E&S*, p. 29; translation altered). Even the abrupt appearance of "the new" – even the "supernatural" power of charisma – never fully ruptures ties to the past, he holds (*E&S*, p. 577; "I," p. 273).

In Weber's sociology, multiple and complex constellations of innumerable groups populate every social landscape. Exclusive reference to familiar dichotomies (e.g., charisma – tradition or charisma – bureaucracy) inadequately captures the diverse, multiple, and substantive ways in which the past perpetually influences the present, Weber's procedures and armament of concepts maintain.[5] Switchbacks, reversals, unforeseen coalitions, and unexpected circumstances characterize his studies rather than a collapsing of regular action and groups into "necessary," directed, and predictable historical developments. "Survivals" and "legacies" are central and frequent (see Kalberg, 1994, pp. 159–64; 2012, pp. 61–66; see Chapter 6); irony repeatedly becomes apparent.

All depictions of history as following linear lines and pursuing an inevitable course stand opposed to Weber's presuppositions. Likewise, his concepts and procedures, it should now be apparent, reject all schools that focus upon overarching themes (the question of social order and "equilibrium," the integration and unity of society, the omnipresence of class conflict), the relationship of micro and macro levels, and positivist assumptions regarding the "lawfulness of society." Patterned action, ideal types, carrier groups, and societal domains, once juxtaposed with broad-ranging and multi-causal procedures and a rigorous orientation to social contexts, articulate a uniquely Weberian "view of history" – one that perpetually and tightly interweaves the past with the present.

These concepts, procedures, and presuppositions central to Weber's methodology and research must be kept in mind whenever his texts are read. The overall contours of *this* volume can now be demarcated. A detailed, chapter-by-chapter overview will serve this purpose. Each chapter will define this study's major themes, goals, conceptual tools, and research procedures.

0.2   An Overview: Themes and Directions

Part I: "The Protestant Ethic Thesis" and *The Protestant Ethic and the Spirit of Capitalism*. Part I shines a deeper light on *PE*. Its many-layered analysis is summarized. *PE*'s "thesis" regarding the possible – at least in part – *religious* origins of a "spirit of capitalism" and *its* possible empirical impact in respect to the unfolding of *modern* capitalism has been frequently misunderstood.

As noted, he maintained that a "Protestant ethic" in the seventeenth century gave birth among the faithful to a systematic approach toward labor, an energetic search for profit, and a methodical pursuit of wealth. This unusually disciplined manner of organizing life – this "ascetic Protestantism" – proved capable of weakening and then shattering a centuries-old, purely "traditional" orientation to work, according to Weber (see *PE*, pp. 15–18, 34–43, 101–05). A successor cluster of values eventually crystallized and became influential in the eighteenth century in secularized manifestations, namely, in a *spirit* of capitalism. This "modern ethos" *assisted* the birth and expansion of a *modern* – industrialized and highly organized – capitalism in the eighteenth and nineteenth centuries in Europe and North America, he insisted.

However, Weber's argument is only partially comprehended in this way. The activity of the faithful, he holds, was firmly separated from the realms of both utilitarian and traditional types of action regularities cultivated in the *Protestant sects*. Indeed, their "breeding" of ethical action contributed in the United States to the Protestant ethic's intensity and endurance (Chapter 2). "Good moral character" among the devout in sects became monitored and "shaped" the believer's behavior. A "methodical-rational organization of life" became widespread in this manner among the faithful. Led by Puritan Divines, these sects became major social carriers of this severe conduct in the eighteenth century.

Chapter 3 turns to the key terminological distinctions central to *PE*'s arguments. Pivotal is the distinction, on the one hand, between capitalism and modern capitalism and, on the other hand, between the "modern economic ethic" (or spirit of capitalism) and the "traditional economic ethic." To Weber, the "shattering" of the latter and the formation and expansion of the modern ethic must be recognized as a long-term transformation, one that endured over generations and even over centuries. Always constituting a "revolution" (*PE*, p. 89), the spirit of capitalism found *its source* in part in the sphere of religion, he became convinced. Its origins can be investigated. In all cases, this modern ethos must be analyzed in reference to its content and influence.

These terminological distinctions paved the way for a consideration in Chapter 3's latter section of the intense debate that surrounded "the Weber thesis" for nearly a century. By summarizing briefly eight major axes of this wide-ranging controversy, this section aims to define its substantive themes and to delineate its boundaries. Many of Weber's critics remained unaware of the various ways in which the Doctrine of Predestination and an Old Testament view of God remained central for seventeenth-century Puritans. Both features eventually formed background aspects that underpinned the legitimation of the *systematic* and values-based orientation by the faithful to work, profit, and wealth. This chapter examines the "psychological dynamic" at the foundation of the Protestant ethic's methodical-rational organization of life and "this-worldly asceticism."

Chapter 4 inquires why a variety of seemingly supportive American schools of thought in Sociology turned away from *PE*. Despite its widespread discussion among sociologists and wide recognition as a true classic, *PE*'s multifaceted *theoretical* contributions to Sociology have been neglected.

This chapter explicitly calls attention to *PE* as *a theoretical treatise* by examining it by reference to four major debates in postwar sociological theory in the United States. *PE* addresses, for example, the relationships between history and sociology, tradition and social change, economic interests and cultural forces, modern capitalism and values, macro and micro levels of analysis, and individual action and the social pressures by groups upon group members. Although all of these familiar controversies stand at the foundation of central discussions in American sociology, *PE* scarcely influenced these debates.

Four major controversies are examined in Chapter 4: the critique of Structural-Functionalism by Conflict theory in the late 1950s and by neo-Marxist theories in the 1960s; the debate between comparative-historical schools and structural-functionalist modernization theory in the 1970s; the opposition of the sociology of culture to comparative-historical perspectives in the 1980s; and the controversy that commenced in the late 1980s between rational choice theorists and sociologists of culture on the one hand and structural sociologists on the other.

Part II: Beyond *"The Protestant Ethic"*: *The Multicausal Sociology of Religion*. This section distinguishes *PE*'s "mono-causal" presuppositions from the multi-causal framework at the foundation of his post-*PE* studies of the "economic ethics" of multiple major "world religions" (Chapters 5 and 6).

We can now link Weber's overarching themes: the uniqueness of the West and the multiple causes of its singularity. His EEWR three-volume series represented in this regard a giant step forward. These chapters explore the EEWR volumes on China (*RofC*), India (*RofI*), and ancient Judaism (*AJ*). Their mode of analysis demonstrates above all Weber's powerful reorientation away from *PE*'s mono-causality and idealism. He now turns toward rigorous comparative strategies and broadly multi-causal procedures.

Hence, Part II alters our focus. It first moves away from a singular orientation to *PE* and then shifts our attention to a sweeping theme, namely, Weber's sociology of religion. Hence, an expansion upon *PE*'s major query is apparent. He now concludes that, in Chapters 6 and 7, his focus upon the EEWR has cast a beam of light upon the ways in which Hinduism, Buddhism, Confucianism, Islam, ancient Judaism, and ancient Christianity call forth patterned and meaningful action. Nonetheless, their rituals and "salvation pathways" fail to give rise to a set of values similar to those of the Protestant ethic. Weber's multi-causality, as he turns away from *PE* and toward the EEWR studies, becomes pivotal.

However, Chapter 6 takes one final glance at his famous work. *PE* concludes with a curious remark: Weber stresses its "one-sided religion-oriented analysis of the causes of culture and history" (*PE*, pp. 178–79). Thus, he acknowledges that *PE* has only incompletely addressed the "causal nexus." A great scholar has written a lengthy volume that closes with a description of a major weakness: his project requires a discussion of *both sides* of the causal equation.

Weber emphasizes his position repeatedly: the *PE* volume expresses exclusively an "idealist" approach; from the outset, a "materialist" mode of investigation is omitted. Nonetheless, in the course of researching and writing his massive *sociology of religion* chapter for *E&S* several years later, Weber expanded his causal analysis: he practiced in this chapter a rigorous and multi-causal comparative-historical strategy that abandoned his "one-sided" methodology. Chapter 6 reconstructs his "ideas *and* interests" analysis of the spirit of capitalism's origins and expansion.

Part III: *The Origins, Uniqueness, and Pathway of the American Political Culture.* In the fall of 1904, Weber travelled for ten weeks throughout the American Midwest, the South, the Atlantic seaboard, and New England (see Scaff, 2011; Kalberg, 2014). Part III's chapters define major aspects of his interpretation of the American political culture. At the forefront stands the question of whether this component of American society will continue to cultivate a vibrant *civic* sphere. If so, on what wide-ranging foundation?

The friendliness and humor of the Americans impressed Weber deeply, as did their high energy. He frequently compared the United States favorably to its more stratified, bureaucratized, and closed European counterparts (see Kalberg, 2014, pp. 59–82). Weber also appreciated its long-term democracy as well as, following Tocqueville, its rare capacity to produce innumerable civil associations "between" the distant and impersonal state and the isolated individual.

However, unlike Tocqueville, Weber traced the unusual density of these associations on American soil back to the Protestant sects of the seventeenth and eighteenth centuries (see "Sects I" and "Sects II"). Moreover, he refused to embrace the French theorist's central thesis: democracies imply a dangerous "tyranny of the majority." The "world-mastery individualism" indigenous to the Puritan legacy significantly ameliorated this possibility, Weber held (see Chapters 7 and 8). His concern is otherwise: he fears that urban and industrial societies will become stagnant and devoid of dynamism.

Chapters 7–9 identify several further characteristics of the American political culture. On the one hand, its singular origins and particular contours are explored, as are the strengths and longevity of this nation's civic sphere; on the other hand, the several ways in which Weber foresees the possibility of an "iron cage" society devoid of a viable civic sphere are investigated.

In sum, Weber possessed a lifelong interest in the ways in which the United States anchored its unique political culture. It did so first with the support of ascetic Protestantism's specific cluster of values. It then did so in reference to their multiple and long-term secular manifestations pivotal to its vibrant civic sphere.

Part IV: *The Sociology of Civilizations*. Commentaries upon Weber's works have often departed from the assumption that the rise of modern capitalism in the West constitutes his major concern. We now see that this posture – Weber must be viewed as a theorist of capitalism – narrows the range of his scholarship. Part IV defines major aspects of his sociology of civilizations. Extremely broad in scope, this feature of his sociology is multifaceted.[6]

Weber argues here that a careful reading of *PE* can assist researchers seeking to evaluate the influence of a civilization's configuration of deeply rooted values (Chapter 10). A re-examination of this classic text can also be helpful wherever religion is viewed as essential to a civilization's cohesion. However, our first step must discuss Weber's analytic opus (Chapters 10 and 11). *E&S* lays out the complex foundation for a comparative-historical sociology of civilizations anchored in interpretive understanding presuppositions. How does it do so?

E&S offers wide-ranging, empirically grounded models. Indeed, it formulates an open-ended analytic framework of sufficient scope to assist civilizations-level research. Hypotheses are formed that facilitate the clear conceptualization of major societal domains and the ideal types specific to them. Their development "directions" (*Entwicklungsformen*) are also formed as hypotheses in *E&S*. Moreover, this treatise offers multiple hypotheses that chart out how these models *may merge* as a consequence of *some* empirical configurations and *may separate off* as a consequence of *other* empirical constellations.

In sum, *E&S* opposes, as diffuse, amorphous, and abstract, all theorizing that stresses history's overarching "progress," "evolution," "cycles," "differentiation," and "inexorable advance." Rather, *E&S* continuously defines patterns of social action and the groups that form from them. Furthermore, rooted explicitly in ideal types, multi-causal presuppositions, and group-based configurational dynamics, the constructs of *E&S* postulate both arrays of "elective affinities" (*Wahl-verwandtschaften*) across groups and arrays of "antagonisms" (*Span-nungsverhaeltnissen*) across groups. Multiple fusions and fissions of groups can be identified and conceptually located with the assistance of the *E&S* framework.

Chapter 11, by reference to five themes pivotal in Weber's sociology of civilizations, examines these presuppositions and procedures in some detail. It also defines by comparing group-based configurations, both the West's singular arrays of groups and those unique to China and India. In addition, this chapter identifies multiple causes at the foundation of each civilization's particular historical development (see Kalberg, 2021).

A different format that facilitates the identification of a civilization's unique group dynamic and pathway of development is introduced in Chapters 12 and 13. Following Weber's procedures, a model is first defined by the author; several short passages from Weber's texts are then selected to illustrate this construct.

Chapter 12 explores the ways in which the *nature of work* varies significantly depending upon its contextual *location*. Does it exist, he queries, in an "old" or "new" civilization? The capacity of Weber's sociology of civilizations, rooted in groups, a wide-ranging theoretical framework, and multi-causal presuppositions to define in detail a civilization's singularity is evident as well in Chapter 12.

Utilizing the same procedures, Chapter 13 addresses *ethnicity* by summarizing his remarks on the ways in which "race" must be conceptualized by social scientists contextually rather than as static and fixed. Salient passages directly from *E&S* and other writings by Weber are here reprinted.

In a preliminary manner, Chapter 14 reconstructs his highly comparative sociology of emotions. Drawing widely from the *E&S*, *PE*, and EEWR volumes and their presuppositions – an orientation to multi-causality and the ideal type level of analysis – Weber's context-based procedures stress the ways in which the emotions in the West became circumscribed. Over centuries, their expansive unfolding was restricted by both "internal" and "external" restrictions.

Chapter 15 defines and discusses a further cross-civilizational construct in his comparative-historical sociology: "routinization." Its existence and dynamic, Weber discovers, is empirically evident across a large number of civilizations. The causes behind its origin and development are evident from *E&S*.

Appendix I comprises an interview with the author. It focuses upon core presuppositions at the foundation of Weber's mode of investigating civilizations.

Finally, Appendix II turns back to *PE*. It documents the ways in which the many flaws in the translation of this classical text by Talcott Parsons prevented adequate comprehension of this volume by social scientists and historians throughout the twentieth century.

Notes

1 The terms research strategies, research procedures, and mode of analysis are used as synonyms.
2 Nonetheless, a systematic discussion of Weber's rigorous mode of analysis does not constitute our major goal here (see Kalberg, 2021).
3 For more in-depth discussion of Weber on this theme, see Kalberg (1994, pp. 50–78).
4 For further examples that demonstrate the centrality of social contexts for Weber, see Kalberg (1994, pp. 38–46, 168–92).
5 Nor will reference to, he would argue, the dichotomous concepts familiar to us today: *Gemeinschaft–Gesellschaft*, tradition–modernity, and particularism–universalism.
6 For a detailed discussion, see Kalberg (2021).

PART I

"The Protestant Ethic Thesis," the Protestant Sects, and the American Reception

1

"THE PROTESTANT ETHIC THESIS"

The Protestant Ethic and the Spirit of Capitalism

Weber wrote the first one-half of *PE* (1904–1905) before departing for a ten-week sojourn in the United States and the latter one-half after his return to Heidelberg. Its thesis regarding the significant role played by values in the development of modern capitalism set off an intense debate that has, remarkably, continued to this day. It is certainly the most enduring controversy in the social sciences.

Both Weber's most famous and most accessible work, *PE* is acknowledged throughout the scholarly world as a genuine classic. Although he comes prominently to the fore in this volume as a theorist who attends exclusively to values, *PE*'s methodology exemplifies a variety of foundational procedures utilized throughout his sociology. Finally, this study constitutes his first attempt to isolate the uniqueness of the modern West and to define its multi-causal origins.

1.1   The Background

PE opposed directly a broad-ranging debate in Germany that sought to identify the causes behind the development of industrial capitalism. Some pointed to technological innovations, the influx of precious metals, and population increases. Other participants insisted that greed, economic interests, and a "desire for riches" in general pushed expansive economic development. Still others saw the role of "economic supermen" – the Carnegies, Rockefellers, and Vanderbilts,

DOI: 10.4324/9781032631813-3

for example – as crucial. Some maintained that the rapid expansion of production, trade, banking, and commerce must be perceived as a societal-wide evolutionary process.

To Weber all of these explanations were incomplete. Above all, they failed to take cognizance of an "economic ethos." Standing "behind" the rigorous organization of the workplace and the systematic pursuit of profit typical of this *modern* capitalism, it implied an "idea of the *duty* of the individual to increase his wealth, which is assumed to be a self-defined interest in itself" (*PE*, p. 79); the notion that "labor [must be] performed as if it were an absolute end in itself" (*PE*, p. 86); the idea that "the acquisition of money, and more and more money, [should] take place...simultaneously with the strictest avoidance of all spontaneous enjoyment of it" (*PE*, p. 80); the view that the "acquisition of money...is ...the result and the expression of competence and proficiency in a calling" (*Beruf*) (*PE*, pp. 80–81); and "the frame of mind...that strives systematically and rationally *in a calling* for legitimate profit" (*PE*, 88; original emphasis). Embodied in these ideas was a *spirit* of capitalism, and Weber insists vehemently that a full understanding of modern capitalism's origins must, first, acknowledge the causal push placed into motion by this "modern economic ethos" and, second, identify its sources (*PE*, 80–81, 108–09).

Thus, rather than a concern with the origins of either modern capitalism or capitalism in general, *PE*'s modest project involved a research agenda focused upon the definition and heritage of this "spirit" (*PE*, pp. 79, 80–81, 96–98, 108–09; 2001, 105–09). After citing numerous passages from the writings of Benjamin Franklin, whose values represent to Weber this "spirit" in a pure form (see *PE*, pp. 77–78), he asserts that he has here discovered an *ethos*, "the violation of [which] is treated not as foolishness but as forgetfulness of *duty*" (*PE*, p. 71; original emphasis). Rejecting the view that capitalism's dominant class, pursuing its economic interests, gave birth to this spirit, *PE* seeks to discern the origins of this new *set of values* (see, e.g., *PE*, pp. 77–98, 245–46; original emphasis).

1.2   The Argument

After observing a frequent orientation of Protestants to business-oriented occupations and their rigorous mode of organizing their daily lives, Weber explored Protestant doctrine. He discovered a "world-oriented ethos" in the Westminster Confession (1647) and the sermons of a seventeenth-century Puritan successor of John Calvin (1500–1564), the activist minister Richard Baxter (1615–1691).

In undertaking revisions of Calvin's teachings, Baxter and other "Puritan Divines" sought, Weber noted, to banish the bleak conclusions implied by Calvin's "doctrine of Predestination": if the question of salvation constituted *the* burning question to believers, if the "salvation status" of the faithful was predestined from the very beginning of history, and if God had selected only a tiny minority to be saved, massive fatalism, despair, loneliness, and anxiety *logically* followed among the devout (*PE*, pp. 117–18, 121–33; 337, note 76). Baxter's alterations sought to ameliorate the harshness of this decree; they formed the Protestant ethic's foundation, according to Weber.

Following Calvin, Baxter acknowledged that the mortal and weak devout cannot know the reasons behind God's decision-making. The complex motives of this majestic, distant, and almighty Deity of the Old Testament remain incomprehensible to lowly terrestrial inhabitants, however great their devoutness (*PE*, pp. 119–22). Nonetheless, Baxter emphasized – again following Calvin – that "the world exists to serve the glorification of God" (*PE*, pp. 119–22) and that this Deity wishes His Kingdom to be one of wealth and one anchored in His Commandments – for abundance and justice in "His Kingdom" would surely serve to praise His goodness and majesty (*PE*, pp. 122–24, 159–61; p. 377, note 39). Hence, systematic and dedicated labor – work in a *calling* – acquired a *religious* significance among the faithful: it became viewed as a means toward the creation of God's affluent and just community on earth.

Entrepreneurial activity as well, Baxter insisted, must be comprehended as *in service to* a demanding God and thus *sacrosanct*. Believers must view themselves as noble instruments – as "tools" – of His Commandments and Divine Plan (*PE*, pp. 122–23, 162–65, 174–75; 377, note 39; 395, note 122). Indeed, those among the devout *capable* of systematic work on behalf of God's Plan could convince themselves that, Baxter argued, the enormous strength required to labor methodically *must* have emanated from the favoring Hand of an omnipotent and omniscient Deity. *And*, the faithful could further conclude, God would favor only those he had chosen as predestined (*PE*, pp. 169–70).

Moreover, continuous work possesses an undeniable virtue for the good Christian, according to Baxter: it *tames* the creaturely and base side of human nature and thereby facilitates a focusing of the mind upon God and supports an "uplifting of the soul" (*PE*, pp. 160–62). Finally, "intense worldly activity" also effectively counteracts the penetrating doubt, anxiety, and sense of unworthiness induced by the Predestination doctrine, Baxter held. In doing so, it bestows the self-confidence upon the devout that allows them *to consider* themselves as among the chosen (*PE*, pp. 124–26). In this manner, the "systematic rational formation of the believer's ethical life" (*PE*, pp. 135–36), as well as methodical work and entrepreneurial activity, became providential.

Nevertheless, the Protestant ethic's singular strength to shatter the ancient and deeply rooted "traditional economic ethic" originated not simply in these ways, Weber maintains, especially if one wishes to explain the Puritan entrepreneur's "uninterrupted self-control" and "planned regulation of...life" (*PE*, pp. 136–37). A further adjustment by Baxter proved salient.

According to the Predestination doctrine, believers could never *know* their salvation status. However, as a consequence of this Deity's admonition – an earthly kingdom of abundance would serve His glory – the faithful could logically conclude that an individual's production of riches for a community constituted a *sign* that God favored this believer. In effect, possession of wealth signified to the devout *evidence* of their salvation: "The acquisition of wealth, when it was the *fruit* of work in a vocational calling, [was viewed] as God's blessing" (*PE*, pp. 167–71; original emphasis). This majestic, omnipotent, and omniscient Deity surely would never allow the condemned to praise His Glory. And in His universe nothing happened by chance.

Thus, owing to seventeenth-century revisions by the Puritan Divines, believers could now seek to *produce proof* – literally through methodical work on the one hand and the acquisition of wealth and profit on the other hand (*PE*, pp. 164–65) – of their salvation. *Psychological certainty* of one's favorable salvation status became the pivotal issue in light of the unbearable anxiety provoked by *the* urgent question: "am I among the saved?" Baxter's revisions to Calvin's dark conclusions, Weber emphasizes, enabled the faithful to comprehend their systematic labor and successful accumulation of wealth and profit as tangible *testimony* (*Bewaehrung*) their membership among the predestined "elect" (*PE*, p. 173; 394, note 115).

Uniquely among Christian believers, a positive *religious* significance was now awarded to riches: because wealth and profit constituted signs that indicated one's favored salvation status, their traditionally suspect character faded. Instead, the steadfast pursuit of wealth and profit became endowed with a "psychological premium." And methodical work now became sanctified and further intensified, for it constituted the most adequate means toward great wealth.

In this way, a set of values heretofore scorned (*PE*, pp. 82–83, 94–95) became of utmost centrality in the lives of the seventeenth-century devout. Neither the efficient adaptation to technological innovations nor the universal desire for riches could call forth the intensity necessary to shatter the traditional economic ethic. Rather, only work motivated "from within by an internally binding" set of religious values was empowered to introduce a "systematization of life organized around ethical principles" and a "planned regulation of one's own life" (*PE*, pp. 133–38). This "Protestant ethic" uprooted economic traditionalism and became a significant source of the spirit of capitalism, Weber contends.

Carried by sects and churches (mainly, the Presbyterians, Methodists, Baptists, and Quakers), this ethic spread throughout several New England, Dutch, and English communities in the sixteenth and seventeenth centuries. Regular adherence to its religious values as a calling marked a person as "chosen." However, as the Protestant ethic spread beyond churches and sects and spread into entire communities, its specifically religious component became, in Benjamin Franklin's more secularized eighteenth-century America, "routinized" in some regions into a "utilitarian-colored ethos" (*PE*, pp. 78–80, 172–74, 176–77), namely, into a *spirit* of capitalism. Rather than perceived as the "chosen elect," adherents of this ethic were viewed simply as upright, respectable, community-oriented citizens of good moral character (see Kalberg, 2014, pp. 33–58).

Weber investigated one "causal origin" of the spirit of capitalism in this way. The *subjective meaning* of devout believers, as manifest in religious values rather than in social structures, rational choices, and economic interests, remains central to *PE*'s argument. Although in the end acknowledged by Weber as unquantifiable (see *PED*, p. 120), this spirit lent a significant push to *modern* capitalism's development in the eighteenth century in Northern Europe and Colonial America, Weber held.

PE's masterful final pages turn to an altogether different dynamic. Once firmly entrenched in the twentieth century, modern capitalism sustains itself on the basis alone of pragmatic necessities, Weber contends. If present at all, a spirit of capitalism "now wanders around in our lives as the ghost of past religious beliefs" (*PE*, pp. 176–77). Indeed, he fears that value-oriented action in the workplace has diminished significantly and a "steel-hard casing," characterized by utilitarian and cold relationships devoid of compassion, is moving more and more to the forefront.

As a case study of one possible source of the spirit of capitalism, *PE* stands to this day as a powerful demonstration of the ways in which social action in the marketplace may be influenced by patterns of noneconomic interaction introduced by people in groups. Weber's message is evident: sociological analysis must not focus exclusively upon the present, nor alone upon material interests, power, technological innovations, demographic transformations, and demographic changes. Value-oriented action, and even "economic ethics," must also be given due consideration. *However*, social scientists must also reject an exclusive focus upon values, Weber warns in *PE*'s classic final paragraph. "*Both* sides" must be acknowledged and a "single formula" must always be avoided (*PE*, pp. 178–79; see Kalberg, 2021; see also Chapter 6).

Hence, he insists in *PE* that a full understanding of modern capitalism's origins in the West requires the investigation of a series of *causal* studies. Values must be scrutinized, but also constellations of political, economic, stratification, legal, and other factors (see *PE*, pp. 178–79; 390–91, note 96). *PE* comprised simply the first step in Weber's larger agenda. EEWR took up this theme and extended it massively to encompass the question of the origins and uniqueness of "modern Western rationalism." His discussion of the influence of the Protestant sects in the West must first capture our attention. They constitute relevant features of "the Protestant ethic thesis."

2

THE PROTESTANT SECTS AND THE "BREEDING" OF ETHICAL ACTION

[The sects]...alone have been able, on the foundation of Protestantism, to instill an intensity of interest in religion in the broad middle class--and especially modern workers--that otherwise is found only, though in the form of a bigoted fanaticism, among traditional peasants. ("SectsI," p. 231)

It is crucial that sect membership meant a certificate of moral qualification and especially of business morals for the *individual*. ("SectsII," p. 212; emphasis in original)

After returning from a whirlwind tour of the United States in November 1904, Weber finished *PE* and wrote a short essay on the Protestant sects ("SectsI"). Significantly revised and expanded in 1920 ("SectsII"), these two studies comment directly on the American political culture and its spirit of democracy.[1]

Less scholarly than *PE* and informal in tone, Weber seeks here to reach a much broader audience. These essays convey his perspicacious observations as he travels through the New England, Midwestern, Southern, and Mid-Atlantic states. His commentary, however, should not be comprehended as offering merely fragmented "impressions of American life." Instead, Weber brings his audience up-to-date in respect to the impact of Puritan beliefs in the United States 250 years after the landing of the Pilgrims. He focuses on two major themes.

DOI: 10.4324/9781032631813-4

First, he explicitly addresses the political culture of the United States. Opposing stereotypes widespread throughout Europe, and especially in Germany, Weber refuses to depict American society as a "sand pile of atoms" – of individuals adrift and without viable social and intimate connections. Rather, he sees multitudes of clubs, associations, and societies as prominent. The origins of these groups, and the vigorous engagement of their members, can be traced back to the Protestant sects in the northern states, he emphasizes.

Second, *PE*'s argument is expanded in "Sects." These essays analyze how a social-psychological dynamic distinct to these organizations accomplish two important tasks: it effectively *carries* the *ethical* action expected by Puritan ministers into the daily lives of the devout *and* transfers consistently ascetic Protestantism's economic ethic into everyday conduct. The faithful became oriented systematically to work, the search for profit, and material success as a consequence of this complex dynamic.

Weber's observations paint a picture of American society as open and energetic, yet stable. Indeed, he perceives the United States as a vibrant nation soon to embark upon a period of great power. And differences are prominent vis-à-vis European societies in respect to both economic and political cultures, he asserts. German society in particular varied distinctly, Weber maintains, and he attempts to convey in "SectsI" and "SectsII" to his countrymen the firm and long roots of the American success story.

In this respect, he aims to confront – and warn against – the dismissive view of American political stability and economic power widespread among German scholars, industrialists, and politicians. Invisible to highly secularized Europeans, a distinct configuration of facilitating religious values stood at the foundation of American growth, power, wealth, and democracy, he holds.

This section turns first to the manner in which multitudes of Puritan sects created, especially in light of social dynamics internal to them, a political culture fundamentally characterized by "exclusivities" practiced by innumerable groups. All insulated Americans against atomistic relationships.

Weber rejected the view in Europe dominant in his era that depicted American democracy as rooted in solitary individuals ("SectsI," pp. 231–32; "SectsII," pp. 214–19). On the contrary, multitudes of associations characterized this society, he argued: churches, sects, social clubs, hobby organizations, and varieties of political and interest groups. Americans formulated groups in an exceedingly quick and nimble fashion. Instead of a "sand heap" of unconnected and lonesome individuals, American democracy must be comprehended as grounded in "joiners," associations, and exclusivities, he insisted:

> American society in its genuine form – and here my remarks explicitly concern also the "middle" and "lower" strata – was never...a sandpile, nor even a building where everyone who sought to enter found open, undiscriminating doors. Rather, it was, and is, saturated with "exclusivities" of all sorts. Wherever this earlier situation still remains, the individual firmly acquires a foundation under his feet, at the university and in business, only when he succeeds in being voted into a *social organization* (earlier almost without exception a church, today an organization of a different sort) and manages, within this organization, to *hold his own*. ("SectsI," pp. 231–32; emphasis original)

> It is still true that American democracy is not a sandpile of unrelated individuals but a maze of highly exclusive, yet absolutely voluntary, sects, associations, and clubs, which provide the center of the individual's social life. (*RCM*, p. 287; see "SectsII," pp. 216–17)

Thus, Weber emphasized an aspect of American life stressed in the strongest terms by Tocqueville: its multiple and multifarious "civic associations." They stand at the foundation of his analysis of the American political culture, its spirit of democracy, and its uniqueness.

However, unlike the French theorist, Weber locates their origins in the realm of religion.[2] Moreover, although he acknowledged that membership provided a sense of belonging and a safe foundation for activity, as had Tocqueville, he emphasized also the capacity of civic associations to bestow social honor. Rather than banished by urbanization, egalitarianism, and industrialization, social honor assumed a new form: no longer given by birth and longstanding tradition, as in feudal societies, it must be *acquired* through admission to groups widely respected in one's community ("Sects2," pp. 212–18; *E&S*, p. 933). Initiative must be taken. In search of an explanation for this foundational aspect of the American political culture, Weber investigated ascetic Protestantism's sects.

2.1 The Protestant Sects: The Social Carriers of Ethical Action in Colonial America

The process of testifying to one's salvation status assumed in America significant new contours in the course of the eighteenth century. It moved away from the Puritan engaged in a lonely struggle to orient his activities to God and to create "evidence" of his salvation, Weber contends, and toward believers situated deeply within a *social* milieu, namely, in *the Protestant sect*. Hence, he now expands his analysis beyond *PE*'s question – how did the faithful prove their devoutness *before God*? – to an investigation of how they testified to their sincere belief *before men* ("SectsII," p. 225; emphasis original). This shift further supported the orientation of the devout to ethical action.

Although believers drew upon an internal strength in order to remain focused upon God and to lead "the moral life," the sect's strict monitoring and unrelenting pressure to conform significantly influenced the ethical conduct of members, Weber argues. This firm organization confirmed the beliefs and psychological rewards enunciated by Puritan doctrine and conveyed them *systematically* to the faithful. In doing so, this tightly knit group carried the ethical action originally expected by the Puritan Divines.

It became manifest in several ways, Weber maintains. The particular manner in which the sect influenced the believer's conduct must first be noted; we then address how this organization must be distinguished clearly from churches. To Weber: "The ascetic conventicles and sects formed one of the most important historical foundations of modern 'individualism'" ("SectsII," p. 225).

A church implies to Weber an inclusive, sacred "corporation." Born into it, all members seek to save the souls of other members. A cultivation of religious beliefs and conduct stands at the forefront. However, this task is not always uncomplicated: because the church exists as a "universal" institution encompassing the righteous and unrighteous alike, membership has no bearing upon a person's spiritual and ethical qualities. This organization allows its "grace [to] shine over all" ("SectsI," pp. 230–32; "SectsII," p. 212; *E&S*, p. 1164).

Sects, as voluntary communities composed of persons with demonstrated religious "qualifications," diverge distinctly. Admission occurs only after a probationary period in which the candidate's sincerity of belief and moral character are scrutinized.[3] Thus, membership implies to believers a sense of belonging to a religious elite and "purity of membership" constitutes a central theme for all sects – for God's majesty would be insulted and dishonored by the presence of the sinful at the Lord's Supper (*E&S*, pp. 1204–05). Moreover, the conviction of sect members that God must be obeyed more than men places a clear demand upon their behavior: it must be in accord with the sacred Word or "righteous."

The "visible church" is now displayed in the exemplary conduct of the faithful (see "SectsI," pp. 230–32; "SectsII," p. 212). Outside a "salvation institution" and cut off from religious officials who administer special means of dispensation, believers are left now entirely on their own:

> ...the idea that the individual, on the basis of the religious qualifications bestowed by God, decided on his salvation status exclusively on his own was important....only the believer's practical conduct mattered: his behavior "testified" to his faith and alone provided a *sign* that he stood on the road to salvation. ("SectsI," p. 231; translation altered; emphasis original)[4]

As Weber quickly emphasizes, the selective admission policies of sects implies that membership, because based on a person's demonstrated capacity to live up to high ethical standards, has the effect of legitimating moral character. It offers, in other words, a "certificate of moral qualification" ("SectsII," p. 212). Also of central interest to him is the sect's greater capacity to convey values to its members and to breed certain forms of behavior. Both the sect's control over admission to communion through membership selection and its character as a self-governing community do so. Now in the hands of laymen, the exercise of discipline, although less centralized and authoritarian, becomes more thorough and encompassing. The sect rivals the monastic order owing to this capacity, Weber contends ("SectsII," pp. 224–26).

However, values and "selected qualities" are mediated by this organization in a further intense manner. A singular *social* dynamic characterizes the sect as a consequence, on the one hand, of its capacity comprehensively to monitor members' action and then to admonish and discipline, and, on the other hand, owing to the enhanced *religious* significance of all conduct: one's very capacity to act in a "respectable and dignified" manner now offers evidence of God's energy within – and God is present only among the saved.

Hence, because activity is now monitored externally as well as internally, the devout *must continuously* act in a righteous manner. Any misstep, which will be surely exposed, will be understood not as a random and forgivable error but as a "fall from grace." And in light of the sect's composition – an exclusive organization of "pure" believers – any exposure of "bad character" will lead immediately to social expulsion, Weber emphasizes.

2.2 "Holding One's Own" and the Methodical-Rational Organization of Life

In this manner, the necessity, under the watchful eyes of peers, to "hold one's own" in the sect – that is, to testify constantly through conduct to one's membership among the elect – became absolute: a collapse of one's entire social existence followed upon the slightest lapse ("SectsII," pp. 224–26; *E&S*, p. 1206). Unlike the authoritarian discipline exercised by churches, this mode of shaping ethical behavior is "unobtrusive," according to Weber, though in the end more comprehensive and intense.[5]

By engaging the entire social being and providing both social honor and social esteem, the sect has the effect of disciplining believers to a unique degree of intensity on behalf of an ethical posture, Weber contends ("SectsII," pp. 225–26). In other words, a powerful social dynamic now supplements ascetic Protestantism's *internal* dynamic revolving around *the* pivotal question: "am I among the saved?"

Weber also refers to a related social-psychological dynamic in order to explain further the unique capacity of the Protestant sects to cultivate and sustain ethical activity. The faithful, as a consequence of the selection of members on the basis of moral qualities, were viewed within their geographical regions as persons of great integrity and even trustworthiness. As the sect – largely for this reason – acquired social prestige, members became subject to enhanced conformity pressures to uphold "good moral character" standards. Supervision and monitoring among the devout was intensified – for the sect's favorable reputation must be maintained.

A further shaping of the believer's conduct took place in this way, Weber contends. Indeed: "According to all experience there is no stronger means of breeding traits than through the necessity of holding one's own in the midst of one's associates" ("SectsII," p. 224; see pp. 221–22; *E&S*, p. 1206).

Finally, the sect constitutes a functional and "impersonal" group, he argues; it is oriented above all *to tasks* in service to God's greater glory and to the construction of His kingdom. By promoting "the precise ordering of the individual into the instrumental task pursued by the group," this "mechanism for the achievement of...material and ideal *goals*" circumscribes affect-laden and tradition-laden relationships among the faithful (*RCM*, p. 286; see *PE*, p. 327, note 34). Neither an emotion-based interaction prevails in the sect[6] nor a warm and comfortable sentimental mode of interaction rooted in familiar and long-standing traditions.[7] All residues of any "mystical total essence floating above [the believer] and enveloping him" were banished (*RCM*, p. 286; see *PE*, p. 327, note 34).[8]

A halo never encompassed the sect – one into which the believer could merge amid a sacred glow. Rather, an orientation by the devout to *tasks* in service to God and high standards of ethical conduct reigned. The stalwart faithful, evaluated exclusively by reference to the "religious qualities evident in [their] conduct," constantly attended to the necessity of "holding their own" (*RCM*, pp. 284–86). And despite the typically intense interaction among sect members, a cultivation of deep emotional ties and an immersion into the group failed to occur, Weber maintains. "Association" (*Vergesellschaftung*) and ethical conduct characterized interaction.

In sum, by juxtaposing an unceasing orientation to activities and tasks, intense conformity pressures, and a hold-your-own individualism, sects pulled the devout away from emotion-oriented relationships, tradition-oriented sentimentality, and all inclinations to attribute a sacred aura to groups. However, far from abandoning believers either to the flux and flow of a daily life anchored by an interest-oriented utilitarianism and the practical-rational mode of organizing life or to an endless random and nihilistic drift, the sect immediately took firm hold of the faithful. It then bound the devout tightly within its own social-psychological dynamic – one that actively cultivated, sustained, and rejuvenated "hold your own" individualism and intense ethical action.

Thus, the *methodical-rational* organization of life typically found among ascetic Protestants arose not only from the individual's *solitary* quest to create "evidence" of his salvation and the psychological rewards placed upon ethical action by the Puritan Divines, as charted in *PE*, but also from its efficient "implementation" through social dynamics typical in the Protestant sect, according to Weber. For all these reasons, high *standards* of conduct must be upheld in the sect. Rewards were apparent – as were punishments. To Weber: "The sect and its derivations are one of [America's] unwritten but vital constitutional elements, since they shape the individual more than any other influence" (*E&S*, p. 1207).

Notes

1 *PE* focuses upon a religious doctrine and a religious tradition dominant in the United States. For the most part, Weber poured his observations regarding the effects of ascetic Protestantism upon American society generally (beyond the predominant work ethic) largely into these essays, as soon will become apparent. For the unabridged essays, see (Weber, "SectsII," pp. 302–22).
2 On Tocqueville on these origins, see Chapter 7.
3 "…admission is preceded by an *examen rigorosum* which inquires about blemishes in [one's] past conduct: frequenting a tavern, sexual life, card-playing, making debts, other levities, insincerity, etc." (*E&S*, p. 1206; see "SectsII," p. 212). Conceivably, the origins of the emphasis in the American occupational sphere upon "passing muster" and in the political arena upon "good character" can be located here.
4 Weber also notes the way in which this idea opposes all "feudal and dynastic romanticism" – or the placing of individualism within a firm hierarchy of relationships – at its core: "The exclusive appraisal of a person purely in terms of the religious qualities evidenced in his conduct necessarily severs off all feudal and dynastic romanticism at its roots" ("SectsI," p. 230).
5 Weber adds: "The Old Methodist confession in the weekly meetings of the small groups set up for this purpose, the class meetings and the mutual control and admonition of the Pietists and Quakers contrast with the Catholic's auricular confession, which in this sense is uncontrolled and serves the sinner's relief but rarely aims at changing his mind" (*E&S*, p. 1206). Weber here sees also a social-psychological dimension readily recognizable today – the issue of self-esteem: "The Puritan sects put the most powerful individual interests of social self-esteem in the service of this breeding of traits. Hence, *individual* motives and personal self-interests were also placed in the service of maintaining and propagating this 'middle class' Puritan ethic, with all its ramifications. This is absolutely decisive for its penetrating and powerful effect" ("SectsII," p. 224; emphasis original).
6 In this regard Weber notes Puritanism's condemnation of personal wants and desires (*Kreaturvergötterung*) – for their satisfaction competes with the believer's loyalty to God – as denying legitimacy to a focus upon the person and all privatized concerns. See (*PE*, p. 328, note 39).

7 Toennies famous *Gemeinschaft–Gesellschaft* dichotomy was well known to Weber. He is here explicitly demarcating an antagonistic position (see *RCM*, pp. 284–86).

8 Weber has here in mind both Catholicism and Lutheranism. Because enveloped by a mystical aura, members of these churches are absolved of an urgent necessity to hold their own. He is critical of this mode of group formation, which he found to be widespread in the Germany of his times (see Mommsen, 1974, pp. 80–81).

3

THE PROTESTANT ETHIC REVISITED

Key Terminological Distinctions and the Debate

The distinction between "capitalism" and "modern capitalism" stands at the foundation of Weber's entire analysis in *PE*. Capitalism, as involving the exchange of goods and calculations of profit and loss balances in terms of money, has existed in civilizations in all corners of the globe and from ancient times to the present. The assessment of balances has been more efficient in some epochs and societies than in others, where it remained "primitive" and approximated guesswork.

However, a calculation of income and expenses, or "capital accounting," has been found universally, as has the "expectation of profit based on the utilization of opportunities for exchange" ("PR," p. 237). Moneylenders, merchants engaged in trade, entrepreneurs investing in slaves, and promoters and speculators of every sort have calculated profits and losses in every epoch (*PE*, pp. 83–84; "PR," pp. 237–41; *GEH*, p. 334; *E&S*, p. 91).[1]

Weber turns quickly away from such "adventure capitalism" and "political capitalism" to a discussion of the distinguishing *features* of *modern* capitalism: a relatively free exchange of goods in markets, the separation of business activity from household activity, sophisticated bookkeeping methods, and the rational, or systematic, organization of work and the workplace in general.[2] Workers are legally free in modern capitalism rather than enslaved. Profit is pursued in a regular and continuous fashion, as is its maximization, in organized businesses (see "PR," pp. 237–41; *GEH*, pp. 275–351; *E&S*, pp. 164–66).

DOI: 10.4324/9781032631813-5

Nevertheless, because it refers to formal aspects only (the *economic form*), Weber insists that this definition of modern capitalism is incomplete; modern capitalism involves *also* the organization of economic activity in terms of an *economic ethic*. This *ethos* legitimates and provides the motivation for the rigorous organization of work, the methodical approach to labor, and the systematic pursuit of profit typical of modern capitalism. It implies "the idea of the *duty* of the individual to increase his wealth, which is assumed to be a self-defined interest in itself" (*PE*, p. 79; emphasis original); the notion that "labor [is] an absolute end in itself" (*PE*, p. 69); the desirability of "the acquisition of money, and more and more money, [combined with] the strictest avoidance of all spontaneous enjoyment of it" (*PE*, p. 40); the view that the "acquisition of money...is...the result and manifestation of competence and proficiency in a vocational calling" (*PE*, pp. 80–81); and a "particular *frame of mind* that...strives systematically and rationally *in a calling* for legitimate profit" (*PE*, p. 88; emphasis original).[3]

Weber designates this "modern economic ethic" the "spirit of capitalism."[4] Its violation, he asserts, involves not merely foolishness but "forgetfulness of *duty*" (*PE*, p. 79; emphasis original). The eighteenth-century American printer, inventor, entrepreneur, businessman, and statesman Benjamin Franklin, embodied this ethos, according to Weber, as apparent from his attitudes toward work, profit, and life in general (*PE*, pp. 77–78). As Weber notes in his "Prefatory Remarks" essay:

> The origin of economic rationalism, [of the type which, since the sixteenth and seventeenth centuries, has come to dominate the West], just as it is dependent upon a rational technology and rational law, is also dependent upon the capacity and disposition of persons to *organize their lives* in a *practical-rational* manner. ("PR," p. 246; emphasis original; see *PERW*, pp. 250–51)

Typically, Weber isolates the distinctive qualities of the spirit of capitalism through comparisons, above all to the *traditional economic ethic*. He does so mainly along two axes: attitudes toward work and the business practices of employers.

Work was perceived as a noble and virtuous activity wherever the spirit of capitalism reigned. Throughout their communities, persons engaged in labor were accorded respect and believed to be of good character. Work played a central role in the formulation even of a person's sense of dignity and self-worth. This "elevation" of work, Weber contends, resulted from an array of historical conditions.

However, adherents to the traditional economic ethic regarded work as involving drudgery. A necessary evil, it must be avoided as soon as customary and constant economic needs had been met. Labor here was approached in an unfocused and lackadaisical manner. Moreover, people understood work as only one arena of life, deserving of no more attention, concentration, or time than activities oriented, for example, to families, hobbies, friendship, and leisure in general.

Those who comprehended labor in this way could not be induced to increase productivity even if employers introduced a piece rate system that provided monetary incentives for faster and more efficient work. On the contrary, because work was viewed negatively and other activities positively, a higher piece rate led to less labor: employees could earn in a shorter period of time the amount of money necessary to fulfill their accustomed needs. More time to pursue leisure activities would then become available. As Weber notes:

> The opportunity of earning more appealed to [them] less than the idea of working less....People do not wish "by nature" to earn more and more money. Instead, they wish simply to live, and to live as they have been accustomed and to earn as much as is required to do so. (*PE*, p. 85; see pp. 84–87; *GEH*, pp. 355–56)

Until relatively recently, the traditional economic "spirit" also held sway over persons engaged in business. Whereas employers imbued with the spirit of capitalism sought profit systematically, organized their entire workforce according to the rules of productive and efficient management, reinvested profits in their companies, and saw themselves as engaged in harsh, competitive struggles, economic traditionalism implied a more comfortable and slow-paced manner of conducting business. Set by long-standing custom rather than by the laws of the market, prices and profits generally remained constant. The circle of customers remained unchanged, and relations between workers and owners were regulated largely by tradition. Because the workday lasted generally only five to six hours, there was always time for friends and long meals. Although capitalist in terms of the use of capital and the calculation of income and expenses, a leisurely ethos characterized the entire approach to moneymaking and to business (*PE*, pp. 22–29).

Weber is proposing that these differences between the traditional and modern orientations toward work and business management are not insignificant. Moreover, although economic forms and economic ethics "exist generally in…a relationship…of 'adequacy' to each other," there is no "'lawful' dependency," and they may exist separately (*PE*, pp. 88–91; "I," pp. 267–68).

On the one hand, even though the spirit of capitalism strongly infused Benjamin Franklin's habits and general way of life, the operations of his printing business followed those typical in handicraft enterprises (*PE*, pp. 88–89). On the other hand, the traditional economic ethic might combine with a highly developed capitalist economy (e.g., Italian capitalism before the Reformation). After comparing the widespread capitalism in Florence in the fourteenth and fifteenth centuries (where activity directed toward profit for its own sake was viewed as ethically unjustifiable) with the economic backwardness of eighteenth-century Pennsylvania (where a spirit of capitalism was "understood as the very substance of a morally acceptable, even praiseworthy way of organizing and directing life"), Weber concludes that capitalism itself did not produce the spirit of capitalism (*PE*, pp. 88–90, 96–98).[5]

How did the "revolution" (*PE*, p. 89) that brought economic traditionalism to an end take place? What are the sources of this monumental shift to a modern economic ethic? And how did it happen that work moved to the center of life? To Weber, the approach to work "as if [it] were an absolute end in itself.…is not inherently given in the nature of the species. Nor can it be directly called forth by high or low wages. Rather, it is the product of a long and continuous process of socialization" (*PE*, p. 86; see p. 297, note 17). He is convinced that, in light of the extreme immutability and endurance of the traditional economic ethic, it could be banished only by persons of unusually strong character (*PE*, p. 29). However, viewed from the perspective of the spontaneous enjoyment of life, such an orientation of activity toward hard work appears fully "irrational" and unnatural (*PE*, pp. 92–99).

This is Weber's concern. Rather than investigating the origins of modern capitalism, the rise of the West, or capitalism as such, this case study seeks to discover the specific religious "ancestry" of the *spirit* of capitalism (see notes 14 and 23). It explores the origins of a "modern economic ethos" and the modern vocational specialist: "My discussion above all *explicitly and intentionally limited* itself to this theme; namely, to the development of the vocational specialist person (*Berufsmenschentums*) as concerns his significance as a component of the capitalist 'spirit'" (*PED*, p. 76; translation altered; emphasis original).

In defining this task, Weber was responding critically to a heated discussion in German scholarship. The unorthodox focus of "the Weber thesis" on the importance of a spirit of capitalism separated *PE* clearly from the major orientation of this debate, namely, toward capitalism as an economic form. In fact, the explorations by his colleagues into the origins of modern capitalism denied the independence of an economic ethic. By explicitly seeking to broaden the boundaries of this controversy in an unwelcome direction, *PE* immediately set off a furor. A glance at the main contours of this debate is indispensable before turning to Weber's analysis. Doing so will situate *PE* within the intellectual currents of its time and further demarcate its uniqueness.

3.1 The Intellectual Context: The Controversy over the Origins of Modern Capitalism and Industrialism

Nearly all participants in the debate on the origins of modern capitalism and industrialism 120 years ago in Germany offered analyses that neglected the role of culture. The dominant explanations can be mentioned only briefly.

The Intensification of Avarice. A number of German scholars argued that in earlier times, the "acquisitive instinct" (*PE*, p. 82) was less developed or even nonexistent. In the eighteenth and nineteenth centuries, however, they saw avarice and greed as becoming stronger. Modern capitalism resulted from an intensification of the "pursuit of gain," they held ("PR," p. 237).

This characterization of more recent centuries as ones in which the "striving for...the greatest profit" ("PR," p. 237) has been more widespread, Weber contends, does not bear up once experimental comparisons are undertaken. The "greed for gain" can be found among "all sorts and conditions of men at all times and in all countries of the earth, wherever the objective possibility of it is or has been given" ("PR," p. 237).

To him, the "*greed* of mandarins in China, of the aristocrats in ancient Rome, or the modern peasant is second to none" (*PE*, p. 82). Because such an *auri sacra fames* (greed for gold) has existed universally and is "as old as the history of man," it fails to offer a causal explanation for *his specific* problem: the rise of a spirit of capitalism in the eighteenth century in the West. Finally, Weber will argue that the rise of modern capitalism involves a "tempering" of all acquisitive desires; indeed, such a "restraining" of avarice – and its channeling into a *methodical* orientation toward work – is indispensable for the systematic organization of work and production in permanent businesses (*PE*, pp. 81–82; "PR," p. 237; *GEH*, pp. 355–56).

The Adventure and Political Capitalism of Charismatic Entrepreneurs. Other scholars in Germany were convinced that the desire of great charismatic entrepreneurs for riches pushed economic development past the agrarian and feudal stages to mercantilism and modern capitalism. Typically engaged in gigantic commercial ventures often involving the continent-spanning trade of luxury items, these unscrupulous and egocentric promoters, financiers, bankers, merchants, and speculators ushered in the modern epoch simply on the basis of their extraordinary energy (*PE*, pp. 79–82).

Again, however, Weber discovered this adventure and political capitalism universally. Yet these types of capitalism never called forth *modern* capitalism. Furthermore, he refused to view the exceptional commercial daring of these sporadically appearing "economic supermen" as implying the continuity of disciplined action requisite for a shattering of the traditional economic ethic. Isolated individuals alone could never call forth this monumental transformation; rather, an organizing of life common to whole "*groups* of persons," all *intensively* oriented toward profit and the rational organization of labor and capital, would be necessary (*PE*, pp. 80, 82; emphasis original).

Evolution and Progress. In *Moderne Kapitalismus* (1902), the economic historian Werner Sombart, Weber's colleague and friend, held that the expansion of production, trade, banking, and commerce could best be understood as clear manifestations of a society-wide unfolding of "rationalism" and progress in general. In this view, crystallization of a spirit of capitalism constituted simply further, and not unusual, evidence of a general evolution. To Sombart, societal progress as a whole deserved explanation rather than the separate component elements in this broad-ranging evolutionary process.

Weber opposed Sombart vehemently. "Society" was too global a level of analysis, he claimed. Instead, the separate societal "realms" (*Lebensbereiche*), "orders" (*Lebensordnungen*), or "spheres" (*Lebenssphären*), which together comprise a "society," must be examined. If one proceeds in this manner, a *nonparallel* development in the various realms becomes evident rather than a general evolutionary process, Weber insists. For example, a systematization or "rationalization" in the sphere of law (in the sense of increasing conceptual clarity and the refinement of the content of the law based upon a foundational written source such as a constitution) reached its highest point in the Roman law of the Middle Ages.

On the one hand, however, this type of law remained far less developed in a number of countries where a rationalization of the *economy* advanced farthest. In England, for example, a less rationalized form of law – Common law – prevailed. On the other hand, Roman law remained strong throughout Southern Europe, an area where modern capitalism developed quite late (*PE*, pp. 96–99). In neither region did the law and economy realms develop in a parallel fashion.

These and similar observations persuaded Weber to reject the notion of "general evolutionary progress" and to focus his attention on a variety of societal orders rather than "society" as an organic unity. He investigated the realm of religion in *PE* and later, in his three-volume analytic treatise, *Economy and Society* (1968), the domains of law, rulership (*Herrschaft*), status groups, "universal organizations" (the family, the clan), and the economy (see Kalberg, 1994, pp. 53–54, 103–17; see Chapters 4 and 8).

The Jews as the Carriers of Modern Capitalism. Sombart's book, *The Jews and Modern Capitalism* (1913), argued that the Jews as a group were the major social carriers of modern capitalism. He viewed the putatively typical business dealings of Jews as decisive: the loaning of money for interest, continuous speculation, and the financing of wars, construction projects, and political activities. In addition, Sombart argued that an "abstract rationalism," which allegedly characterized Jewish thinking, was identical with the "spirit of capitalism" of English Puritans. The wish to make money dominated in both groups.

Weber disagreed forcefully on all points both in *PE* and in later writings (see *PE*, pp. 165–66; 382–83, notes 68 and 69; *GEH*, pp. 358–59; *E&S*, pp. 611–23, 1202–04).[6] He viewed the innovation-averse economic ethos of the Jews as "traditional" and noted their absence among the heroic entrepreneurs in the early stages of Western European capitalism. Furthermore, he saw the capitalism of the Jews as a form of the speculative capitalism that had existed universally rather than as involving a systematic organization of production, labor, and the workplace in general (*PE*, pp. 382–83, note 66).

Finally, Weber argued, the outcaste social position of the Jews in Europe kept them outside the pivotal craft and guild organizations of the medieval period, and their double ethical standard, which followed from this outcaste position (strong ethical obligations to other Jews, yet quite different practices in economic relationships with non-Jews), hindered the unfolding of measures of economic efficiency across the economy.

Historical Materialism, Economic Interests, and the Power of the Dominant Class. Although the "internal contradictions" of capitalism constituted the major concern of Karl Marx, his writings clearly yield an analysis of its origin. For him, the rise of modern capitalism can be equated with the overthrow of the feudal aristocracy and the hegemonic rule of a new class: the bourgeoisie. Ownership of the means of production (property, factories, technology, tools, etc.) by this class as well as its economic interests and sheer greed were believed to be crucial; they stood as foundational ingredients in the quest of capitalists to acquire more and more wealth. As the bourgeoisie became larger and more powerful, trade, banking, production, and commerce expanded. Eventually, factory-based capitalism came into being.

A "spirit of capitalism" could play no part in the historical materialism of Marx. Had he been alive to address the Weber thesis, Marx would have viewed this ethos as arising directly out of the economic interests of the bourgeoisie; the set of values it implied would be understood as nothing more than an expression, in abstract form, of the economic interests of this class. Such an "ideology" served, Marx argued frequently, to justify the hegemony of the dominant class and to sedate workers into accepting their misery and exploitation.

PE rejects this analysis completely. The economic interests of this class, Weber insists, did not give birth to the spirit of capitalism.

Franklin himself offers evidence against this position: his economic ethos far preceded the formation of a bourgeoisie (*PE*, pp. 19, 32–33). Moreover, Weber rejected a pivotal Marxian assumption: the capacity of social groupings to call forth uniform action.

> The assumption is…by no means justified *a priori*…that, on the one hand, the technique of the capitalist enterprise and, on the other, the spirit of "work as a vocational calling," which endows capitalism with its expansive energy, must have had their *original* sustaining roots in the same social groupings. (*PE*, p. 298, note 24; emphasis original; see "I," pp. 268–71, 292)

As noted, even those members of the bourgeoisie who proved to be economic supermen were incapable, Weber maintained, of the sustained and group-based thrust necessary for a rupturing of economic traditionalism. Finally, he found that the spirit of capitalism was formulated and cultivated above all by self-made parvenus from the modest circumstances of the middle classes rather than by the entrepreneurs of a commercial elite (the "patrician merchants"; see *PE*, pp. 88–89, 243–46). To him, the "youth of these ideas – the capitalist spirit – is altogether more thorny than was assumed by the 'superstructure' theorists" (p. 82 *et passim*).[7]

Miscellaneous Forces. Many historians and economists emphasized the importance for economic development of technological innovations, geographical forces, the influx of precious metals from the New World, population increases, and the growth of cities and science. Weber examined all of these arguments. Through scrutiny of comparative cases, he deduced that favorable scientific inventions, population and climatological changes, urban expansion, and other factors had existed in the Middle Ages in the West, in the ancient world, and in a number of epochs in China and India – yet modern capitalism had failed to appear first in these civilizations.[8]

* * *

In these ways,[9] *PE* sought fundamentally to recast an ongoing debate toward an exploration of the spirit of capitalism's origins (*PE*, pp. 82–98). Weber laments the exclusion of such a discussion and the dominant orientation to an economic form. By insisting that any explanation of modern capitalism's early development must acknowledge a rational economic ethic as a sociologically significant causal force and that an investigation of its source must take place, Weber seeks (1) to bring values unequivocally into the debate and (2) to legitimize an exploration of their causal origins.

He is attempting, in other words, to persuade his readers that "cultural values" must no longer be neglected. However complicated it may be to investigate their sources and to assess their influence, values should not be regarded, Weber holds, as passive forces generally subordinate to social structures, power, classes, evolution and progress, and economic and political interests. The spirit of capitalism had significant noneconomic and nonpolitical roots, he contends.

3.2 Empirical Observations: The Turn Toward Religion and the Aim of *The Protestant Ethic*

A trial-and-error pathway never characterized Weber's search for the religious sources of the spirit of capitalism. Rather, at the outset he upheld a view not uncommmon in the Germany of his time: *religious belief* influenced work habits and approaches to business as well as life in general. Hence, queries regarding differences between Protestants and Catholics appeared to him a quite plausible and natural orientation for his research (see Nipperdey, 1993). Indeed, since his teenage years, Weber had been reading theological literature, including the American Unitarians William Ellery Channing and Theodore Parker (see Roth, 1997).

Although relationships between occupational status, educational attainment, Catholicism, and Protestantism were acknowledged among journalists and the educated public in Germany in the 1890s as well as earlier,[10] very little social science research had addressed this theme. As he pondered English and American Puritanism in the mid-1890s, Weber read the massive study by economic historian Eberhard Gothein, *Wirtschaftsgeschichte des Schwarzwalds* (1892) (*Economic History of the Black Forest*), which called attention to Calvinism's strong role in spreading capitalism (pp. 9–10). Although greatly impressed by Gothein (pp. 9–10), Georg Jellinek's *The Declaration of the Rights of Man and of Citizens* (1979 [1895]) inspired Weber "to take up the study of Puritanism once again."[11]

The centrality of devout Dissenters in seventeenth-century England for the emergence of fundamental political rights and liberties had been documented by Jellinek: "[His] proof of religious traces in the genesis of the Rights of Man...gave me a crucial stimulus...to investigate the impact of religion in areas where one might not look at first" (cited in Marianne Weber, 1975, p. 476).

In the late 1890s, Weber encouraged a student to examine the influence of religion on social stratification in the Southwest German state of Baden. Martin Offenbacher's statistical investigation concluded that distinct differences existed between Protestants and Catholics in regard to occupational choices and levels of education: Protestants dominated as owners of industrial concerns, while Catholics were more often farmers and owners of businesses utilizing skilled labor. Protestants' generally higher levels of education accounted for their disproportionately high employment as state civil servants and for their unusually high earnings if they remained in the working class (1900, pp. 63–64).[12]

The publication in 1902 of Sombart's two-volume work, *Moderne Kapitalismus*, appears to have motivated Weber to intensify his own research (see Lehmann, 1987). In his chapter on the origin of the capitalist spirit, Sombart had dismissed the role of Protestantism, especially Calvinism and Quakerism, as "too well-known to require further explanation." Instead, he discovered "empirical proof" of capitalism's origins in the high esteem accorded to the possession of money, indeed to the addiction to "sparkling gold" that appeared in the European Middle Ages. To Sombart, "the Protestant religion was not the cause but the result of modern capitalist thinking." He provoked his readers to discover "empirical proof of *concrete-historical contexts* to the contrary" (1902, vol. 1, pp. 380–81; emphasis in original; see vom Brocke, 1987; Lehmann, 1987 and 1993, pp. 196–98; Marshall, 1982, pp. 36–40).[13]

Weber took up the challenge, and he most likely completed his research for *PE* by the end of 1903. Against Sombart, he responded vigorously. Even external social structures of extreme rigidity, such as those typical of religious sects, Weber asserts, should not be viewed as themselves calling forth homogeneous beliefs and patterns of action (see "I," pp. 268–71, 292). How then could capitalism do so? The studies he had read in the 1890s pointed in a different direction. As well, Weber noted the unusually methodical and conscientious work habits of young women from Pietistic families in Baden (*PE*, p. 87). Even this:

> Analysis derived from [early twentieth century] capitalism has indicated to us yet again that it would be worthwhile simply to *ask* how these connections between people's capacity to adapt to [modern] capitalism, on the one hand, and their religious beliefs, on the other, could have been formulated during the youth of [modern] capitalism. (*PE*, p. 87; emphasis original)

He then explicitly states his aim in *PE*:

> It should here be ascertained only whether, and to what extent, religious influences *co*-participated in the qualitative formation and quantitative expansion of this "spirit" across the globe. (*PE*, p. 108; emphasis. in original)

Whether religious beliefs constitute the "specific ancestry" of the spirit of capitalism must be investigated.[14]

Weber's description of his step-by-step procedure responds to Sombart's provocation even more directly. He will first investigate whether an "elective affinity" (*Wahlverwandtschaft*) exists between certain religious beliefs of the Reformation and a vocational ethic (*Berufsethik*). If this "meaningful connection" can be established, he will then be able to clarify the "way" and "general direction" in which religious movements, as a result of this elective affinity, influenced the development of *material culture*, or practical, workaday life.[15] Only then will it be possible to assess "to what degree the historical origin of the values and ideas of our modern life...can be attributed to religious forces stemming from the Reformation, and to what degree to other forces" (*PE*, p. 109).

Weber's complex and multilayered analysis in *PE* can be broken down into two major stages: (1) his investigation on the origins of the Protestant ethic and (2) his linkage of the Protestant ethic to the spirit of capitalism.

3.3 Modern Capitalism: The Decline Today of the Methodical-Rational Organization of Life and the Hegemony of Means-End Rational Action

Although Weber holds that his concern remains the spirit of capitalism's religious origins, a further theme unavoidably looms throughout *PE*: the sources of modern capitalism. Indeed, he addresses this theme directly in several passages in *PE*. Weber's articles in response to his critics do so even more (see *PE*, pp. 256–71).

Ascetic Protestantism called forth the organized, directed life at the very root of today's "economic man," he contends (*PE*, p. 172). As the "only consistent carrier" of a methodical-rational life *in* the world, the Puritans "created the suitable 'soul' for capitalism, the soul of the 'specialist in a vocation'" (*PED*, p. 73; see *PE*, pp. 130–31, 176–78). The spirit of [modern] capitalism provided the "ethical style of life 'adequate' to the new capitalism" (*PED*, p. 95) and the "economic culture" that served to legitimate modern capitalism.

More generally, an *elective affinity* exists between the ethically rigorous devoutness of ascetic Protestants on the one hand and "the modern culture of capitalism" and "economic rationalism" on the other hand, he insists (*PE*, p. 75; see *E&S*, pp. 479–80): "[The] spirit of [modern] *capitalism*... finds its most adequate form in the modern capitalist company and, on the other hand,...the capitalist company discovers in this frame of mind the motivating force – or spirit – most adequate to it" (*PE*, pp. 88–89). To Weber, the rational work ethic of Puritans and their style of life generally gave a boost to the development of modern capitalism:

> It is clear that this style of life is very closely related to the self-justification that is customary for bourgeois acquisition: profit and property appear not as ends in themselves but as indications of personal ability. Here has been attained the union of religious postulate and bourgeois style of life that promotes [modern] capitalism. (*E&S*, p. 1200)

Indeed, the "significance of the modern capitalist spirit for the development of [modern] capitalism is obvious" (*PE*, p. 169; see *E&S*, pp. 1200, 1206).[16] ["Puritanism had revealed] the psychological aspect of modern economic development" (*PED*, p. 72).

PE's last pages leap across the centuries in order briefly to survey a new theme: the "cosmos" of modern capitalism. In broad strokes and unforgettable passages, Weber briefly explores the fate today of "this-worldly" directed action and the life organized methodically by reference to a constellation of ethical values. The question of *how we can live* under modern capitalism preoccupied him for his entire life.

Firmly entrenched after the massive industrialization of the nineteenth century, "victorious capitalism" now sustains itself on the basis of *means-end rational* action alone, Weber argues. In this urban, secular, and bureaucratic milieu, neither Franklin's spirit nor the Protestant ethic's asceticism endows methodical work with subjective meaning. As these value configurations so significant at the birth of modern capitalism collapse and fade, sheer utilitarian calculations move to the forefront (*PE*, p. 175). Modern capitalism today unfolds on the basis of an inescapable network of pragmatic necessities (*PE*, pp. 176–78).

Whether employees or entrepreneurs, people born into this "powerful cosmos" are coerced to adapt to its market-based functional exchanges in order to survive. The motivation to work in this "steel-hard casing" involves a mixture of constraint and means-end rational action. A "mechanical foundation" anchors the modern era and "the idea of an 'obligation to search for and then accept a vocational calling' now wanders around in our lives as the ghost of beliefs no longer anchored in the substance of religion" (*PE*, p. 177). In one of his most famous passages, Weber tersely captures this significant transformation at the level of subjective meaning and motives: "The Puritan *wanted* to be a person with a vocational calling; we *must* be" (*PE*, p. 177).

This new epoch ushers in a further *type of human being*, he maintains. Intimately linked to capitalism's internal workings, the frame of mind of *the specialist* varies distinctly from that of the "cultivated man" of the eighteenth and early nineteenth centuries (see *E&S*, pp. 998–1002). Now lost, this epoch of the multitalented Wolfgang von Goethe (1749–1832) is longed for by many. Capitalism will not vanish, however, Weber maintains, and he mocks the many nostalgic thinkers of his day in Germany who expected a return to the past (*PE*, pp. 176–77).

Moreover, material products today, owing to modern capitalism's oft-praised capacity to create high standards of living, acquire "an increasing and, in the end, inescapable power over people – as never before in history" (*PE*, p. 177). The striving for their possession takes the form of a vigorous "pursuit of gain," yet one now "stripped of its religious-ethical meaning." Ruling instead are "purely competitive passions" (*PE*, p. 177).

This theme connects directly to a theme familiar to us, one underlying the entire expanse of *PE*. Methodical-rational lives organized rigorously on the basis of internalized value configurations appeared with Puritanism's "ascetic saints." The devout tamed the *status naturae* and owing to intense *belief*, severed their action from the firm grip of tradition on the one hand and all sheer utilitarian, practical-rational orientations to given tasks on the other hand. The *directed* life replaced the life flowing to the beat of a random succession of events. The sincere faith of the devout – who lived *in* but not *of* the world – enabled these unusual and complex achievements, for their rigid focus upon God's decrees implied a firm guiding of activities by *ethical* values.

However, this dignified life – the life directed comprehensively "from within" – now appears to Weber endangered. Amidst the dependency today of most persons upon a modern economy characterized by sweeping coercion, practical rationalism, impersonal exchange relationships, and narrow specialization, a cultivation on a broad societal scale of the life organized by reference to ethical values seemed utopian. The person unified internally by core values – "the personality" – will soon disappear, he feared. Modern capitalism – this "grinding mechanism" – will "[determine] the style of life....with overwhelming force..., perhaps...until the last ton of fossil fuel has burnt to ashes" (*PE*, p. 177).[17]

This summary of his brief commentary upon capitalist societies today reveals Weber's analysis in *PE* as characterized by four discrete stages (see chart on page 84).[18]

3.4   The Protestant Ethic Debate

Controversy surrounded *PE* immediately after its publication. While at times quiescent, generations of critics and defenders have debated vehemently "the Weber thesis" up to the present. A substantial study would be required to do justice to this controversy.[19] Arguably, no other volume in the social sciences in the English-speaking world has generated a more intense and long-term discussion.[20] As will become apparent, most of Weber's critics never mastered his complex argument.

Some commentators have failed to see either the centrality of the *certitudo salutis* question or its powerful capacity – grounded in the doctrine of predestination, an Old Testament view of God, and pastoral care concerns – to provide an impetus to religious development from Calvin to seventeenth-century Puritans. Others never acknowledged that conduct oriented to disciplined work, despite the logical consequences of the doctrine of predestination, was understood by the Puritans as *testifying* (*sich bewähren*) to intense belief, which was believed to emanate originally from God.

Many interpreters neglected Weber's analysis of how believers seek to serve God as His "tool" – and then to systematize to unusual degrees their entire lives around work, material contributions to His community, and His laws. Still others were unaware of the several ways the devout discovered signs of God's favoring hand and the manner in which these "indications" motivated the organization and direction of their activity.

Weber's early critics, as well as many later commentators, refused to take cognizance of his pivotal distinction between action guided by *values* and oriented to the supernatural, and other, basically utilitarian, action. Furthermore, Weber's analysis of how motivations for action, and even an unintended ethos, may arise through religious beliefs and practices, and how belief may further call forth "psychological premiums" that direct action (see note xx above), was often omitted from the commentary. The major themes of the controversy must be adumbrated here in succinct form.[21]

Weber is an Idealist. Many commentators have argued that *PE* exaggerates the causal influence of religion. Some have seen an "idealistic determinism" (Tawney, 1954); others contend that the Protestant ethic arose out of capitalism and must be seen as an epiphenomenon of economic transformation.

These critics have ignored Weber's own direct statement regarding the limitations of *PE*: "...it can not be, of course, the intention here to set a one-sided spirtualistic analysis of the causes of culture and history in place of an equally one-sided 'materialistic' analysis. *Both are equally possible*" (*PE*, p. 179; see pp. 399–400, notes 142, 143). Commentators have also neglected his massive comparative studies on the uniqueness of the West (*GEH, E&S, RofI, RofC, AJ*), all of which attend *both* to "ideas" and "interests" (see Chapter 6 below and Kalberg, 2021).

The Rise of Modern Capitalism is Not Explained. A vast array of critics has misunderstood the aim of *PE*. They have comprehended this volume as designed to offer an analysis of the rise of modern capitalism – and then dismissed it as sorely incomplete. The commentators at this point divide into two groups.

Some discover Puritanism (e.g., in France or Hungary), yet conclude that its presence failed to introduce capitalism, thereby misunderstanding Weber's "more modest" aim (see below). Other critics fault Weber for omitting the role of, for example, population changes, technological innovations, the discovery of the new world, the circulation of precious metals in a world economy, and the growth of the modern state and modern law. The Kiel historian of Germany and Holland, Felix Rachfahl (1867–1925), was the earliest critic to argue that *PE* had not explained the consequences of either the Protestant ethic or the spirit of capitalism for economic development. However, Weber states his more modest aim repeatedly[22]: as noted, he sought to examine the extent of *religious* influences upon the formation and expansion of the *spirit* of capitalism (pp. 108–09; see also pp. 177–79).[23]

Weber Misinterprets Doctrines. Church historians in particular have been critical of Weber's discussions of Catholic, Lutheran, and ascetic Protestant doctrines. Others have dissected John Calvin's teachings and failed to discover an emphasis upon work in a vocation. These latter scholars have failed to note Weber's distinction between Calvin's doctrines and the ascetic Protestantism of the sixteenth and seventeenth centuries. He locates the source of the Protestant ethic in the Puritanism of this latter period rather than in Calvin's teachings, and he emphasizes the many revisions of Calvin's thought introduced by Richard Baxter and the Puritan Divines (see *PE*, pp. 27–32). Moreover, Weber held that Calvin recommended "steadfast faith" to believers rather than methodical work in a vocation (see *PE*, pp. 123–26).[24]

Capitalism is Universal. Commentators frequently insisted that capitalism predated Puritanism. They discovered it to be significantly widespread in the ancient and medieval worlds in the West as well as in China and India. Although Weber maintains that his main concern in *PE* involved the origins of a Protestant ethic and the extent of its influence upon the spirit of capitalism, capitalism's general origins, as discussed, are also of interest to him. His discussion of this theme, however, distinguished sharply between modern capitalism on the one hand and political and adventure capitalism on the other hand. While the former arose only in the early modern West, the latter two types of capitalism appeared universally, he holds.

Elongating and Relativizing the Weber Thesis. Many critics have expanded and relativized the Protestant ethic thesis. They have located the origin of the major groupings Weber attended to in much earlier epochs. Some discovered "Protestant asceticism" in medieval Catholicism – hence they argued that it predated Puritanism and constituted its foundation.

At this point, however, the critics neglected Weber's distinction between Puritanism's "this-worldly" asceticism and the medieval monk's "otherworldly" asceticism. Others located a "capitalist spirit" much earlier than did *PE* and emphasized its capacity to mold the evolution of Puritanism. Weber contends that these critics equated his definition of the spirit of capitalism with the charisma of great "adventure" and "political" capitalists (see next paragraph). Against this school of "relativizing critics," he also maintained that a weakening of economic traditionalism did not itself imply the birth of either a Protestant ethic or a spirit of capitalism.

Fugger and Alberti Carried a Spirit of Capitalism. A long list of critics has maintained that the great medieval entrepreneur Jacob Fugger and the Renaissance thinker Leon Battista Alberti possessed a spirit of capitalism essentially similar to Benjamin Franklin's. These commentators further hold that the spirit of capitalism blossomed forth exclusively out of practical interests and utilitarian business astuteness. A religious source must be seen as both superfluous and historically inaccurate, they insisted.

In endnotes added in 1919 and 1920 to *PE*, Weber counters this attack by repeating and elaborating upon his defense against the "relativizing" critics. While noting that Alberti and Fugger had accommodated to, rather than changed, the economic conditions of their time, Weber insists that the central issue here involves a distinction – pivotal for him yet unacknowledged by the critics – between means-end rational action on the one hand and value-rational action oriented to a testifying to belief on the other hand. Motives vary, he emphasizes, and the "practical-rational" approach to life is not dominant in all groupings in all historical epochs (see "PR," p. 246).

The ways in which values may motivate action was neglected by this commentary, he maintained. Indeed, a *methodical* aspect – an element indispensable for the birth of the spirit of capitalism – was *alone* introduced by action oriented to values, Weber holds. He discovers its source in the Protestant ethic. Moreover, this constellation of values proved central in a further, also unacknowledged, manner: at the foundation of this-worldly asceticism and a methodical-rational organization of life, it alone manifested the systematic intensity requisite for a shattering of the traditional economic ethic. Finally, through the spirit of capitalism, it placed into motion a significant push toward modern capitalism.

These critics neglected, in other words, *PE*'s emphasis upon the ways in which – owing to certain circumstances related to religious belief, the certainty of the salvation question, and the necessity among the devout to testify to their own salvation in their vocational callings – motives became fundamentally altered *and*, in reference to values held dear, *intensified*. Sanctified activities must be distinguished from utilitarian endeavors just for this reason, he contends: they are oriented beyond the realm of pragmatic considerations to large and crucial questions that concern one's destiny in the next life and relationship to the supernatural. The *PE* analysis and its particular *psychological* dimension cannot be fully comprehended without a recognition that motives, in this manner, are sociologically significant. This response by Weber relates directly to a further frequent criticism of *PE*.

Anxiety is Too Thin a Thread. Further critics have summarized the Protestant ethic thesis in a manner that reduces drastically its subtlety and complexity. The most frequent commentary in this regard understands Weber's answer to his query – the religious origins of the motivation to work methodically in a vocational calling – as one that focused exclusively upon the overwhelming anxiety and uncertainty caused by the Predestination doctrine.

Work, it is held, constitutes a mechanism to address this severe anxiety (*PE*, p. 125); it effectively focuses energy upon tasks given by God and hence away from anxiety regarding one's personal salvation. Commentators then ask Weber *how work* became elevated to the forefront. His putative main answer – work alleviates anxiety – has been criticized as obscure, doubtful, and incomplete. Anxiety must be seen as too thin a thread, they then insisted, to explain the Protestant ethic's origin.

However, this manner of summarizing *PE*'s argument left out too much. It omitted one of Weber's crucial points: he sought to provide an explanation for the origins of *an ethos*, that is, a "Puritan style of life." Moreover, the critics neglected the ways in which a *variety* of motives stand at the center of Weber's analysis and the context that, he stresses, sanctified work: an omnipotent, omniscient, and wrathful God possessed an array of specific wants and wishes. They omitted also his crucial distinction between these wishes and the essential revisions undertaken by Baxter and other Puritan Divines, all of which enabled believers in search of the *certitudo salutis* to move beyond their anxiety and to engage in the sanctified action that constituted to them a *sign* of membership among the elect.

Furthermore, the critics omitted discussion of the entire psychological dynamic that first pulled the devout away from the *status naturae* on the one hand and utilitarian activities on the other hand. This dynamic awarded premiums to work, profit, wealth, and the conviction by the faithful – God is "operating within" – that called forth this-worldly asceticism, the methodical-rational organization of life, and the Puritan style of life.

Finally, the critics ignored that which, according to Weber, distinguishes ascetic Protestant believers: they live *in* but not *of* the world. For this reason, a "natural" mode of living is reversed, indeed to such an extent that a trajectory toward this-worldly asceticism is then placed into motion. The anxiety of the faithful plays only a limited part in Weber's argument.

In sum, a multidimensional and dynamic tapestry characterizes the *PE* analysis. Anxiety must be understood as comprising a single link on the complex pathway that elevated work in a vocation and the search for profits and wealth to the center of believers' lives.

Historians versus Sociologists. *PE* has been discussed in depth, and for generations, by historians and sociologists alike. From this commentary, clear disciplinary patterns have emerged.

A preference for the empirically testable statement and a dislike for the sociologist's typical attention to patterns within and across large groups has been manifest among historians. In generally focusing upon *PE*'s discrete points, they have faulted Weber either for inappropriately selecting his sources or failing to offer adequate empirical evidence.

His use of a construct – the ideal type – to investigate a single case has been met with massive criticism. The generalizations Weber formed on the basis of this heuristic tool have been uniformly greeted with suspicion; exceptions to his "broad strokes" have been frequently discovered. His "errors" have then been utilized as evidence to refute his general position. In addition, many historians have failed to appreciate that Weber's study addressed the question of the origins of *modern* capitalism rather than of capitalism as such.

Sociologists, denigrated by historians as unqualified to assess Weber's research, fall at the other end of the spectrum. They have often avoided serious evaluation of Weber's specific points and focus instead upon *PE* as a treatise that provides a provocative "modernization theory."[25] Moreover, sociologists have too frequently addressed criticisms by historians regarding particular aspects of Weber's research by noting first their unawareness of his related comparative project on the economic ethics of the world religions and second their misunderstanding – or rejection – of his ideal type-based methodology and interpretive sociology of subjective meaning. These two camps, in addressing Weber's classic investigation, have starkly unveiled their lack of common ground. Gordon Marshall saw at this point a clear message: "...sociology and history must move forward together – or not at all" (1982, pp. 10–12, 133–40, 170–73).

In sum, Weber's many critics have often misunderstood and simplified his analysis.[26] Despite regular indictments, "the Weber thesis" survives to this day and must be confronted by scholars seeking to understand the rise of modern capitalism in the West. "[*PE*] has lost nothing of its power to fascinate". Indeed, its reception has expanded over the last 40 years beyond Germany, the United States, England, France, and Italy, and now extends throughout Asia. Arguably, it remains "the most famous and widely read [text] in the classical canon of sociological writing" (*PED*, p. 1). The influence of *PE* has been manifest both through its generation of studies that seek directly to test the Weber thesis and its capacity to stimulate a wide variety of research.

Notes

1 Weber fairly frequently returns to arguments formulated originally in *PE*. At times, his points are more clearly rendered in the later texts. When this occurs, reference to the later relevant passage is provided.

2 Weber uses "rational" in many ways. This usage – indicating a systematic, or methodical, aspect – is frequent. The term does not imply "better" or "superior" (see *PED*, pp. 57–72).

3 The commentary upon *PE* has frequently insisted that capitalism predated seventeenth-century Puritanism. On this point, argued originally by his critic Rachfahl in 1909 (see *PED*), Weber acknowledged his failure in *PE*'s 1904–1905 version to emphasize clearly his interest in the origins of *modern* capitalism. See Weber's response to Rachfahl (*PED*, pp. 61–88 [notes 34 and 36]). His 1919–1920 revisions added frequently "modern" in front of "capitalism." However, he was not thorough in doing so; hence, when appropriate, "modern" has been added in brackets.

4 Following Weber, the terms *modern economic ethic, rational economic ethic*, and *spirit of capitalism* will be used as synonyms. *Ethos* and *ethic* are also synonymous terms.

5 Weber's critics past and present have attacked this position repeatedly. See below, pp. 51–63.

6 In order to strengthen his argument against Sombart, Weber significantly expanded the endnotes on this theme in his 1920 revisions. These endnotes are marked. In a letter to Sombart in 1913, Weber states: "...*perhaps not a word* is correct [in your book] concerning Jewish religion" (see Scaff, 1989, p. 20, note 3). On Sombart and Weber generally, see Lehmann (1987, 1993).

7 See also, for example (*E&S*, pp. 70, 341, 480, 577, 630; *PED*, pp. 31, 171); Otsuka (1976). Sombart supported also this Marxian analysis. Weber's rejection in *PE* of "developmental laws" (or "laws of economic development") as explanations for historical change is directed against Marx, though also against an array of German and English scholars.

8 These themes are rarely discussed in *PE*. They appear in numerous passages throughout Weber's other writings (see, e.g., *GEH*, pp. 352–54; *E&S*, p. 1180). His rejection of such causal forces as alone adequate constitutes a foundational point of departure for his Economic Ethics of the World Religions series (see Chapter 6).

9 These positions were central in the debate on the origin of modern capitalism during Weber's time. In *PE*, he also argued against minor streams

in this ongoing controversy (especially in the endnotes added in 1920), such as Lamprecht's biology-based evolutionary determinism (p. 352, note 133), all proponents of "national character" (pp. 106–07), the many theorists who understood social change as resulting from changes in laws, and finally, Hegelians who viewed ideas as causal forces. Weber insists that Hegelians neglected the crucial questions. Did social carriers crystallize to bear the ideas? Did they exist as cognitive forces only? Or did ideas also place "psychological premiums" upon action. See Kalberg (2021) *et passim.*

10 A pamphlet written in 1887 by Weber's uncle, the Reformation and Counter-Reformation historian Hermann Baumgarten, who was very close to his nephew, notes this theme in a vivid passage: "Where Protestants and Catholics live together, the former occupy predominantly the higher, the latter the lower rungs of society....Where the Catholic population flees higher education or cannot attain it, the Protestants must inevitably gain a considerable lead in public administration, justice, commerce, industry, and science" (Marcks, p. 16).

11 Weber deleted this remark when he revised *PE* in 1919–1920. It appeared originally in the second installment (1905) of *PE*.

12 Chapter 1 of *PE* borrows its title "Religious Affiliation and Social Stratification" from Offenbacher's book.

13 On the background to the writing of *PE*, see Lehmann and Roth (1993). Weber's interest in this theme extends at least back to a lecture course offered in 1898.

14 Weber resists quantification of this influence (see *PED*, p. 120). For Weber's restatement of this aim at the end of *PE*, see pp. 176–78. See also pp. 78–82, 96–98, 107–09, 114–15. See further the numerous statements in the essays in response to his early critics. Here, Weber restates his goal in *PED*; see pp, 163, 169, 173, 286. Many of these passages illustrate his awareness of the multiplicity of causes for historical developments as well as the necessity to view single factors contextually (see Kalberg, 1994, pp. 39–45, 98–102, 168–76). Fischoff's formation of Weber's aim is succinct: "Weber's limited thesis was merely that in the formation of this pattern of rationally ordered life,...the religiouscomponent must be considered as an important factor" (1944, p. 63).

15 This is nearly a literal rendering. See (*PE*, pp. 106–09).

16 "[The effect of] the stricture against consumption with this unchaining of the striving for wealth [led to] the formation of capital....[which] became used as investment capital...Of course, the strength of this effect cannot be determined exactly in quantitative terms" (*PED*, p. 120; emphasis original; see also p. 391, note 97).

17 This theme will be visited at various points throughout this volume.

18 Significantly, the value-rational action – the spirit of capitalism – of Franklin is oriented as the Protestant ethic, *both* to individuals (their salvation status in the ascetic Protestant groups) *and* to a community, while the means-end rational action of the individual entrapped within

the "powerful cosmos" of industrial capitalism is oriented merely to the individual's survival. For recent discussions of this significant shift, see Bellah et al. (1985), Etzioni (1997 and 1998), Hall and Lindholm (1999), Putnam (2000), and Chapters 7–9.

19 See the listing below of studies dedicated to this debate (note 26). Marshall's (1982) volume is by far the most ambitious.

20 Zaret calls this debate "the longest-running in modern social science" (see 1994, p. 245).

21 Themes will be our focus here rather than a discussion organized either chronologically or in terms of major players. The criticisms against Weber have been ordered differently by Sprinzak (1972) and Nelson (1973, p. 84).

22 Hence, Weber's response to Rachfahl: "This is not my theme" (see *PED*, p. 100).

23 Weber stressed that the spirit of capitalism has many origins; *PE* constitutes simply its major *religious* source (see pp. 48–49). Further, modern capitalism's rise does not unequivocally require, he argues, either the presence of a Protestant ethic or its "functional equivalent" (as many interpreters believed in the 1950s and 1960s). His goal in the post-*PE* series on the economic ethics of Hinduism, Buddhism, and Jainism in India and Confucianism and Taoism in China is to understand the reasons behind the development of *modern* capitalism *earlier* in the West than in India or China. See Kalberg (2021, pp. 173–200).

24 Nelson notes that "the many criticism of Weber by unsympathetic American church historians can readily be shown to go far beyond the evidence" (1973, p. 97).

25 Some sociologists have been engaged in historical-sociological work that takes a pathway "between" the two groups. See, for example, the classical studies by Bendix (1956); more recently, see Kaelber (1998), and Gorski (2003).

26 Writing more than 60 years ago, Fischoff came to the same conclusion (see 1944, pp. 57–59, 71–73). More recently, Nelson (1973, pp. 77–85), Marshall (1982, pp. 9–12, 168–73) agree. After his wide-ranging review of the controversy, Marshall holds that the entire debate has "been dogged from the outset by the grinding of particular religious, political, or theoretical axes; by a widespread tendency to oversimplify Weber's argument through increasing reliance on inaccurate secondary expositions of it and by the routine employment of certain rhetorical devices...in order to disguise intellectual and empirical weaknesses..." (1982, p. 169). He sees both sociologists and historians as emerging from this controversy with little credibility in tact (p. 171).

4

AMERICAN SOCIOLOGY'S NEGLECT OF *THE PROTESTANT ETHIC* AS A THEORETICAL TREATISE

Demarcating the Parameters of Postwar American Sociological Theory

Max Weber's *The Protestant Ethic and the Spirit of Capitalism* has been recognized for more than 90 years as one of sociology's few true classics. Its acclaimed analysis regarding the rise of a "spirit" of capitalism immediately called forth an intense controversy (see *PED*). Scarcely interrupted, debate over "the Weber thesis" has endured to this day.[1]

However, *The Protestant Ethic* offers much more than an analysis of the origins of a modern economic ethos and even much more than a study of the manner in which ideas influenced the unfolding of modern capitalism in the West. Written by one of the discipline's major founding theorists, this classic must be comprehended as well in terms of its many theoretical contributions to sociology. *The Protestant Ethic* addresses, for example, the relationships between history and sociology, tradition and social change, economic interests and cultural forces, capitalism and values, micro and macro levels of analysis, past and present, and individual action and social groupings. Curiously, although all these familiar themes stand at the foundation of central controversies in postwar American sociology, *The Protestant Ethic* has scarcely influenced these debates.

This study examines *The Protestant Ethic* through the lens of four familiar controversies in postwar American sociological theory. Doing so not only allows the contrasts and comparisons indispensable for a precise identification of its theoretical contributions, but also fulfills

DOI: 10.4324/9781032631813-6

a further purpose: to demarcate a number of major parameters of postwar American sociological theory. Hence, this investigation offers a new perspective upon *The Protestant Ethic*, and in calling attention to its expansive theoretical capital, seeks to throw into clear relief the unique contours and dichotomies of American sociological theory.

The conclusion addresses the puzzling fact that Weber's *Protestant Ethic*, despite the massive attention accorded to it as a study of the "role of ideas" in economic development, has never been understood in the United States as a multifaceted contribution to sociological theory. I ask whether the widespread neglect of this volume's theoretical capital can be understood in part by reference to the major parameters of sociological theory in America. Were theorists in the United States engaged in a style of theorizing that, in a sense, precluded acknowledgment of this classic's theoretical lessons? If so, for what reasons?

Four major debates are examined: the critique of structural functionalism by conflict theory in the late 1950s and by neo-Marxist theories in the 1960s; the debate between comparative-historical schools and structural functionalist modernization theory in the 1970s; the opposition of the sociology of culture to comparative-historical perspectives in the 1980s; and the debate between rational choice theorists and sociologists of culture, on the one hand, and structural sociologists, on the other, that commenced in the late 1980s and endures to the present.[2] The discussion of each controversy follows a common format: a brief summary of the theoretical debate in American sociology; a more extensive examination of the potential theoretical contributions of *The Protestant Ethic* to the debate; and a brief assessment of *The Protestant Ethic*'s actual influence upon each debate.

4.1 The First Major Debate: Conflict Theory versus Structural Functionalism

The first major debate involved a broad critique of the dominant school in the 1940s and 1950s – structural functionalism – by conflict theory in the late 1950s and neo-Marxist theories in the 1960s. Structural functionalism was attacked for downplaying power, rulership, conflict, social change, economic interests, and class.

Of course, the relative neglect of these central aspects of social life was not accidental; rather, it followed directly from a Durkheimian understanding of societies as basically unified and holistic. This societal organicism emphasized, especially in the works of Parsons, the "functional prerequisites" of social order, the harmonious inter-locking of societal sectors and "systems," slow and gradual change, and "equilibrium" as the normal state of societies – at the expense of those aspects noted above. The criticisms of structural functionalism by Conflict theorists and neo-Marxists were powerful, and sociolo-gists in the United States today generally accept them as legitimate.

How does *The Protestant Ethic* address societal organicism? Is its analysis compatible with a mode of theorizing that acknowledges the significance of power, rulership, class, social change, conflict, and eco-nomic interests?

First, *The Protestant Ethic* does not focus upon "society" as an organic unity or upon a particular "society" that calls forth mod-ern capitalism. Rather, a demarcated societal domain or sphere of life (*Lebensordnung, Lebensbereich, Lebensphäre*) – the domain of religion – and developments taking place within it captures Weber's attention. The manner in which a specific religious doctrine influences action is his focus, especially action oriented to the economy. Weber never views societies as organic and holistic entities with delineated boundaries. The centrality of societal domains – which immediately distinguishes his sociology from structural functionalism – becomes directly manifest in Weber's criticism of his colleague Werner Sombart (see *PE*, pp. 95–98).[3]

Weber contests Sombart's view that the development of the funda-mental feature of modern capitalism – its "economic rationalism" – can be explained by reference to a general, all-encompassing, and evolu-tionary growth of "rationalism" in Western societies. A *nonparallel* "rationalization" in *various* domains of action has occurred in the West, according to Weber. For example, rationalization in the domain of law – increasing conceptual clarity and the differentiation of the content of the law based upon a fundamental written source, such as a Constitution – reached its highest point in the Roman Law of later antiquity, and remained far less developed in a number of countries where a rationalization of the economy advanced farthest, most obvi-ously in England where Common Law prevailed.

On the other hand, Roman Law remained strong throughout Southern Europe, an area where modern capitalism developed quite late. Such observations persuaded Weber to focus his attention on a variety of societal domains rather than "society" as an organic unity, for example, religion in *The Protestant Ethic* and later in *Economy and Society*, the law, rulership, economy, religion, status groups, and "universal organizations" (the family, the clan) domains (see Kalberg, 1994, pp. 53–54, 103–17).

However, Weber opposes societal organicism in *The Protestant Ethic* in a further manner: his investigation of the religion societal domain emphasizes the role of "social carriers" (*soziale Träger*). Such carriers of patterned action oriented to interests, values, and traditions (see Kalberg, 1994, pp. 50–78, 103–04), that is, primarily status groups and organizations, were central to him, not "society" and least of all "society" as an organic unity comprised of putatively integrated "subsystems" (see Parsons, 1951; Parsons and Shils, 1951; Parsons and Smelser, 1956).

This pivotal aspect of Weber's sociology is already apparent in his emphasis in *The Protestant Ethic* upon two organizations: ascetic Protestant churches and sects. Both "carried" patterns of social action oriented to values. Indeed, even though he takes the individual's social action as the basic unit of his sociology, the question "within what carrier status group or organization social action occurs" remains fundamental in all his studies. For Weber, the social action of individuals becomes sociologically significant action *only* when located in demarcated groups of individuals (see *PE*, pp. 81–82; *E&S*, pp. 48–50, 52–53, 302–07, 356–69, 468–518, 926–39, 941–1211; "I," pp. 268–69).

Thus, Weber again rejects a mode of analysis that focuses upon society – its holism, organic unity, and interconnecting "systems" – and the question of social order. Even in *The Protestant Ethic* as well as *Economy and Society* and the Economic Ethics of the World Religions series (see *RofC*, *RofI*, *AJ*, "I,"; "IR"), empirical social reality is, for Weber, always tenuously constituted from continuously moving social carriers jockeying for position against a series of other social carriers. Continuous fluctuation – here a new coalition, there competition and struggle – characterizes social reality for Weber.

The emphasis in *The Protestant Ethic* upon societal domains and social carriers naturally and easily provokes questions regarding the circumstances under which social carriers compete and clash, as well as an acknowledgment, when the outcomes of these conflicts are examined, of power and rulership. Moreover, Weber's attention in *The Protestant Ethic* to societal domains and social carriers and their relationships to one another, not to mention the entire dynamic placed into motion by Calvinism and then Puritanism, leads also to a concern with social change.

Indeed, a view of social reality that includes power, rulership, conflict, and social change was embraced in the 1960s and the 1970s American sociology after a long concern with Parsonsian "system requisites," "normative orders," and "societal integration."[4] Yet, Weber's *Protestant Ethic* exercised no discernable influence upon the conflict theorists who articulated this criticism against structural functionalism. Indeed, the entire debate ignored this classic text.

4.2 The Second Major Debate: Comparative-Historical Sociology versus Structural Functionalism Modernization Theory

A second major debate appeared in American sociology in the mid-1960s and endured for more than a decade. Intense criticism was again directed against structural functionalism and in particular against its modernization theorists. These opponents, however, focused upon its general downplaying of history.

The emphasis of structural functionalism upon "system needs," the "functions of institutions," and the "prerequisites of social order" was condemned strongly as implying a static mode of analysis that attended to the immediate present alone. It thereby neglected the impact of the past upon the present: an illegitimate banning of historical development from sociology was lamented. Moreover, the dichotomies of this school – tradition and modernity, particularism and universalism, ascription and achievement, specificity and diffuseness, and function and dysfunction – were all viewed as too global and nonempirical to be able to conceptualize the complex and pulsating flow of history. Its evolutionary assumptions, apparent in its major "differentiation," "adaptive upgrading," and "value generalization" concepts, became suspect for the same reason.

Less "general theory" and more historically grounded case studies were demanded. Loosely knit groupings of neo-Marxian, neo-Weberian, and Braudellian comparative-historical and historical sociologists congealed. All heeded a call to "bring history into sociology," whether more influenced by Immanuel Wallerstein's world-systems theory

(1974, 1979, 1980, 1984, 1989), Barrington Moore's neo-Marxism (1966), Skocpol (1979); see also Skocpol and Somers (1980), Reinhard Bendix's neo-Weberian studies (1956, 1978), and Charles Tilly's narrative works (1964, 1978).

What are *The Protestant Ethic*'s theoretical contributions to this debate? Weber adamantly refused to separate history from sociology. Indeed, history was indispensable to sociological explanation in this case study.[5] He scrupulously avoids all abstract, nonempirical formulations and concepts, rejects any concern with "system prerequisites" and "the question of social order," and offers an empirically informed analysis.[6]

Weber's stress in *The Protestant Ethic* upon social carriers of value-oriented action, means-end-oriented action, and tradition-oriented action had pushed him in this direction. He not only identified a variety of carriers of patterned action, but also emphasized that some were always more powerful than others: some fade quickly, others survive longer periods, indeed far beyond the epochs of their origin. Furthermore, some fade and then, owing to an alteration of *contextual* forces, become reinvigorated, influential, and long-lasting.

This is not surprising in light of Weber's dynamic view of empirical social reality as comprised of multiple and competing status groups and organizations. At times, coalitions are formed; at other times, these carriers are clearly antagonistic. Puritanism, the major carrier of the Protestant ethic in the United States, illustrates how patterned social action changes its carrier status group or organization and in doing so, survives into a subsequent epoch, influencing it distinctly and substantively.

Weber's magisterial concluding passages – "...the idea of an obligation to search for and then accept a 'vocational calling' now wanders around in our lives as the ghost of past religious beliefs" and capitalism, "ever since it came to rest on a mechanical foundation, no longer needs asceticism as a supporting pillar" (*PE*, p. 177) – imply that he understood Puritanism in the contemporary epoch as banished fully by secularization and the sheer external constraints indigenous to industrialization. Were this the case, Weber's analysis could be correctly captured by reference to a "tradition/modernity" dichotomy; an inventory of the "system needs" of the "modern society" could then be offered. However, although Weber believed that ascetic Protestantism had in a certain sense died out, his strong focus upon several intermediate stages renders any such dichotomy a clear misrepresentation of his analysis. How is this the case?

Weber argues in the above passages that the religious roots of ethical action had been weakened and even abolished. Long before this occurred, however, the ethical values of religious origin "migrated" from their original carriers – ascetic Protestant churches and sects – to another carrier organization: Protestant families. Consequently, these values re-remained central in childhood socialization. In a manner heretofore scarcely imaginable,[7] children were taught to revere upward mobility, heroic individual achievement, self-reliance, honesty and fair play in business transactions, the just price, ascetic personal habits, methodical work, and hard competition.

They were socialized as well to oppose worldly authority, avoid all ostentatious display, and distrust the state (see *PE*, pp. 158–79). Even as they gradually lost their explicitly religious roots through secularization and industrialization, these values became firmly anchored in the family and were taught in intimate, personal relationships to children. In other words, they were cultivated further – or carried – by this organization as binding ethical values and hence continued to influence social action.[8]

Thus, action-orientations toward a set of values originally cultivated in ascetic Protestant sects and churches survived and endured in a more secularized epoch, long after these sects and churches had become weakened. Indeed, and even though their religious ancestry is seldom acknowledged, the values of the ascetic Protestant "sect spirit" have remained integral in the United States to this day: a self-reliant individualism, a distrust of the state (especially the strong state), unambivalent support of capitalism, an orientation to the future and the "opportunities" it offers, a traditional intolerance of perceived evil, a high rate of regular giving to charity organizations, and a strong belief in the capacity of individuals to set goals, shape their own destinies, and even to be upwardly mobile (see *PE*, pp. 158–79; Kalberg, 2012, pp. 227–48).[9]

Hence, Weber refused in *The Protestant Ethic* to conduct sociological analysis by reference either to the immediate present alone or to abstract concepts. On the contrary, this empirically anchored ideal types and his focus upon the social carriers of patterned action both rejected in principle all modes of analysis based upon a disjunction of past and present and offered procedures that unveiled and explicated their interwovenness. Indeed, he insisted in *The Protestant Ethic* and elsewhere that cognizance of a historical dimension was necessary to understand the present: the past penetrates deeply into the present.

Because very few sociologically significant developments, Weber argues, have ever died out fully, recourse to an immediate present of "system needs," "functional prerequisites," and "the question of social order" can serve sociological analysis only in a preliminary manner (see *E&S*, pp. 14–18). Even when lacking strong carriers in the present, past sociologically significant developments leave *legacies* that can become influential. This occurs especially when social carriers for them appear as a result of universal organizations shifting configurations of forces related to the economy, rulership, law, status groups, religion, and domains.

The principled intertwining of past and present in *The Protestant Ethic* contrasts sharply with the general neglect of history by structural functionalists, nearly all of whom examine societies ahistorically. Their sharp present/past disjunction, global and nonempirical categories, and evolutionary assumptions were sharply denounced by comparative-historical sociologists in the 1970s. Many American sociologists then began widely to acknowledge the interlocking of past and present and to formulate empirically based comparative-historical procedures oriented to the investigation of specific historical cases. Yet none of these comparative-historical sociologists took their cues from *The Protestant Ethic*. On the contrary, the theoretical contribution of this classic text was again neglected and had no impact upon this major debate.

4.3 The Third Major Debate: The Sociology of Culture versus Comparative-Historical Sociology

By the early 1980s, criticism was no longer directed against structural functionalism. Rather, the various neo-Marxist and structuralist comparative-historical sociologists of the 1960s and 1970s, all of whom had opposed structural functionalism, were now judged as having omitted a crucial causal dimension: culture. World-systems theorists focus upon the power of the international economy to influence domestic political and economic development and the interests of economic and political actors in the core: Barrington Moore saw classes, class structures, and the interests of ruling classes as central;

Skocpol's state-centered theory emphasized national politics and the capacity of the state to act independently.

All these approaches failed to acknowledge a clear causal capacity for values and beliefs. A loud clamor rang out across the discipline critical of these perspectives: "bring culture in" (see, e.g., Swidler, 1986). However, this transformation could not take place in the organicist, amorphous, and ahistorical manner heretofore advocated by the structural functionalists.[10]

The theoretical capital of *The Protestant Ethic* supports strongly the call to retrieve culture. Unlike the neo-Marxist and structuralist comparative-historical sociologists of the 1960s and 1970s, Weber argues that empirical social reality unequivocally includes a sociologically significant cultural dimension. This dimension can never be conceptualized as merely passive, reacted upon by economic and political forces. Noting the unusually methodical work habits of young women from Pietistic families and the high percentage of Protestants who elected a business-oriented education (see *PE*, pp. 67–75), *The Protestant Ethic* argues forcefully that a sociology limited to social structures on the one hand or economic interests and power on the other hand is theoretically inadequate.

At the outset, Weber rejects the assumption that the origins of an "economic ethic" – the "traditional" economic ethic[11] on the one hand or the spirit of capitalism on the other hand – can be explained by reference to social structures. For him, even external structures of rigidity, such as those typical of religious and political sects, let alone the factory, fail to call forth homogeneous patterns of action. The Calvinist, Methodist, Pietist, and Baptist sects all advocated distinct doctrines, as did sects in India (see *PE*, pp. 115–57; "I," p. 292). The same must be said of churches as well as, Weber is convinced, strata[12] and classes (see *PE*, pp. 95–96).[13]

He saw diverse possibilities in regard to, for example, the "economic form" of capitalism and the traditional and rational "economic ethics": the traditional ethic might combine with a highly developed capitalist economy (Italian capitalism before the Reformation) or with irrational capitalism (the medieval textile entrepreneur) and the rational economic ethic – the spirit of capitalism – might appear in combination with either modern capitalism (nineteenth-century laissez-faire and industrial capitalism) or without a modern capitalist economy (the printing business of Benjamin Franklin, the Quaker sects in eighteenth-century Pennsylvania (see *PE*, pp. 88–91, 95–96; *E&S*, p. 480).

Precisely such observations convinced Weber of the complex relations between social structures and constellations of values; they underpin the entire organization of *The Protestant Ethic*. Most important, they led directly to conclusions about the origins of *modern* capitalism.[14] After comparing the widespread capitalism in Florence in the fourteenth and fifteenth centuries (where activity directed toward profit for its own sake was viewed as ethically unjustifiable) with the economic backwardness of eighteenth-century Pennsylvania (where a "spirit" of capitalism was "considered the essence of moral conduct, even commanded in the name of duty"), Weber argued, in this "positive critique of historical materialism," that capitalism alone – or its dominant class – could not have given birth to a "spirit" of capitalism (see *PE*, e.g., pp. 81–82, 86, 88–89, 95–96; 369, note 225; "PR," pp. 246–50; *E&S*, pp. 70, 480, 630). He then investigated whether cultural forces, such as the orientation of action to certain religious doctrines, might be causally significant in respect to the origins of the "spirit" of capitalism.

The very core of *The Protestant Ethic*'s major argument calls attention to the centrality of cultural factors in a further manner. Weber did not seek in this study to explain the origins of modern capitalism or capitalism in general; rather, his project was more modest. He argued vehemently that the sources of that form of capitalism of interest to him – *modern* capitalism in the West – could not be comprehended fully without cognizance of a spirit of capitalism or "*modern* economic ethic" (*PE*, pp. 88–89; see, e.g., p. 108). The purpose of his study was to investigate the specific ancestry of this "spirit" (see *PE*, pp. 79, 95–98, 108–09; see Weber, 1972, pp. 302–07).

This central aim opposed the evolutionists of his time, all of whom saw the rise of modern capitalism as an inevitable outgrowth of the general, society-wide unfolding of "progress" (*PE*, pp. 96–98). It also opposed the economists and historians who explained modern capitalism simply as a consequence of gradually increasing economic exchange, trade, mercantilism, commerce, and the development of banking, commercial law, and new technologies (*PE*, pp. 79, 95–96; 1972, pp. 323–24; *GEH*, pp. 352–56).

Vehemently rejecting both explanations, Weber argues that the origin of modern capitalism in the West cannot be fully understood without reference to a new ethos and conduct of life (*Lebensfuehrung*)[15] – a new *set of values*. According to this "rational economic ethic":[16] the "idea of the *duty* of the individual toward the increase of his capital" became an end in itself (*PE*, p. 79; emphasis in original; see also pp. 80–82), as did the systematic, rational pursuit of profit. After citing numerous passages from Benjamin Franklin, who represents the "spirit" of capitalism in a pure form (see *PE*, 76–79), Weber notes that he has here discovered an *ethos*, and "its violation is treated not simply as foolishness but as a sort of forgetfulness of *duty*" (*PE*, p. 79; emphasis in original).[17]

This ethos, Weber argues, had clear noneconomic and nonpolitical, namely, religious, roots. *The Protestant Ethic* discovered these roots neither in the power of a specific class nor in "social structures," "society" as such, or sweeping evolutionary developments, but alone in the religious beliefs of delineated groupings of individuals: the ascetic Protestant churches and sects, especially the seventeenth-century Puritanism formulated by the English minister Richard Baxter. This classic case study reconstructed the anxieties, beliefs, and values of an ideal-typical Puritan in such a way that the *subjective meaningfulness* to this believer of methodical, intense work became plausible and "understandable" to the social scientist, however "irrational," strange, and suspect it may appear from the vantage point of the secularized modern (see *PE*, p. 178 and 1972, p. 33) and Catholic medieval epochs (see *PE*, pp. 95–96) as well as to all Eastern religions (see "PR," p. 245; "IR," pp. 325–26).

Thus, *The Protestant Ethic* offered a notion of culture that recognized the religious realm's independent causal significance while avoiding the holistic, amorphous, and nonempirical concept of culture advocated particularly by Parsonsian structural functionalism. It opposes directly all approaches, such as World-systems theory and the state-centered perspective, that emphasize economic interests, power, and political hegemony at the expense of cultural forces and supports strongly the attempt in the 1980s to "bring culture in." Again, this major debate, too, was uninfluenced by *The Protestant Ethic*. Indeed, the theoretical contributions of this classic were totally neglected.

4.4 The Fourth Major Debate: Rational Choice Theory versus the Sociology of Culture and All Schools of Social Structures

The recent ascendance of rational choice theory to a strong position in American sociology (see, e.g., Coleman, 1990; Hechter, 1987; Friedman and Hechter, 1988, 1990; Cook, 1990; Kiser and Hechter, 1991) has led to a fourth major debate. Rational choice theory opposes two significant perspectives in the discipline, one of recent vintage – the emphasis upon culture that arose in the 1980s – and one of older provenance: sociology's long-term focus upon social structure, whether indebted more to the Durkheimian or Marxian traditions.

At first glance, Weber might appear to share a great deal with rational choice theorists. Like him, this school departs from single actors and the manner in which they perceive the world. It attempts then to understand action from the actor's point of view. However, the fundamental difference – aside from the fact that Weber links his "microsociology" unequivocally to a "macrosociology" that emphasizes social contexts (see Kalberg, 1994, pp. 39–46, 98–102, 168–77) – lies in how this action is conceptualized. According to rational choice theorists, actors are fundamentally calculators of gains and losses, advantages and disadvantages – and little more. They choose one course of action over another by undertaking cost-benefit analyses. In other words, the rational choice school theorizes by reference to only one of Weber's four types of social action: means-end rational (*zweckrationales*) action.

Long before he defined these types of action in the "Basic Concepts" chapter of *Economy and Society* (pp. 3–62), Weber offered an analysis in *The Protestant Ethic* of the *spirit* of capitalism's origins that rested upon plural types of social action. Moreover, his central argument cannot be comprehended without acknowledging a further foundational assumption that separates him again from rational choice theory: the types of social action are not of equal *intensity*. The opposition of *The Protestant Ethic* to rational choice theory becomes apparent only if major aspects of Weber's argument are scrutinized.

The Protestant Ethic opposes rational choice theory in a fundamental manner. Weber holds that, as stated most succinctly in the "Basic Concepts" chapter of *Economy and Society*, most action is not rational. Rather, "in the great majority of cases actual action goes on in a state of inarticulate half-consciousness or actual unconsciousness of its subjective meaning [and] in most cases ... action is governed by impulse or habit" (*E&S*, p. 21; emphasis in original). Thus, according to Weber, "rational action" must be understood alone as a heuristic device, one that helps the researcher *conceptualize* "actual" social action – through comparison – rather than, as for rational choice theorists, as empirical action itself.

Weber's four types of social action, including the value-rational and means-end rational types of action, constitute ideal types or models rather than empirical reality, as is action for rational choice theorists. Moreover, Weber's mode of conceptualizing action, unlike that of rational choice theorists, enables acknowledgment of the rarity of *some* rational action, such as the Puritan's methodical action. Rational choice theorists, on the other hand, able to see rational action only in terms either of its expansion into arrays of groups or circumscription, deny the possibility of a rational action that is qualitatively unusual.

In investigating the sources of the spirit of capitalism – the "idea of the *duty* of the individual to increase his wealth, which is assumed to be a self-defined interest in itself" (*PE*, p. 79; emphasis in original); the notion that "labor is an absolute end in itself, or a 'calling'" (*PE*, p. 86):

> ...the view that the "acquisition of money, and more and more money, takes place...simultaneously with the strictest avoidance of all spontaneous enjoyment of it....[and] is the result and the expression of virtue and proficiency in a calling (*PE*, pp. 80–81) and a frame of mind) that, *in a calling*, strives rationally and systematically for legitimate profit. (*PE*, p. 88; emphasis in original)"

This frame of mind places Weber's mode of analysis explicitly in opposition to all explanations resting upon a linear "proliferation" of means-end rational action.

The shattering of the traditional economic ethic required a qualitatively different type of action, one more systematic and intense than means-end rational action oriented to economic interests and profit making alone. After all, the desire for and pursuit of wealth, trade, and commerce, Weber reasoned, have been apparent universally (*PE*, pp. 83–84; see "PR," pp. 236–37), but "economic rationalism" arose exclusively in one civilization and one epoch. The indispensable *methodical* orientation toward work could be provided, according to Weber, only by *value*-rational action: it alone proved able to uproot the traditional economic ethic.

Weber discovered "psychological rewards" for this value-rational action in the "world-oriented ethos" overt in the Westminster Confession (1647). It was also apparent in the sermons of a Puritan successor of John Calvin: Richard Baxter. For Weber, Baxter's alterations of Calvin's teachings sought above all to banish the bleak conclusions rationally implied by his "doctrine of Predestination": If the question of salvation constituted the burning question to believers (see *PE*, 123–25),[18] if the "salvation status" of the faithful was preordained from the very beginning, and if God had selected only a tiny minority to be saved, massive fatalism, despair, loneliness, and anxiety among the devout logically followed (see *PE*, pp. 115–22; note 76, pp. 337–39). As Calvin's sect of "virtuosi" developed into large groupings in churches and as the original fervor and inspiration of the first generations of the faithful waned, these consequences of the Predestination decree became more unbearable. Baxter knew well that the harshness of this doctrine precluded its continued endorsement by most believers (see *PE*, p. 124).[19]

Accordingly, Baxter undertook a revision that, Weber argues, launched the Protestant ethic.[20] Along with Calvin, Baxter recognized that the mortal and weak devout cannot know God's judgment, for the motives of this majestic, distant, and almighty deity of the Old Testament remain incomprehensible to lowly terrestrial inhabitants (*PE*, pp. 117–19). However, that "the world exists to serve the glorification of God" (*PE*, p. 122) and that God wishes His Kingdom to be one of wealth, equality, and prosperity cannot be doubted, for abundance among "His children" would surely praise His goodness and justice. The "City on the Hill" must be built by believers *in majorem gloriam Dei* (see *PE*, pp. 160, 169).

Understood as a means toward the creation of God's earthly community, regular and dedicated work – or "work in a calling" – now acquired a religious significance. Hence, among the devout, it became subjectively meaningful. Whether workers or entrepreneurs, believers comprehended their worldly social and economic activity as *in service to* a demanding God, and they could view themselves as noble instruments or "tools" (*PE*, pp. 135–36) of His commandments and

His Divine Plan: "Labor... in the service of all impersonal societal usefulness to promote the glory of God – and hence to be recognized as desired by Him" (*PE*, p. 123; see also pp. 122–23, 126–27; 377, note 39; *E&S*, p. 546). As Weber notes, work in a calling "is commanded [by God] to all" (*PE*, p. 377, note 39). To him, "the entire ascetic corpus of literature...is highly pleasing to God" (*PE*, p. 175).

Indeed, those believers *capable* of systematic work on behalf of God's Plan could convince themselves that their strength to do so emanated from the favoring Hand of an omnipotent God – and the believer could conclude, God would favor only those he had chosen to be among the predestined: "...the religious value placed upon tireless, continuous, and systematic work in a vocational calling was defined [by the Puritans] as absolutely the highest of all ascetic means for believers to testify to their elect status" (*PE*, p. 170; see also *E&S*, p. 573).

Moreover, according to Baxter, continuous and systematic work possessed an undeniable virtue for the good Christian: it tames the creaturely and base side of human nature and thereby facilitates the concentration of the mind upon God and the "uplifting" of the soul (*PE*, pp. 160–61). Finally, "intense worldly activity" also counteracts the penetrating doubt, anxiety, and sense of unworthiness induced by the Predestination doctrine and instills the self-confidence that allows believers to consider themselves among the chosen (see *PE*, pp. 124–25). In this manner, systematic work as well as the "systematic rational formation of the believer's ethical life" (*PE*, p. 136) became hallowed: "Unusually capable of working, these employees attached themselves to their labor, for they understood it as bestowing a purpose on life that was desired by God" (*PE*, p. 174).

However, Weber argues that the singular power of the Protestant ethic to upset the traditional economic ethic originated in other ways besides these, especially if one wishes to understand the "constant self-control" and "methodical rationalization of life" (*PE*, pp. 136–38) of entrepreneurs. A further adjustment by Baxter of Calvin's Predestination doctrine proved significant as well.

Although believers, according to the Predestination doctrine, could never *know* their salvation status, they could logically conclude, in light of God's desire for an earthly kingdom of abundance to serve His glory, that the actual production of great wealth for a community by an individual could be viewed as a sign that God favored this individual. In effect, personal wealth itself became to the faithful actual *evidence*

(*Merkmal*) of their salvation status. Omnipotent and omniscient, God surely would never allow one of the condemned to praise His Glory, yet "...the acquisition of [wealth], when it was the *fruit* of work in a vocational calling, was a sign of God's blessing" (*PE*, p. 170; emphasis in original; see also "Sects II," p. 226; *E&S*, pp. 1199–200).[21] In His universe, nothing happened by chance.[22]

Thus, although the devout could never be certain of their membership among the elect, more business-oriented believers could seek to produce the evidence – literally, wealth and profit[23] – that alone would convince them of their "chosen" religious status. Weber emphasizes that a psychological certainty of salvation is the crucial issue. Baxter's revisions allowed the business-oriented faithful to understand the accumulation of wealth, and its reinvestment for the betterment of God's community,[24] as tangible proof of their chosen status:

> ...religious asceticism gave to the employer the soothing assurance that the unequal distribution of the world's material goods resulted from the special design of God's providence. In making such distinctions, as well as in deciding who should be among the chosen few, God pursued mysterious aims unknown to terrestrial mortals. (*PE*, p. 174; see also pp. 394–95, note 117)

Riches now acquired among believers, uniquely, a religious significance: because they constituted signs that indicated[25] one's membership among the elect, they lost their traditionally suspect character and became endowed with a positive "psychological premium." Methodical work became viewed as the most adequate means toward great wealth.

In view of the unbearable anxiety provoked by the central religious question – "am I among the saved?" – in sixteenth- and seventeenth-century England, a psychological certainty mattered most. On the one hand, the believer's sheer capacity to "lead... a life organized around ethical principles" oriented to work in a calling could establish this certainty; on the other hand, great wealth could do so. In this manner, a set of work-oriented values heretofore scorned (see *PE*, pp. 82–83, 95–96) became central in the lives of the devout and even called forth a *methodical-rational* conduct of life. Weber vehemently argues that not the desire for riches or adaptation to economic forces, but only work motivated "from within" by an "internally binding" set of religious values was empowered to introduce a "systematization of ethical conduct" (*PE*, p. 134) and a "deliberate regulation of one's own life" on behalf of work (*PE*, pp. 136–37). This *ethical*[26] *conduct of life rooted in values* alone was endowed with the sheer methodicalness and intensity necessary for an uprooting and banishing of the traditional economic ethic.

Hence, Weber's argument in *The Protestant Ethic* rests upon a theoretical framework grounded in plural models of social action. The origin of a methodical-rational life that places work at its center cannot be comprehended as simply a manifestation of the universal desire for great wealth and its means-end rational pursuit, as rational choice theorists would argue, or even a putative accentuation of this desire as a consequence of greater trade, new banking techniques, or new technologies. Rather, the critical ethical aspect of this activity lay in the radical orientation of believers beyond all practical and economic concerns to the supernatural.

The *certitudo salutis* question suffused the consciousness of the devout thoroughly and thus uprooted them internally from all immediate concerns. Remarkably, the obsession with the religious question in Baxter's Puritanism – "am I among the saved?" – had the unique and unexpected effect of radically organizing and focusing action in the world: the crucial issue of salvation could never be addressed by this Calvinist through a withdrawal from the world, but only through worldly, particularly economic, activity. God's glory – the mastery of the world (*Weltbeherrschung*) on behalf of His sacred aims – deserved nothing less. Puritan believers "sought to reorganize practical life into a rational life *in* the world rather than, as earlier, in the monastery. Yet this rational life in the world was *not of* this world or *for* this world" (*PE*, p. 157; emphasis in original; translation altered; see also pp. 129–30; 373, note 20).[27]

Thus, far from merely a pragmatic, means-end rational and "naive affirmation of the world," as widespread in Antiquity and lay Catholicism (see "I," p. 291), the economic activity of the Calvinist must be understood as motivated by and steadfastly oriented to a religious ethic of conviction (*Gesinnungsethik*) – and hence, given the urgent and all-encompassing character of the question of salvation, as far more intense and focused than sheer practical activity.[28] This extreme focus implied to Weber a conduct of life and an "inner-worldly asceticism" in which all natural drives and spontaneous impulses became controlled and directed on behalf of the acquisition of the subjective *certitudo salutis* state:

> As can be said for every "rational" asceticism, Puritan asceticism... worked to render the devout capable of calling forth and then acting upon their "constant motives," especially those motives that the believer, through the practice of asceticism itself, "trained" against the "emotions." In contrast to a number of popular ideas, the Puritan goal was to be able to lead an alert, conscious, and self-aware life. Hence the destruction of the spontaneity of the instinct-driven enjoyment of life constituted the most urgent task. (*PE*, p. 131)

A "Protestant ethic" originated in this manner. Carried, above all, by Puritan sects and churches, it spread throughout several New England, Dutch, and English communities in the sixteenth and seventeenth centuries. Both the disciplined, hard labor in a calling and the wealth that followed from a steadfast adherence to its religious values marked a person as "chosen." By the time of Benjamin Franklin's more secularized America a century later, the Protestant ethic had spread beyond churches and sects and into entire communities. In the process, however, its specifically religious component became weakened and transformed into a utilitarian-colored ethos (*PE*, pp. 79–80, 172–74, 176–77): a *spirit* of capitalism.[29] Rather than believed to be among the "chosen elect," adherents of this ethos, like Franklin, were viewed simply as righteous, respectable, community-oriented "citizens" of good moral character.

In sum, Weber's investigation of the Protestant ethic's origin involves a causal analysis rooted thoroughly in four types of action. This plural framework is apparent as well when he turns away from his major theme – the *origins* of the "spirit" of capitalism – to, in the concluding pages of *The Protestant Ethic*, a characterization of modern capitalism in the twentieth century (see also *PE*, p. 81). Once a "spirit" of capitalism had assisted the growth of modern capitalism and this "economic form" became firmly entrenched amid massive industrialism, modern capitalism sustains itself, Weber argues, on the basis of *means-end* rational action alone. In this contemporary urban, secular, and bureaucratic milieu, neither Franklin's spirit of capitalism nor Baxter's Protestant ethic endows methodical work with subjective meaning.

Rather, an inescapable network of pragmatic necessities overwhelms the individual; persons born into this "immense cosmos" are coerced simply to adapt to capitalism's "rules of action" in order to survive. In this "iron cage" of "mechanized ossification" and formal rationality (*PE*, pp. 176–78; see Chapter 6), the motivation to work – its *subjective meaning* – is simply means-end rational and "the idea of an 'obligation to search for and then accept a vocational calling' now wanders around in our lives as the ghost of past religious beliefs (*PE*, p. 177; see pp. 173–74; emphasis in original)." The Puritan, Weber proclaims in one of his most famous passages, "*wanted* to be a person with a vocational calling; … we *must* be" (*PE*, p. 177; emphasis in original).

Of course, some may today still invoke the spirit of capitalism's values, yet one must now inquire whether they are sincerely or cynically upheld. For the latter person, reasons of pure expediency prevail, as was the case for the young man whose baptism in North Carolina Weber personally witnessed. As Weber's relative explained, the young man wished to open a bank and membership in an ascetic Protestant church would establish the customer trust requisite for its successful competition against other banks (see "Sects I." pp. 304–05). These four stages of Weber's argument can be diagrammed as follows:

The Protestant Ethic and the Spirit of Capitalism: Stages of Weber's Analysis

	Period	*Organization*	*Type of action*	*Devout*
I. Calvin: Fatalism follows from Pre-destination Doctrine	15th and 16th c.	Small sects	Value-rational	Yes
II. Baxter: The Protestant Ethic	16th and 17th c.	Churches and sects	Value-rational (methodical worldly activity)	Yes
III. Franklin: The Spirit of Capitalism	18th c. American Colonies	Communities	Value-rational (a utilitarian-colored ethos)	No
IV. The "specialist": Capitalism as a "cosmos"	20th c.	Industrial society	Means-end Rational	No

Hence, three of Weber's four models of action are indispensable to his argument: means-end rational,[30] value-rational, and traditional action. Furthermore, Weber's analysis requires acknowledgment of their differing capacities to endow action with intensity: the extreme strength of the traditional action that upheld the traditional economic ethic, the incapacity of sheer means-end rational action to banish this ethic, and the capacity of the Protestant ethic, owing to its origin in a set of *religious* values and its consequent methodical character, to do so. Conducting his argument by reference to a discrete case, Weber demonstrates the inadequacy of any theory of action rooted alone in means-end rational action to provide a conceptual framework adequate to explain the origin of the spirit of capitalism in Western Europe and North America.

Thus, *The Protestant Ethic* argues that all theories of action based exclusively upon interests and pragmatic choices, such as rational choice theory today, neglect an array of distinctions crucial for an understanding of economic development. Once again in a major postwar debate, the theoretical contributions of this classic text were neglected. Rational choice theorists remained uninfluenced in their theorizing by *The Protestant Ethic* and indeed quite oblivious to its theoretical argument.

4.5 Barriers Against *The Protestant Ethic*?

Scrutiny of *The Protestant Ethic* as a multifaceted theoretical treatise rather than simply an investigation of the role played by "ideas" in the unfolding of modern capitalism provides a provocative slant not only upon Weber's classic study, but also upon central theoretical debates in postwar American sociology. Indeed, when examined from this unorthodox perspective, *The Protestant Ethic* serves as a powerful heuristic tool that demarcates many of the parameters of these debates. Moreover, comparisons between mainstream schools of American sociology and this classic have not simply revealed that the diverse theoretical contributions of *The Protestant Ethic* have never been acknowledged; they have demonstrated as well that Weber's text has stood squarely in opposition to major American theoretical currents.

This conclusion deserves further discussion in light of the enduring attention otherwise given to *The Protestant Ethic*. Did a style of theorizing in the United States erect barriers against the theoretical lessons offered by this work – even effectively dismissing central aspects of its argument? Or can the limited influence of *The Protestant Ethic* upon American sociological theory be attributed, despite its *de rigeur* status among theorists, simply to happenstance, a poor translation (see Appendix II), and unfortunate misinterpretations? Some general ruminations on these questions suggest reasons for the neglect of its theoretical contributions. They will further illuminate the central contours of American sociology.

The orientation of Weber's sociology to the causal analysis of unique cases rather than the formulation of general laws (see Chapter 1, pp. 28–32) surely appeared to American sociologists in the 1940s and 1950s as offering an agenda too modest to sustain the development of a strong discipline. Sociology in the United States, following the French example, had by this time embarked energetically upon an ambitious quest to define itself as a rigorous science and to imitate the procedures of the natural sciences (see Oberschall, 1972). Indeed, despite clearly anti-positivist aspects in Parsons's own theorizing, the fit between American positivism and structural functionalism's societal organicism was comfortable (see Wiley, 1990, p. 395).

This imitation of a natural sciences model led mainstream American sociologists, unlike sociologists in Germany, to distance themselves from history, which became viewed as a "soft" science in alliance with the humanities.[31] It also led to the rejection of those features of Weber's sociology less amenable to a positivist model of science, for example, the concern both with power and economic interests as well as the stubborn endurance of traditions and values, both change and continuity, both history and the present, both religion and culture on the one hand and power and rulership on the other hand, and a methodological individualism that stresses subjective meaning, interpretive understanding (*Verstehen*), and the ways in which values become grounded (*Wertbezogenheit*) in specific historical epochs. In addition, the apogee during this period of American world power and confidence in capitalism, as well as its own values generally, ill-disposed sociologists in the United States to bring power, rulership, conflict, and economic interests deeply into their theoretical ruminations (see Gouldner, 1970; Buxton, 1985).[32]

Perhaps, in the end, a Max Weber other than the ahistorical advocate of a timeless "systematic theory of society," "general theory," and "evolutionary universals" presented by Parsons would never have created an echo of any sort in American sociology (see Zaret, 1980, 1994, pp. 342–44). The infrequent alternative voices of the 1940s, such as those of the German refugees Ephraim Fischoff (1944), Hans Gerth (1946), and Albert Salomon (1934, 1935a, 1935b, 1945; see Kalberg, 1993), all of whom discussed Weber as a non-positivist theorist who combined history and sociology, rejected societal organicism, awarded culture with significant standing in his theorizing while emphasizing also rulership, power, conflict, and social change, and articulated a methodology rooted in subjective meaning, interpretive understanding, and the various orientations of individual action, remained unheard.

Extensive cross-national influence from Germany that might have introduced a different Weber into American sociology also could not occur in the 1940s or 1950s. As a consequence of the horrendous events of the 1933–1945 period, Germans turned *en masse* away from their own traditions and toward the "safe" and "uncorrupted" style of sociology offered by the ahistorical theories (structural functionalism and urban ecology) and procedures (quantitative methods, field methods, and a rigidly operationalizing empiricism) popular in the United States[33]

The protest in the 1960s and 1970s in the United States against the positivist model, structural functionalism's societal organicism, and timeless, abstract theorizing offered, perhaps, a singular opportunity for a viable turn on American soil to the theoretical lessons of *The Protestant Ethic*. However, in the spirit of the times, the wave of dissent turned more to Marx than to Weber.

The enthusiasm for Marx, however, proved more fanfare than substance. Even as younger sociologists in the United States called out loudly for the incorporation of history and the central Marxian concepts, strong schools defended the positivist and quantitative orientations of American sociology. In addition, they discovered severe shortcomings in all attempts to "bring history in" and to define sociology by reference to power, conflict, economic interests, and capitalism. Although Parsons's sacrifice of these dimensions in favor of organic holism was widely condemned, the pivotal aspects of his project – symmetrical syntheses of micro and macro and culture and structure – retained an enduring appeal to theorists in the United States. Despite the political tumult of the 1960s and 1970s, the vociferous targeting of capitalism, and the discipline's severe splintering, a broad and sustained cultivation of neo-Marxist paradigms did not occur.[34]

Nonetheless, a strong "radical"/"conservative" split did crystallize. Weber, although far more widely read in the 1970s than earlier (not least owing to the availability in 1968 of a full translation of *Economy and Society*), fell between these poles. To some, still following Parsons's misinterpretations, Weber appeared closely allied with the universalizing, abstract, evolutionary, and "bourgeoise" tendencies of Parsons, to others his concern with power, rulership, conflict, and stratification proved attractive. To still others his sociology remained simply a fragmented collection of ideal types and endless typologies (Skocpol and Somers, 1980; see Parsons, 1963, pp. Ixii–lxvi). As the plea to bring culture in" rang out in the 1980s, the weaknesses of the Parsonsian interpretation of Weber again became apparent: this "theorist of culture" had never articulated Weber's sociology as a non-holistic sociology of culture.

Not surprisingly, many of Weber's main interpreters of the 1970s and 1980s, falling victim to the discipline's polarization, were also unable to do so: addressing sociology's major divisions, they attempted to establish Weber, against the Parsonsian reading, securely as a conflict theorist – and hence focused too much upon the power and rulership themes (see Bendix, 1962, 1965; Bendix and Roth, 1971; Roth, 1968, 1971, 1976; Collins, 1975). On the other hand, Wolfgang Schluchter, diverging from his German traditions, offered in the 1980s too much of a Parsonsian and taxonomic reading of Weber to be influential in the American landscape (1981, 1989; Roth and Schluchter, 1979).

The proponents of a more culture-oriented sociology in the 1980s and 1990s, deprived of a Weberian theoretical framework, unable to coalesce with the offspring of structural functionalism – "neofunctionalism" (see Alexander, 1985, 1990) – that embraced culture yet remained tarnished with the broad brush of "Parsonsian conservatism," and unwilling to become allied with neo-Marxist and state-centered perspectives, were left only an atheoretical route: to conduct empirical studies underinformed by rigorous sociological theory.[35] Finally, the emphasis in *The Protestant Ethic*, and in Weber's sociology as a whole, upon value-oriented and tradition-oriented action on the one hand and the contextual understanding of social action on the other, could scarcely be attractive in the 1980s and 1990s to a style of sociological theorizing that viewed individuals as unrestrained and endowed with autonomous choices, as does rational choice theory.

As a theoretical treatise, Weber's *Protestant Ethic* has never found a home in American sociological theory.[36] Frequently viewed exclusively as an investigation into the influence of "religious ideas" upon the rise of modern capitalism and minutely dissected by both Weber specialists and sociologists of development and modernization, its contributions to sociological theory in the United States have scarcely been mined. I have attempted to demonstrate this volume's multifaceted theoretical capital. More than a century after its original publication, *The Protestant Ethic and the Spirit of Capitalism* should now be fully acknowledged not only as an analysis of the rise of a spirit of capitalism, but also as a bountiful resource for sociological theory.

However, in addition to analyzing this classic as a theoretical treatise and suggesting reasons for its neglect by American theorists, this study has also sought to call attention to the many ways in which the theoretical lessons articulated by *The Protestant Ethic* reflect vividly the contours of pivotal controversies in postwar U.S. sociology. The diverse theoretical capital offered by Weber's volume throws into stark relief the styles and substance of theorizing common in American sociological theory. Indeed, *The Protestant Ethic* has articulated a particular view of the empirical world, one far distant from the major dichotomies that have structured the perception and understanding of this world among American theorists: history and sociology, conflict and equilibrium, society and the individual, culture and economic interests, social order and social change, individual interests and social structure, tradition and modernity, and micro and macro levels of analysis.

Although each of these dichotomies has been called into question by schools prominent in the postwar debates noted here (as well as others) and by Weber's *Protestant Ethic*, they endure and continue to set the parameters for theorizing in the United States. Understood as a theoretical treatise, this text argues that a sociology rooted in traditional, affectual, value-rational, and means-end rational types of action, conflict, power, and social change, "carrier" organizations, the interpretive understanding of subjective meaning, an array of analytically equal societal domains, the ineluctable intertwining of past and present, and the ubiquitous penetration of economic and political interests by cultural forces offers a viable alternative view of the empirical world and a style of theorizing in opposition to major parameters of American sociological theory.

Notes

1 For summaries of this debate, see, for example, Parsons (1928, 1935), Knight (1928), Fischoff (1944), Green (1973), Besnard (1970), Nelson (1973), Otsuka (1976), Marshall (1982), Poggi (1983), Dülmen (1989), MacKinnon (1993), and Lehmann and Roth (1993).

2 I do not suggest that these four were the only significant debates. See, for example, Wiley (1985, 1990); Ritzer (1990).

3 On Weber's "methodological individualism" and "four types of social action" (affectual, traditional, value-rational, and means-end rational), see ("Obj," pp. 100–38); see also *E&S* (Chapter 1) and below, pp. 5–17 and 195–202.

4 An assumption of societal organicism appears indispensable if one of structural functionalism's crucial concepts – the notion of role – is to remain viable. Roles become central in sociological analysis only where a high overlap of societal domains is presupposed. Only on the basis of such interlocking can the learning of roles in "socialization processes" take place with continuity. If such organicist assumptions are rejected, the analysis of social processes will with greater likelihood involve concepts as well as an entire level of analysis more capable of addressing conflict and power, such as class or status group. These concepts have their origins in a tradition of sociological theory which has, with only one exception (Tönnies), rejected societal holism fundamentally: the German tradition. The ubiquitous influence of German Romanticism upon sociology in Germany until 1940 (and even in some schools to this day), with its emphasis upon the uniqueness of the individual and the inexorable tension between the autonomous individual and society (see, e.g., Simmel 1917 [1950], pp. 58–86; 1908 [1971], pp. 227–34; 1913 [1971], pp. 217–26; 1918 [1971], pp. 375–93), prevented the reception of role theory. Not surprisingly, German sociology seriously acknowledged the concept of role only during its short-lived period of infatuation with American sociology in the 1950s (see Kalberg, 2007). Ironically, the major proponent of role theory at this time in Germany, Ralf Dahrendorf (see 1968), is known in the United States exclusively as a conflict theorist (see 1959). For the definitive *German* critique of role theory, see Tenbruck (1987).

5 Although ambitious in scope, it should not be forgotten that *The Protestant Ethic* is a case study investigating the extent to which religious

sources can be discovered for the spirit of capitalism in England's six-teenth and seventeenth centuries. In this sense, this classic is consistent with the aim of Weber's sociology: to explain causally unique cases and developments or the "historical individual" (see "Obj," pp. 113–14; *AG*, p. 385; *E&S*, p. 10).

His opposition to a positivist sociology that defines the formulation of ahistorical general laws as its goal is unequivocal. Even *Economy and Society*, Weber's systematic treatise, does not seek to formulate general laws. Instead, its project involves the formulation of (empirically based; see next note) ideal types, all of which, rather than capturing "social re-ality," serve alone as heuristic tools that assist researchers to carry out causal analyses of cases (see, e.g., "Obj," pp. 103–04, 113–21; Kalberg, 1994, pp. 81–142; Zaret, 1980, 1994).

The attempt by numerous interpreters to generalize *The Protestant Eth-ic*'s argument beyond a particular geographical region and to formulate, from this study, "universal laws" of economic development runs against the grain of Weber's entire methodology, not to mention the firm com-mitment in his sociology to contextual analysis: "…the totality of *all* the conditions uncovered must 'act in conjunction' in that way and no differ-ently…" ("Obj," p. 183; emphasis in original).

Hence, strictly viewed, the search for "equivalents" of ascetic Prot-estantism, as occurred in the 1960s (see, e.g., Bellah, 1957; Eisenstadt, 1968), in non-European developing countries also opposes Weber's aim to explain the causal origins of specific cases as well as his contextual methodology. Further, this literature neglects the crucial distinction in *The Protestant Ethic* between the indigenous development of a "spirit" of capitalism and the capacity of societies to "import [technical economic rationalism]" (*E&S*, p. 630). Weber never doubted that this capacity was widespread (see "PR," pp. 237–42; *E&S*, pp. 629–30). Of course, the "spirit" of capitalism does not itself imply asceticism (as did the Protes-tant ethic), as proponents of this approach have often argued, though it does imply a set of values or an ethos (see Chapter 1).

6 Ideal types rather than "society" constitute Weber's level of analysis. Moreover, these heuristic research tools, although synthetic constructs, are always grounded empirically (see Weber, "Obj," pp. 121–38; Burger, 1976, pp. 115–40; Kalberg, 1994, pp. 81–91). On Parsons's misunder-standing of the ideal type, see Burger (1976, pp. 138–39).

7 These values were widely viewed as reprehensible (see, e.g., *PE*, pp. 96–97).

8 Weber argues that the teaching of *ethical* values, if it occurs, necessar-ily involves a strong personal bond (see, e.g., *E&S*, pp. 346, 585, 600, 1186–87; *GEH*, pp. 357–58; "IR," p. 331).

9 Weber notes as well the manner in which the "sect spirit" influenced purely social configurations of American life. See "Sects I"; "Sects II"; *E&S*, pp. 1205–08; 2001; see Chapters 7 and 8.

10 Parsons in particular (see 1951; Parsons et al., 1951; Parsons and Shils, 1951), though also Merton (see, e.g., [1949] 1968, pp. 185–214), strongly

integrated culture into their overall theorizing. To Parsons's critics, however, he understood culture in a manner too diffuse, organicist, and nonempirical.

11 The spirit of capitalism opposes directly the traditional economic ethic. In this orientation to work, workers and alike view labor in the "traditional" manner as a necessary evil that must be accepted to fill constant basic needs. Because time spent in leisure and with one's family and friends is more highly valued than work, an increase in wages or profits encourages the worker or entrepreneur to labor less: once minimum subsistence requirements are met, no further incentive to work exists. Higher or lower wages, Weber is convinced, will never evoke the notion that "labor must be … performed as if it were an absolute end in itself, a calling" (*PE*, p. 87; see also pp. 83–92; *GEH*, pp. 355–56).

12 Regarding the capacity of a particular to call forth a "spirit" of capitalism: "The assumption is by no means justified *a priori* … that on the one hand the technique of the capitalistic enterprise and on the other the spirit of 'professional work,' which gives to capitalism its expansive energy, must have had their original sustaining roots in the same social strata" (*PE*, p. 298, note 24; see also "I," pp. 268–70).

13 The analytic separation of "structure" and "action" runs as a foundational theme throughout Weber's sociology. This point is at times obscured by his model-building, particularly with models that chart an elective affinity between daily practical activities and religious beliefs (see "I," pp. 268–69; *E&S*, pp. 468–500). Regarding the incapacity of a particular class to call forth a "spirit" of capitalism, see (*PE*, pp. 88–89; "I," p. 270).

14 Capitalism, Weber states repeatedly, can be found in all epochs and societies (see *PE*, p. 79). Its origin is not his concern in *The Protestant Ethic* (see p. 108), as both early and later critics have frequently asserted. Rather, his interest focuses on *the origins of the* spirit of capitalism that played a significant causal role in respect to – or "stands generally in an 'adequate' relationship to" (*PE*, p. 88) – the rise of *modern* or *rational* capitalism (see Chapter 1). This type of capitalism involved not simply "an expectation of profit based on the utilization of opportunities for *exchange*" ("PR," p. 237), but also relatively free market exchange, "the maximization of profit in continuous productive enterprises," a systematic pursuit of profit, the separation of the business (corporate property) from the household (personal property) (see *E&S*, pp. 164–66; "PR," pp. 236–40), rational bookkeeping, *and* "the rational-capitalist organization of (formally) *free labor*" ("PR," p. 236; emphasis in the original; *E&S*, p. 91; *GEH*, pp. 275–351), or a "frame of mind" (*Gesinnung*) that, *in a calling*, seeks profit rationally and systematically (*PE*, pp. 88–89; emphasis original; see also *GEH*, pp. 352–69). Weber argues this point more forcefully in "PR" and in his essays against his earliest critics (see 2001) than in *The Protestant Ethic* itself.

15 Literally, the "leading of a life." Hence, *Lebensfuehrung* implies an ordering principle to life and a consistency of action in terms of the ordering principle.

16 Weber uses this expression synonymously with "modern economic ethic" and "spirit of capitalism."

17 Weber makes this point even more vividly in a later essay: "...the origin of economic rationalism depends not only on an advanced development of technology and law but also on the capacity and disposition of persons to organize their lives in a practical-rational manner" ("PR," p. 246; see "I," p. 293).

18 Weber emphasizes that "we moderns" can scarcely imagine the urgency of this question to these believers (see, e.g., *PE*, pp. 92–93, 177–80; 1972, p. 33).

19 Weber notes the quite practical interests Baxter may have had in mind (see *PE*, pp. 337–39, note 76).

20 Weber points out on several occasions that Baxter's revisions were "irrational": the doctrine of Predestination had already offered a fully rational answer to the dilemma that drove the development of *religious* thinking: the problem of suffering (*PE*, pp. 97–98, 115–19, 156–74; see "IR," pp. 358–59; *E&S*, pp. 518–26; see also Tenbruck, 1980; Schluchter, 1979; Kalberg, 1979, 1990, 2021, pp. 57–72). Thus, Weber argues that Baxter's Protestant ethic, which stood in a relationship of "elective affinity" to the spirit of capitalism, had irrational origins (see *PE*, pp. 97–98).

21 Similarly, the opportunity to compete with others for a profit did not appear by chance; rather, it constituted an opportunity given by God to acquire wealth. A positive "religious premium" is here bestowed upon economic competition, and the "natural" attitude toward competition – of ambivalence: someone will win, but someone will also lose – is shattered.

22 And thus the devout could likewise understand an "unwillingness to work [as] symptomatic) of a lack of grace" (*PE*, p. 161). Similarly, those living in poverty could not possibly be among the saved (see *PE*, pp. 164; 394–95, note 117), and hence being poor indicated not laziness alone but also a poor *moral* character.

23 "Most important, the usefulness of a vocational calling is assessed mainly in moral terms, as is its corresponding capacity to please God. A [yet further] criterion, one clearly the most important at the practical level, is also central in assessing a calling's usefulness: its economic *profitability* for the individual. For if his God, whom the Puritan sees as acting in all arenas of life, reveals a chance for turning a profit to one of His faithful, He must do so with clear intentions in mind. Accordingly, the believer must follow this opportunity and exploit it" (*PE*, p. 163; emphasis in the original; see also *E&S*, p. 1200).

24 This emphasis upon the community's "common good" stands alongside an emphasis upon "one's own" good (see *PE*, pp. 163, 169–70, 173–74) or attention to one's salvation status. That reinvestment, in the community, in fact, occurred rather than individual-oriented and ostentatious consumption, provided, according to Weber, (a) an incredibly strong and unique sustaining thrust to economic growth (see *PE*, pp. 170–71, 174–75) and (b) clear evidence of the Protestant ethic's deep *religious* roots

and genuine asceticism: because the faithful were convinced that wealth was received only through an omnipotent God, the extreme temptation it presented – to be used for one's personal enjoyment – could not be acted upon. All covetousness – "the pursuit of riches for their own sake" – and frivolous indulgence must be condemned as idolatry (see *PE*, pp. 159, 169–71).

25 It is surprising how infrequently the secondary literature notes the importance in Weber's analysis of the believer's search for a *sign* from God. As a rule, commentators stress instead the attempts by the devout to ameliorate the anxiety, doubt, and sense of unworthiness called forth by the doctrine of Predestination as the single source of the "intense worldly activity" and systematic work characteristic of the Protestant ethic (see, e.g., Bendix, 1962, pp. 60–64, 275–76; 1971, pp. 189–90; Marshall, 1982, pp. 75–76; Poggi, 1983, p. 64). Poggi focuses even more upon the attempt by the believer to serve as an "instrument" of God's will (see pp. 64–67), and Marshall also notes the manner in which the believer, if capable of systematic and continuous work, comes to believe this very capacity as "evident proof of rebirth" (see Marshall, 1982, pp. 80–81; *PE*, p. 170).

26 Weber defines an "ethical" standard as "… a specific type of value-rational belief among individuals which, as a consequence of this belief, imposes a normative element upon human action that claims the quality of the 'morally good' in the same way that action which claims the status of the 'beautiful' is measured against aesthetic standards" (*E&S*, p. 36; translation altered; emphasis in original). Social action, Weber contends, can be influenced by an ethical standard even if "external" support for it is lacking and even, at times, in spite of opposing "external" action patterns.

27 Weber here refers to inner-worldly asceticism as "Janus-faced" (*Doppelgesicht*): To focus upon God and the question of salvation, a turning away from the world and even rejection of this random "meaningless…natural vessel of sin" (see, e.g., *E&S*, p. 542) was called for. On the other hand, a turning toward and mastering of the world was necessary on behalf of ethical values and the creation on earth of God's Kingdom (see "IR," p. 327). This Janus-faced character of action in the world itself bestowed a methodicalness to this action that separated it from worldly action motivated by practical concerns or economic interests.

28 In answering a criticism by Sombart (see [1913] 1967), Weber argues that the manner of life and "worldly wisdom" of Leon Battista Alberti (1402–1472), a "versatile genius of the [Florentine] Renaissance," must be understood as entirely different from that of Puritans, whose action was oriented by religious questions, and from that of Benjamin Franklin, whose action was oriented by a "utilitarian-colored" ethos (see *PE*, pp. 79–80, 292–96 [note 12]). The "adventure capitalism" of the heroic medieval entrepreneur Jakob Fugger must be also clearly distinguished (see *PE*, p. 79).

29 Rather than a "determinative" relationship, Weber sees an "elective affinity" (*Wahlverwandtschaft*) between the Protestant ethic and the "spirit" of
capitalism (Parsons's translation of *Wahlverwandtschaft* as "correlation"
is inadequate; see Appendix II below). This "weak causal" manner of stating the relationship results in part from Weber's position that the sources
of the spirit of capitalism are many and that religious sources constitute
only one – however significant and not to be neglected – possible source:
"We only wish to ascertain whether and to what extent religious influences
co-participated in the qualitative formation and the quantitative expansion
of this spirit across the globe" (*PE*, p. 108; emphasis in original). He further notes: "...one of the constitutive components of the modern capitalist spirit and, moreover, generally of modern civilization was the rational
organization of life on the basis of the *idea of the calling*. It was born out
of the spirit of *Christian asceticism*" (*PE*, p. 176; emphasis in the original).

30 Significantly, the value-rational action – the spirit of capitalism – of
Franklin is oriented, as the Protestant ethic, to both individuals (their
salvation status in the Protestant ethic case) and to a community (see *PE*,
e.g., pp. 163, 170), while the means-end rational action of the individual
entrapped within the "immense cosmos" of industrial capitalism is oriented simply to the individual's survival. For a contemporary discussion
of this significant shift, see Bellah *et al.* (1985).

31 The traditional exclusion of historical analysis from sociology in the
United States can also, if one moves to a cultural and sociology of knowledge level of analysis, be understood partly as a legacy of an ascetic Protestant religiosity that places a strong emphasis upon the capacity of the
self to be shaped and molded apart from traditions and historical constraints and in reference alone to the individual's self-defined will, aims,
and aspirations. In this religious tradition, the future is open and offers
abundant opportunities (originally to create the "evidence" that would
convince the faithful of their salvation status), while the past and traditions in general are unconstraining and unimportant.

32 The noted exceptions, of course, were Gouldner, Mills, and Coser.

33 This did not change until the late 1960s when sociologists in Germany
began cultivating their indigenous traditions: the Frankfurt School in the
1960s, Weber in the 1970s and 1980s, and Georg Simmel in the 1980s
and 1990s.

34 Indeed, although the "bring culture in" movement of the 1980s cannot
be understood as a surreptitious attempt to "bring Parsons back in," the
Parsonsian concern with cultural forces appears to this day to have more
deep and enduring roots in American sociology than does a concern with
economic interests, power, rulership, and conflict (see, e.g., Bellah et al.,
1985; Lamont and Fournier, 1992; Swidler, 1986).

35 Had Weber's *verstehende* sociology exerted a strong influence upon the
development of Symbolic Interactionism (see Zaret, 1994, pp. 350–57),

perhaps his impact upon the new sociology of culture literature would have been greater.

36 Zaret's conclusion is more general: "Weber's entire sociology has had no significant effect ... on the various traditions of American sociological theory" (1994, p. 356).

PART II

Beyond *The Protestant Ethic*

The Multicausal Sociology of Religion

5

FROM *THE PROTESTANT ETHIC* TO THE ECONOMIC ETHICS OF THE WORLD RELIGIONS

Weber's broad-ranging Economic Ethics of the World Religions studies on Confucianism and Daoism (*RofC*), Hinduism and Buddhism (*RofI*), and ancient Judaism (*AJ*) expand upon themes explored in *PE* in 1904/1905. Do major religions possess an "economic ethic?" If so, are they capable of contributing to the development of a spirit of capitalism? These volumes, through rigorous comparisons between the modern West and China, India, and ancient Israel along multiple axes, seek to define the uniqueness of each civilization. More generally, they attempt to define the singularity of subjectively meaningful patterns of action in the West, China, India, and ancient Israel.

PE forcefully demonstrates how variation in the meaning clusters of actors implies diverging consequences for economic activity. However, as discussed, its idealist focus and omission of comparative cases restricts its contribution to Weber's comparative-historical and multi-causal procedures. EEWR signifies a giant step on just this score.

Nonetheless, as he moved beyond an assessment of ascetic Protestantism's impact upon the development of a spirit of capitalism and traversed millennia East and West in his quest to define precisely the uniqueness of Western rationalism, Weber never abandoned *PE*'s core concern: action oriented toward religion. Moreover, both EEWR and *PE* opposed in principle all explanations rooted exclusively on the one hand in political power, structural and demographic variables, and

DOI: 10.4324/9781032631813-8

economic interests, and on the other hand, all explanations anchored in overarching, general "evolutionary" processes.

Weber stressed the powerful influence of carrier groups (e.g., intellectuals, the feudal aristocracy, and civil servants) upon the formation and spread of religious doctrines (see *E&S*, pp. 468–517). However, he argued as well that belief could not be viewed as a mere function of stratum-specific interests (see *PERW*, pp. 238–41). Likewise, rejecting in principle all schools that assert the uniform causal primacy of social structure, an "economic ethic" could not be understood "as a simple 'function' of a form of economic organization," or even of a religious organization (*PERW*, p. 239), he held. Structurally identical religious sects existed in Hinduism as well as in Christianity, as mentioned. Nonetheless, their contrasting sacred values "pointed [the social action of believers] in radically different directions" (*PERW*, p. 250).

The *multiple* obstacles erected by Eastern civilizations to a Western path of development must be also recognized, Weber maintains in the EEWR volumes. An array of nonreligious hindrances to economic development were widespread in China, India, and ancient Israel, he notes. Extremely rigorous sib ties were apparent in China, and "a formally guaranteed law and a rational administration and judiciary" were absent (*RofC*, p. 85; see also pp. 91, 99–100). And the caste system in India placed constraints upon migration, the recruitment of labor, and the availability of credit (*RofI*, pp. 52–53, 102–06, 111–17).

By the same token, the expansive presence in the modern West of groups of formally trained jurists should not be understood as originating alone from economic interests – for then a salient query is quickly formed: why did "...capitalist interests [not] call forth this stratum of jurists and this type of law in China or India" ("PR," p. 245). Indeed, an entire host of conducive economic interests failed to bring about *modern* capitalism in China, such as freedom of trade, population growth, occupational mobility, an increase in precious metals, and the presence of a money economy (*RofC*, pp. 12, 54–55, 99–100, 243). Throughout, the EEWR studies locate causal significance in a variety of societal domains and organizations, and assume that facilitating patterns of action must always be weighed against groups carrying obstructing patterns of action.

Although cognizant of the qualitatively new ground explored in the EEWR studies, many commentators comprehend these investigations as concerned exclusively with the *economic ethics* of the great world religions. They comprise a direct extension of *PE*, it is argued. EEWR confirms "the Weber thesis"; these interpreters then conclude: because a "functional equivalent" of the Protestant ethic proved absent from Confucianism, Taoism, Hinduism, Buddhism, and ancient Judaism, and because China, India, and ancient Israel all failed to give birth to modern capitalism, the West can be said to have developed *as a consequence* of Puritan asceticism. A particular religious ethos is here perceived as the necessary causal force behind the development of modern capitalism.

5.1   *Both* Sides of the Causal Question

This interpretation misconstrues fundamentally Weber's analysis. Rather than exclusively oriented to economic ethics, the EEWR volumes, unlike *PE*, examine "*both* sides of the causal equation" (see *PE*, pp. 178–79). A *variety* of pivotal components of civilizations are investigated in China, India, and ancient Israel, including social status constellations, the strength of universal organizations (families and clans), and the predominant forms of law, rulership, and the economy. Variations in respect to types of cities are also examined (see also *E&S*, pp. 1212–372). Hence, the EEWR studies offer complex, *multi-causal* investigations. This new focus broadened Weber's mode of analysis qualitatively.

Thus, his research methodology in the EEWR volumes stands opposed to the view that the absence of this-worldly asceticism in Asia explains the absence of modern capitalism in this region. Although his scrutiny of Confucianism, Taoism, Buddhism, Jainism, and ancient Judaism explores whether "psychological premiums" were bestowed upon methodical economic activity, he holds throughout that *constellations* of patterned action by persons in multiple groups constitute the appropriate level for a causal analysis (see Introduction, pp. 5–18; Chapter 1, pp. 28–32; and Chapter 6).

Weber's insistence that groups perpetually interact *conjuncturally* within contexts of further groups is also apparent throughout the EEWR studies (Kalberg, 1994, pp. 98–102, 143–92; 2012, pp. 108–12, 145–78). He identifies diverse arrays of regular action located in groups in the rulership, religion, economy, social status, family, clan, and law domains in various civilizations. The many *clusters* of social action conducive to the unfolding of modern capitalism in China and India in the seventeenth and eighteenth centuries were in the end outweighed by a complex series of opposing patterns of action in groups, he concluded.

Finally, Weber was convinced that modern capitalism could be *adopted* by – and would flourish in – a number of Eastern civilizations. Indeed, he identified the many patterns of action that would allow this to occur (on Japan, see *RofI*, p. 275; on China, see *RofC*, p. 248). Adoption, however, involved different processes than his concern, he stressed: the *origin* in a specific region of a *new* economic ethos and a *new* type of economy.

Hence, Weber renounced any search for a single, encompassing causal equation: "This sort of construction," he held, "is better left to that type of dilettante who believes in the 'unity' of the 'social psyche' and its reducibility to *one* formula" (*PE*, p. 400, note 142; original emphasis). As will become apparent in Chapters 6 and 10, *E&S* further confirms Weber's commitment to multi-causal analysis and his interest in comprehending and analyzing the uniqueness of civilizations.

6

"IDEAS *AND* INTERESTS"

From *The Protestant Ethic* to the Later Sociology
of Religion

Max Weber acknowledges at the end of *The Protestant Ethic and the Spirit of Capitalism* that he has addressed only "one side of the causal question." This volume has provided a "religion-oriented analysis" of the "spirit of capitalism's" origins, he holds. Some of its significant roots are traced back to the ideas and values that constitute "a Protestant ethic" (*PE*, pp. 178–79).

Weber insists that his "case study" must be viewed as simply the "beginning stage" of a larger causal investigation focused upon the spirit of capitalism's sources. An *adequate* research methodology must stress *both* the "material and ideal sides of the equation" (*PE*, pp. 178–79).[1] One of his most famous passages captures this aim:

> Not ideas, but material and ideal interests, directly govern men's conduct. Yet very frequently the "world views" that have been created by "ideas" have, like switchmen, determined the tracks (*Gleise*) along which action has been pushed by the dynamic of interests. ("I," p. 280)

Weber never lost sight of his goal to investigate "both sides." Hence, a serious query must be formulated: did he actually pursue an "ideas *and* interests" agenda distinct from *PE*'s presuppositions in his post-*PE* sociology of religion?

DOI: 10.4324/9781032631813-9

This question assumes great urgency once we recognize that several of Weber's discussions in his post-*PE* writings attend closely to ideas and values: they offer analyses of the causal capacity of worldviews (*Weltbilder*), salvation doctrines, and "rational thought." These discussions capture our attention in Part I. They would seem to separate Weber further from the multi-causal – ideas *and* interests – research procedures so abundantly praised in *PE*'s concluding pages. Our query remains: did he abandon the multi-causal goal pronounced in *PE* (*PE*, pp. 178–79)?

Weber's post-*PE* sociology of religion presents a complex picture: albeit not easily visible, it places at its core *both* ideal and material analyses (Part II). Three concepts in Weber's writings demonstrate the importance for him of *interests*, namely, "carrier groups," the "routinization of charisma," and "lay rationalism."[2] The conclusion to this chapter maintains that Weber's post-*PE* sociology of religion emphatically supports an "ideas *and* interests" causal methodology.[3]

6.1 World views, "Rational Thought," Salvation Doctrines, and Weber's Post-*Protestant Ethic* Attention to Ideas and Values

Worldviews and Rational Thought. Worldviews imply a coherent set of values, Weber argues. Although they span a wide spectrum in terms of their content and internal cohesiveness, these "ethical orders" always address ultimate questions. What is the meaning of life? What purpose does our existence serve? How do we best live our lives?

Hence, rooted in shared cultural presuppositions, worldviews demarcate a moral universe and a cosmological vision. Both offer instructions regarding the meaningfulness – or lack thereof – of mundane activity. Meaning constellations are articulated in strict opposition to diffuse and random action, traditional action, and the practical-rational, utilitarian "flow of life." Weber especially attends to whether religion-based worldviews direct the devout to "adapt to" the world (China) or to orient their social action "toward" (as in the West) or "away from" (as in India) the world. And does a worldview imply modes of social action that can be realistically pursued and fulfilled by the laity as well as by elites?

Both the *world and religion realms* may ground a worldview's expansive value constellation, Weber maintains. Secularized intellectual, social, and political groups may define broad-ranging sets of values. In other words, wherever worldviews congeal and become influential, social action becomes concerted and directed – perhaps even toward ethical values.

Thus, a disjunction is apparent; although varying in intensity depending upon the worldview's values and the forcefulness of their articulation, this "meaningful order" always sets standards in reference to which pragmatic action is evaluated. Adherents now query: is my social action consistent with the unified ethical purpose expressed by the worldview's value constellation? Indeed, the *discrepancy* between an "ordered totality" and "irrational" earthly events itself places an *ideal thrust* into motion, Weber holds. To the extent that persons *cognitively* evaluate the degree to which their social action logically conforms to their perception of a worldview's values, a thrust is placed into motion toward patterned, value-oriented social action. For example:

> To the prophet, both life and the world, both social and cosmic events, have a certain systematic and coherent "meaning" to which man's conduct must be oriented if it is to bring salvation and after which it must be patterned in an integrally meaningful manner.... [This meaning] always contains the important religious conception of the "world" as a "cosmos" which is challenged to produce somehow a "meaningful," ordered totality, the particular manifestations of which are to be measured and evaluated according to this postulate. (*E&S*, pp. 450–51)[4]

In sum, Weber stresses that the integrated values of a worldview provide a deep cultural legitimation and ideational thrust for values-based patterned action – even for a comprehensively organized, "methodical-rational" directing of life (*methodisch-rationale Lebensführung*). Group formation, significant events, and history's development arise not only from the economic, legal, political, and status interests of daily life, he contends, nor alone from traditions, mundane values, organizations, power considerations, and rational choices. The transformation, for example, of Christian religious doctrine throughout the Middle Ages and from medieval Catholicism to Lutheranism and then to seventeenth-century ascetic Protestant sects and churches cannot be comprehended by reference alone to worldly action oriented to the rulership, law, economy, family, clan, and social status domains (see Kalberg, 2012, pp. 43–72).

Christianity's worldview, for example, offers a set of below-the-surface values that justify innumerable historical developments, Weber insists. The birth of the notion of universal citizenship in the West's medieval cities took Christianity's rejection of all dualistic, insider-outsider ethics as its deep cultural point of legitimation (see *E&S*, pp. 1226–50). Furthermore, the ethos of radical equality and "brotherhood" in the congregation is scarcely conceivable, Weber argues, without the emphasis in Christian doctrine upon an "equality before God" and the *shared* status – as His children – of all. And the development of individualism in the West finds its ideational point of reference in Christianity's commanding and awesome God who proclaimed His children as "tools" for His Will and *demanded* ethical behavior of *each* person (see *GEH*, pp. 315–37; *E&S*, pp. 1236–62).

Similarly, the impetus for the unfolding of modern science becomes comprehensible only if the attempt by sixteenth and seventeenth century scientists to prove the existence of God through the discovery of the laws of the universe is included in the multi-causal explanation; however hidden, their presence would offer proof of a superior intelligence, it was believed (see "SV," p. 142). In China, the respect for ancestors and authority cultivated in the family mirrored the call for such respect and deference in Confucian values. And in India, the aim of the Buddhist monk to withdraw from the world in order to silence the inner being through meditation, and then to merge into the Deity, can be comprehended only in light of this figure's particular perception of the supernatural realm, namely, as constituted from a cosmic and immanent All-One Entity (see Kalberg, 2012, pp. 77–78).

In these ways, worldviews as moral universes stand "behind" surface-level occurrences and justify particular patterns of social action. If cultivated by powerful carrier groups, they cast broad shadows across millennia and across civilizations. They then contribute coherence to history's unfolding. As well, they oppose all schools oriented exclusively to, for example, secular traditions, sheer power, and utilitarian axioms (see Kalberg, 1990, pp. 61–63). Constituted from configurations of values, worldviews directly extend *PE*'s "idealism."[5]

Attention to values and ideas is manifest in Weber's post-*PE* sociology of religion in another manner: in some worldviews, severe tension exists across their values. A "dynamic autonomy" arises as a consequence and arguments rooted in logical deduction become overt as "theoretical rationalization processes."[6]

Weber addresses in this regard the problem of theodicy. To the extent that the universe is conceptualized as rationally ordered, unified, and a totality of "universal meaning," continuing misery becomes increasingly difficult to explain. "Undeserved" woe is now recognized as frequent ("I," p. 275). If the universe has been created as a meaningful and unified cosmos by an omniscient ethical Force,[7] how can all forms of internal and external suffering continue to exist (*E&S*, p. 519)?

This conundrum became the concern above all of prophets, priests, theologians, and monks. Solutions were formulated on a regular basis and believers altered their behavior to conform to new admonitions. Nonetheless, because hardship and injustice persisted, *rational thought* led repeatedly to one conclusion: the nature and wishes of the supernatural Being had been misunderstood. Further scrutiny of the worldview's values led to new definitions and new proposals for *ethical* action – yet, distress endured ("IR," p. 353; *E&S*, p. 519).

In this manner, a dynamic was placed into motion, one that sought repeatedly to order and unify a worldview's constellation of values through logical deduction. Cognitive thought – a rational "theodicy of misfortune" – again and again came to the fore to seek "rationally satisfactory answers to the questioning [regarding] the basis of the incongruity between destiny and merit" ("I," p. 275). Rather than involving simply a varying response to "the social conditions of existence" or fluctuating economic and political forces, this dynamic followed an "imperative of consistency," Weber insists:

Religious interpretations of the world and ethics of religions created by [religion-oriented] intellectuals and meant to be rational have been strongly exposed to the imperative of consistency (*Gebot der Konsequenz*). The effect of the *ratio*, especially of a teleological deduction of practical postulates, is in some way, and often very strongly, noticeable among all religious ethics. This holds however little the religious interpretations of the world in the individual case have complied with the demand for consistency and however much they might integrate points of view into their ethical postulates which could *not* be rationally deduced. ("IR," p. 324 [emphasis in original]; see also "I," p. 286)

The development of ideas regarding the supernatural realm's features and contours was pushed by just this *religious* question as articulated by those in search of salvation: given the unity of the cosmos, why does suffering continue? As Weber stressed: "The rational need for a theodicy of suffering and of dying has had extremely strong effects" ("I," p. 275) and "this problem belongs everywhere among the deciding forces determining religious development and the need for salvation" (*E&S*, p. 519; translation altered). It also served as an impetus for the *constitution* of social groups: the dilemma presented by the problem of theodicy itself has the effect of drawing together persons concerned about this puzzle, Weber argues. Group formation arises not only from the economic, political, and status interests of daily life, nor from secular traditions alone, utilitarian action, power searching, or mundane values. Confrontations with the transcendent sphere also play a causal part.

In sum, Weber's post-*PE* attention to values and ideas is manifest in his discussion of worldviews. Driven by an "imperative of consistency," prophets, priests, monks, and theologians, as well as secular thinkers, search for clues to explain distress and to unveil hints that offer strategies to alleviate terrestrial misery and injustice, he maintains.[8]

Salvation Doctrines and Rational Thought.[9] The effect of salvation doctrines upon the social action of the devout differs distinctly in *intensity* from the influence of the ideal thrusts of worldviews, all of which involve cognitive assessments of whether action stands in a relationship of teleological consistency with the ideal thrusts. An entirely new dimension comes into play with salvation religions, Weber insists, namely *psychological rewards*.[10]

As mediated generally by doctrines, these incentives are placed directly upon action that, if properly executed, promises salvation to the believer. In Weber's analysis, the capacity of these rewards to convince the faithful of their redemption from this-worldly suffering and evil endows them with a *far greater* influence upon action than does a cognitive pondering of the consistency between mundane action and the values of a worldview (see *PE*, pp. 114–15; *GEH*, p. 364; Kalberg, 1990, p. 64).

All salvation religions involve, as a means of specifying their promises of a release from suffering and responding to the discrepancy between the "rational" supernatural realm and a terrestrial sphere saturated by unexplained misery, at least a minimum of religious doctrine (*E&S*, p. 563). As "rational religious systems of thought," doctrines generally originate from the theoretical rationalization processes undertaken by priests, monks, and theologians in reference to the problem of theodicy (see Kalberg, 2012, pp. 18–25, 43–72; 1990; Levine, 1985). They constitute ethical claims, according to Weber, rooted in a stable body of related teachings that are accepted as "revealed" knowledge. Doctrines, as constellations of values, prescriptions, laws, and norms internally consistent with one another to a greater or lesser extent, endow all thinking regarding God and sin with a further "rational element" (*E&S*, p. 426). In doing so, they fulfill the demand that Weber sees as the "core of religious rationalism":

> Behind [the great varieties of doctrines] always lies a stand towards something in the actual world which is experienced as specifically "senseless." Thus, the demand has been implied: that the world view in its totality is, could, and should somehow be a meaningful "cosmos." This quest [is] the core of genuine religious rationalism... The avenues, the results, and the efficacy of this metaphysical need for a "meaningful" cosmos have varied widely. ("I," p. 281; see also "IR," pp. 325, 351; *E&S*, pp. 427, 450–51, 458, 540, 563)

> The rational religious pragmatism of salvation, flowing from the nature of the images of God and of the world, [such as the Indian doctrine of Kharma, the Calvinist belief in predestination, the Lutheran justification through faith, and the Catholic doctrine of sacrament], have under certain conditions had far-reaching results for the fashioning of a practical way of life. ("I," p. 286)

Owing to their capacity to bestow psychological rewards upon action, salvation doctrines became endowed under certain circumstances with the potential to combine *on a continuous basis* the comprehensive ideal thrusts of worldviews, the quest for salvation, and the daily action of the devout, Weber maintains. In these cases, a methodical-rational organization of life congeals (see Kalberg, 1990).[11] The devout and the sincere as well as the much smaller group of "true believers" will continue to orient their action to religious doctrines *even* when their interests oppose doing so.[12] For him, a dynamic autonomy originating from ideas placed a "religious developmental process" into motion.[13]

In this manner, his religion-oriented analysis answers a question pivotal to him: How, and to what extent, do worldviews, salvation doctrines, and rational thought regarding suffering and the problem of theodicy assist the development of salvation religions? However, as evident from *PE*'s last pages, Weber wished to offer not only an "ideas" and "values" answer to this query; rather, he sought to provide a multi-causal analysis. We are now prepared to evaluate whether his analysis of the development of salvation religions includes sustained consideration of *both* ideas *and* interests.

Our orienting query should now be restated: did Weber, in his post-*PE* sociology of religion, fulfill his goal of offering causal analyses that investigated "both sides of the equation?" Or did he remain focused on ideas, values, a "systematization of thought," and an "imperative of consistency?"

6.2   The Attention to Material Factors

The above discussions on worldviews, salvation doctrines, and "rational thought" have charted an *expansion* of *PE*'s orientation to ideas and values. Indeed, these sections appear to lead to a clear conclusion: Weber downplayed material factors in his later sociology of religion and awarded priority to ideas and values. With the above queries in mind and now searching for the "other side," a turn to Weber's post-*PE* sociology of religion is again necessary. Does he, in fact, investigate *both* an "autonomous religious development" *and* the "materialist side of the causal equation?"

Weber stresses in Chapter 6 of *Economy and Society*, as well as throughout the Economic Ethics of the World Religions volumes, that the influence of worldviews upon social action remains extremely fragile. Although the impact of salvation doctrines is greater, a series of facilitating patterns of action by followers in groups is indispensable if worldviews and salvation doctrines are to call forth an internally unified, methodical-rational organization of the believer's life. They are also necessary if this action is to circumscribe sheer utilitarian patterns of action (2012, pp. 81–86).

A central lesson from Weber's post-*PE* sociology of religion is already evident: the thrusts set into motion by worldviews and the psychological premiums of salvation doctrines may both be drastically weakened by *interest*-oriented actions emanating from, for example, the economy, political, law, and status spheres. This *may* even occur in a widely pluralistic manner. Weber's far-reaching multi-causality will become apparent.

This "other side" – the "material side" – of his post-*PE* writings on religion is visible throughout the "Religious Rejections" ("IR") and "Social Psychology" ("I") essays as well as *Economy and Society*'s chapter on the sociology of religion. Multiple examples could be offered. Particularly illustrative, in light of this chapter's sociology of religion focus, are his multi-causal analyses that chart the origins of carrier strata, the routinization of charisma, and lay rationalism. We now turn to these analyses and explore Weber's *mode of procedure*; it calls attention to "both sides of the causal nexus." Indeed, these later writings seek to implement the goal articulated at *PE*'s conclusion: researchers must integrate "ideas and interests" if causality is to be adequately established (*PE*, pp. 178–79). Perhaps our attention to *PE*'s ideas and values has neglected the full array of research strategies utilized in Weber's sociology of religion.

Social Carriers. Weber attends repeatedly in his post-*PE* sociology of religion to the groups, strata, and organizations that "carry" the values of worldviews and the values and doctrines of salvation religions. This orientation constitutes a significant turn away from *PE*'s presuppositions.

To influence conduct, worldviews and salvation doctrines must possess cohesive and powerful social carriers. Their contours must not only be articulated by charismatic figures and their immediate disciples, Weber holds; in addition, powerful and demarcated groups with amenable interests and values must cultivate and carry them. Followers must congeal into lay circles and these groups must expand in size and internal organization into churches, mosques, synagogues, temples, and sects. Only then can the prophet's basic ideas and values be consistently defended; only then can a religion endure and remain viable (*E&S*, pp. 439–67, 500–03).

Indeed, the values and interests of powerful social strata significantly influence the formation and definition of a religion's belief configuration and teachings (see "I," p. 270). The impact of an intellectual stratum was particularly strong in the world religions of the East, Weber maintains. Confucian teachings in China were influenced significantly by the status ethic of a cultured stratum of intellectuals (see *RofC*, pp. 107–70; "I," p. 268). In India, the formation of Hinduism's salvation doctrine was strongly imprinted by a hereditary caste educated in Vedic ritual, and the teachings of early Buddhism were influenced significantly by contemplative, itinerant, and mendicant monks (*RofI*, p. 215; "I," pp. 268–69). The religions of China, India, and ancient Greece involved "representations appropriate to any cultivated intellectual stratum," as did ancient Judaism (*AJ*, p. 352, note 5).

The transformation and rationalization in ancient Israel of old oracles and promises and the introduction of the "characteristically different and independent conceptions" that formulated the intellectual traditions of this religion could not have occurred if an "independent cultured stratum" had been absent (*AJ*, p. 205). The situation has been entirely different wherever strata practically active in life influenced the development of a religion: "Where they were chivalrous warrior heroes, political officials, economically acquisitive classes, or, finally, where an organized hierocracy dominated religion, the results were different than where genteel intellectuals were decisive" ("I," p. 282).

To Weber, the interests and values of itinerant artisans, journeymen, petty bourgeois merchants, and more generally, urban civic strata shaped significantly Christianity's belief system in Antiquity. And the fact that functionaries held bureaucratic offices in the later Church itself influenced the character of its ecclesiastical lawmaking. The impact, Weber further contends, upon ascetic Protestantism's doctrines by the typical patterns of action, interests, and ways of directing life found in the middle and lower bourgeoisie is generally clear (see "I," pp. 268–69; *E&S*, pp. 479–80, 828, 1180).

The influence of a carrier stratum's ethic and interests upon religious belief is also readily visible whenever a world religion changes its carrier stratum. As Weber notes: "[A] change in the socially decisive strata has usually been of profound importance" ("I," p. 270). Carried in its classical period by Brahmins educated in the Vedas, Hinduism, for example, became a sacramental religion of ritual, belief in saviors, magic, and even orgiasticism in India's Middle Age when its carriers became plebeian mystagogues and the lower strata

("I," p. 269; see *RofI*, p. 176). Weber succinctly indicates the importance of carriers for religious ways of life in general:

> The various great ways of leading a rational and methodical life
> have been characterized by irrational presuppositions, which have
> been accepted simply as "given" and which have been incorporated
> into such ways of life. What these presuppositions have been is his-
> torically and socially determined, at least to a very large extent,
> through the uniqueness of those strata that have been the carriers of
> the ways of leading a life during its formative and decisive period.
> ("I," p. 281; translation altered; see pp. 279–85)

Throughout his post-*PE* sociology of religion, Weber attends to the
interests and values of the strata that influenced the formation of various salvation religions and served as their major carriers. This orientation constitutes a strong break from the focus in *PE* upon values in a
worldview, salvation doctrines, and "rational thought."

The Routinization of Charisma: Interests and Values.[14] The attribution of charisma to leaders plays only a minor role in *PE*. However, charismatic personalities – above all exemplary and emissary
prophets – play a large role in Weber's sociology of religion generally,
especially in respect to the origins of salvation religions. Disciples uphold and cultivate the prophet's original message.

Nonetheless, also prominent in his post-*PE* considerations of the
world religions are opposing groups pushing toward a "routinization
of charisma." Absent from *PE*, this concept breaks decisively from its
analysis. Just as Weber's discussion of social carriers, the routinization of charisma analysis moves distinctly away from *PE*'s procedures.
Interests – "the other side of the causal equation" – assume a pivotal
part in this ideas *and* interests imbroglio.

Weber insists that the faithful experience the transcendent realm
in different ways. Charismatic figures, all of whom are believed to
possess unusual qualifications, do so in a direct manner. An intense
"relationship to the supernatural"[15] infuses these "virtuosi" (*Virtu-
osen*). Conversely, the lay devout are endowed with "religious qualifications" of lesser intensity. Also oriented to the supernatural realm's
ideas and values, they operate in a manner less compelling than occurs

for the virtuosi (*E&S*, pp. 468–517; see Kalberg, 1990, pp. 67–70). Conflicts rooted in ideas *and* interests become regular.

As non-elites, members of churches, mosques, synagogues, temples, and sects regularly demand from elites' *revisions* of the prophet's extemporaneous and imprecise pronouncements involving routes to salvation. His inspirational sayings and speeches must be clearly comprehensible and rendered in systematic form. The devotion of the laity must be awakened and, if to be influential, their conduct must be directed; salvation paths must be demarcated and, not least, "adjusted" to meet the religious qualifications of the laity (*E&S*, pp. 439–67). Disciples, followers, priests, ministers, and theologians all undertake the task of interpreting the prophet's worldview and original ideas. The growth of religious organizations follows in part this conflictual pathway, Weber insists.

However, these interpreters perform their tasks not only in reference to variations in respect to ideas and qualifications, he stresses. Owing to frequent competition with other religious groups and sheer survival issues, salient also are economic, status, and political *interests*. They become in some cases central. Religious groups wish to insure a livelihood in *this life as well as* salvation in the next, Weber maintains (*E&S*, pp. 452–67, 486–88).

He designates this conflict-ridden process the "routinization of charisma" (*E&S*, pp. 246–54, 1121–25; see Kalberg, 1994, pp. 124–27). As religious groups and organizations become cohesive and firm, charisma becomes more and more cultivated not only in order to rejuvenate and sustain the founder's message but also to strengthen the capacity of organizations and groups to "institutionalize" charisma. "Office charisma" (*Amtscharisma*) comes into existence. Simultaneously, a *dynamic interaction* of interests, beliefs, values, ideas, power, and rulership congeals among both elite and lay groups (see *E&S*, pp. 1121–23, 1139–41; Kalberg, 1994, p. 126). Status groups, each defending its own social, economic, and political agenda, as well as values-based aims, also crystallize. Charisma's "creative aspect" now becomes absorbed – to varying degrees – into the permanent institutions of everyday life (see *E&S*, pp. 1131–33, 1156; "EK," p. 470).

The interest of followers in legitimizing positions of prestige and rulership, as well as to secure economic resources, plays a central role, Weber argues. Indeed, especially important at each stage of charisma's routinization has been the search for economic advantage (see *E&S*, pp. 148, 262, 1120, 1146, 1156). Those holding economic and social power seek, with the aim of legitimating positions of privilege, to "capture" the charismatic movement and to utilize its ideas, energy, and aura for their own ends (see *E&S*, pp. 252, 1121–23). Concomitantly, now impersonal and transformed into routinized forms, firm hierarchies appear within the religious organizations. These developments further influence the charismatic founder's pronouncements and enable persons in possession of authority to view their superior positions as legitimate (*E&S*, pp. 1122–23, 1126–27).

Weber's analysis of charisma's routinization pathway is central to his post-*PE* sociology of religion. Absent from *PE*, it qualitatively diverges from this classic study's framework and presuppositions. Weber has here expanded his sociology of religion to include "the other side" of the causal equation, namely, a "materialist" analysis that takes the role of economic, status, and political interests directly into account.

Lay Rationalism. Weber's post-*PE* sociology of religion moves distinctly beyond *PE*'s attention to ideals and values in a further overt manner: his later writings include discussions of the ways in which interests become intertwined with "lay rationalism."

The founders of salvation religions interacted with lay believers "located" in varying social contexts, he insists. This population, locked within encompassing magic, ritual, and age-old traditions and ethnic dualisms, was in some regions highly insulated from, and resistant to, new beliefs and utilitarian conduct. In other regions, a lay rationalism was widespread: here, the devout were urban dwellers less rooted in magic and tradition and more anchored in guilds as well as in production and exchange activities.

This rationalism implied a significant break from magic, ritual, traditions, and ethnic dualisms, Weber holds. A more mobile population could arise. Moreover, a more active posture vis-à-vis religious doctrines, rituals, and sacred traditions could now crystallize. In this context, the laity's corresponding rationalism was endowed with a greater capacity to evaluate and challenge a worldview's values, as well as salvation doctrines, on a regular basis (see *E&S*, pp. 452–57, 464–67). Pressure for their alteration also arose externally, namely from transformations of action patterns oriented to the economy, social status tensions and conflicts, and political struggles.

Interests could more frequently become manifest in this milieu. Indeed, this elevation of diverse interests in Weber's post-*PE* sociology of religion relocates his mode of analysis distinctly away from *PE*'s orientation to values and ideas and toward multi-causal research procedures – ones that acknowledge a range of political, economic, and status interests.

6.3   "Ideas *and* Interests"

Where does Weber stand? He instructs his readers in a concerted manner that even when understood as strongly interactive, the economic, political, and status interests of daily life, as well as traditions and mundane values, fail to constitute for his sociology of religion the *full spectrum* of potentially causal patterns of action. The directed action of the devout toward religious values and ideas, albeit at times without consistency despite orientations to worldviews and salvation doctrines, must not be neglected. This social action at times even stands firm against the utilitarian "flow of life." To Weber, confrontations with the transcendent sphere also imply causality.

Moreover, he stresses that an "imperative of consistency" influences the patterned social action of the faithful and particularly of religion-oriented elites: prophets, priests, monks, and theologians. The problem of theodicy in the end *can* burden their souls, in certain contexts, to such an extent that an alteration of their social action occurs in consistent ways. Nevertheless, and although the capacity for "rational thought" must never be omitted from "the causal equation," Weber's sociology of religion *also* charts the impact of mundane interests.

Thus, despite his attention to ideas and values in *PE* and in many of his post-*PE* writings, as noted above, Weber cannot be categorized as a theorist oriented exclusively to these factors. Rather, he must be viewed as attending to *both* ideal and material causes. He seeks perpetually to combine "ideas *and* interests" throughout his sociology of religion and unrelentingly attempts to do so in spite of his repeated acknowledgment of the complexity of this task.

Perhaps Weber's unending struggle to interlock tightly, if causality is to be established, "*both sides* of the causal equation" accounts in part for the well-known difficulty of his texts. This unfortunate feature of his mode of analysis and research procedures seems invariably to render "a Weberian analysis" multi-causal and nonlinear. To him:

> Neither religions nor men are open books. They have been histori-cal rather than logical or even psychological constructions without contradiction. Often they have borne within themselves a series of motives, each of which, if separately and consistently followed through, would have stood in the way of the others or run against them head-on. In religious matters "consistency" has been the ex-ception and not the rule. The ways and means of salvation are also psychologically ambiguous. ("I," p. 291)

Notes

1 The full passage deserves attention: "This study has attempted, of course, merely to trace ascetic Protestantism's influence, and the particu-lar *nature* of this influence back to ascetic Protestantism's motives in re-gard to one – however important – point. The way in which Protestant asceticism was in turn influenced in its development and characteristic uniqueness by the entirety of societal cultural conditions, and especially *economic* conditions, must also have its day....Of course it cannot be the intention here to set a one-sided religion-oriented analysis of the causes of culture and history in place of an equally one-sided 'materialistic' analysis. *Both* are *equally possible*. Historical truth, however, is served equally little if either of these analyses claims to be the conclusion of an investigation rather than its beginning stage" (*PERW*, pp. 178–79; trans-lation altered).

2 It is evident from the quotation above (note 1) that Weber's reference to "materialistic analysis" implies a strong rejection of the Marxian under-standing of this term, especially its broad usage and reductionist features. Hence, any reference to "materialism" and "interests" as synonyms is pre-cluded (see also Weber, e.g., *E&S*, p. 341; "Obj," p. 113; 1988, p. 456). Although Weber never offers a systematic discussion of "interests" (see the abbreviated treatment at *E&S*, pp. 29–32), his usage is clear: the *vary-ing* interests of people in diverse groups are emphasized (whether, e.g., economic, status, or political groups) *as is* the capacity of interests to be-come causally significant *in a specific context* (as opposed to Marx's clear elevation of material factors to central epistemological status). Weber's passage at the end of *PE* follows this pattern (see again note 1). This usage is compatible with the "ideas and interests" pluralism he calls for, that is, a multi-causal framework anchored in a variety of societal domains (the economy, law, rulership, religion, status groups, and family spheres (see Kalberg, 2012, pp. 97–112, 129–40) legitimize values and ideas on the one hand and interests on the other hand.

3 Unfortunately, this chapter cannot undertake the enormous task of exploring the major aspects of "the material side" as discussed in *Economy and Society, General Economic History*, and the Economic Ethics of the World Religions series on China (*RofC*), India (*RofI*), and ancient Judaism (*AJ*). However, it should be noted that these more historical writings address the theoretical issue of concern here in an irregular manner. The *analytic* sources for Weber's post-*PE* sociology of religion provide a more suitable terrain for an analysis of the "ideas and interests" relationship: The "Introduction" ("I") essay, the "Religious Rejections of the World" ("IR") essay, and Chapter 6 ("The Sociology of Religion") in *Economy and Society*. Our focus will be upon the *concepts and modes of analysis* prominent in these texts. Nonetheless, the omission of an analysis rooted also in Weber's investigations on China, India, and ancient Judaism, it must be stressed, render this study a *preliminary* investigation only.

4 The "correctness" or "superiority" of a worldview can never be scientifically proven, Weber argues (see *RCM*, p. 331). The subjective meaningfulness of beliefs to a group of people alone establishes its legitimacy.

5 For a more detailed discussion of worldviews, see Kalberg (2012, pp. 73–92).

6 "Dynamic autonomy" is the author's term. See Kalberg (2012, pp. 79–81).

7 That is, monotheism on the one hand and the immanent, impersonal All-One of Buddhism and classical Hinduism on the other hand.

8 For more detail on this "religious development" to ethical salvation religions and then to ethical salvation religions that devalue the world, see Kalberg (2012, pp. 43–72).

9 The following four paragraphs are indebted to Kalberg (2012, pp. 81–83).

10 On the critical distinction between the influence of cognitive consistency as opposed to the effect of psychological rewards (*Prämien*) on action, see *PE*, pp. 114–15; 327–29, notes 39, 40; 376–77, note 37; "I," p. 267; "IR," p. 338; Kalberg (2012, p. 67, note 31). Weber employs the terms "psychological impulse" (*Antrieb*) and "psychological strength" (*Kraft*) synonymously.

11 This very complex process, which relates to the salvation goals and salvation paths articulated by the doctrine, is examined in detail at Kalberg (2012, pp. 47–62; see also pp. 73–92).

12 For example: "The power of [a fully developed ecclesiastic hierarchy] rests upon the principle that 'God must be obeyed more than men,' for the sake of spiritual welfare both in the here and the hereafter. This has been the most ancient check on all political power, the most effective one up to the great Puritan Revolution and the Declaration of the Rights of Man" (*E&S*, p. 1175).

13 Weber stresses that a clear difference remains between worldly interests and religious values in regard to his "autonomy" theme: owing to the omnipresent and enduring question of salvation, religious development retains a *highly consistent* focus – the supernatural and the problem of suffering – quite separate from the flux and flow of mundane reality, all

the more whenever religion-oriented groups crystallize into cohesive organizations and even social strata. Interests, however, whenever unencumbered and hence able to "follow their own laws," do so alone on the basis of power coalitions. Thus, while an *internal* consistency and continuity of development in reference to the problem of suffering characterizes the dynamic autonomy of religious ideas and their accompanying values, interests follow a different course: they remain subject to the push and pull of power configurations. They follow various routes simply as a consequence of history's perpetually shifting alliances and antagonisms across groups (see Tenbruck, 1980).

14 A more detailed discussion can be found in Kalberg (1994, pp. 124–26).

15 This is Weber's definition of religion (see *E&S*, p. 424; see also pp. 399–400).

PART III

The Origins, Uniqueness, and Pathway of the American Political Culture

7

TOCQUEVILLE AND WEBER ON THE SOCIOLOGICAL ORIGINS OF CITIZENSHIP

The Political Culture of American Democracy

Alexis de Tocqueville's *Democracy in America* (1945) is considered today to be perhaps the most profound analysis of American society ever written.[1] Far more than a "political commentary," this classic focuses upon the "manners and mores" – the customs – at the very foundation of its political culture.[2] Two major themes, both of which originate from Tocqueville's focus upon the far-ranging differences between "aristocratic and democratic nations" and the ways in which the "equality of conditions" widely influences American society, stand at the center of his analysis: a concern regarding a potential "tyranny of the majority" dander and an emphasis upon, if democracy is to remain stable, the necessity of widespread civil associations.

Max Weber also sojourned in the United States and retained a life-long interest in this nation. Although far less well known and broadly scattered throughout his works, his commentary upon the American political culture addresses the two major themes of concern to Tocqueville. An examination of these writings and a comparison of their conclusions to Tocqueville's, in respect to these themes, constitutes the major task of this investigation.[3]

Tocqueville attempts to capture the political culture of the United States largely be reference to its widespread egalitarianism and the tyranny of the majority theme, as well as the nimble capacity of the Americans to formulate civil associations. While cognizant, as Tocqueville, of a debilitating tendency toward rigid social conformism

DOI: 10.4324/9781032631813-11

in American life, Weber focuses upon a counterbalancing "world-mastery" individualism and the development of a distinct *civic sphere* penetrated by a specific constellation of values.

In comparing Tocqueville and Weber, this study seeks to define their distinct perspectives upon the American political culture, to contrast Tocqueville's more structural and interest-based mode of analysis to Weber's emphasis upon the significance of values and beliefs, and to demarcate the underlying axes of the American political culture. On the basis of insights offered by both theorists, this investigation hopes to comment upon an array of significant sociological forces at the origin of modern citizenship.

7.1   A "Tyranny of the Majority" in the United States?

Alexis de Tocqueville. After a nine-month journey, Tocqueville left the United States with a favorable impression (see, vol. 1, p. x). Convinced that democratic governance would eventually come to European shores and seeking to impart the lessons he had learnt to his countrymen, he hoped to assist the development of democracy in Europe and, in particular, in France (see vol. 1, pp. ix–x, 3, 14–15, 338–42). Nonetheless, he remained skeptical in a major respect: unless a series of distinct "safeguards" existed, he feared that democracies would unavoidably call forth a tyranny of the majority.[4] He based this conclusion upon his observation of the American political culture.

Democracy in the United States, Tocqueville argues, is rooted in the overarching assumption that majority opinion has a *moral* authority. It is widely believed "that there is more intelligence and wisdom in a number of men united than in a single individual" (vol. 1, p. 265), and hence "the interests of the many are to be preferred to those of the few" (vol. 1, p. 266). "All authority," he asserts, "originates in the will of the majority" (vol. 1, p. 268) and "the majority understands itself as a 'superior intelligence'" (vol. 1, p. 265).

Tocqueville calls attention to the "germ of tyranny" that arises from the simple fact that the "right and means of absolute command" (vol. 1, p. 270), conveyed to the majority, is not restrained by a countervailing force. If "no obstacles exist [to] impede…its progress" (vol. 1, p. 266; see also pp. 270–71), to whom then can the wronged individual appeal? A legislature represents the majority and the executive is elected by the majority – even judges are in many states elected. "When I see that the right and the means of absolute command are conferred on any power whatever, be it called a people or a king, an aristocracy or a democracy, a monarchy or a republic, I say there is the germ of tyranny, and I seek to live elsewhere, under other laws" (vol. 1, p. 270).

Tocqueville argues that the great powers of majority rule are especially visible in respect to the "exercise of thought." Wherever the majority constitutes the legitimate court of last appeal, individuals become extremely aware of and sensitive to the opinions of their fellow citizens. Indeed, once pronounced by the majority's vote, decisions entail an end to all discussion and silence. Debates involving broad-ranging and fundamental issues are curtailed.

Thus, Tocqueville proclaims he "knows of no country where there is so little independence of mind and real freedom of discussion" (vol. 1, p. 273). A certain narrowness of opinion prevails, even to the extent that the question arises whether viable political liberties can be said to exist. Whoever entertains positions and opinions opposed to those of the majority soon realizes that political careers cannot be followed, and they also often experience social ostracism.

The lesson is clear to Tocqueville: wherever government is "self-made" and individuals feel themselves equal to one another, a conformity of opinions will result. Wherever citizens are without clear social standing by birth and must create their social positions, as in democracies unlike feudal societies, they become, merely to avoid scorn, inordinately sensitive to the opinions of others (see vol. 1, pp. 274–77). Whereas the aristocrat's superiority is never questioned of weakened in spite of the most outrageous pronouncements and behavior, for it is founded securely in noble birth, citizens in egalitarian societies must continually create and recreate their social standing, always doing so by reference to the opinions of their peers. Moreover, a currying of favor and extreme timidity very often become widespread.

Unlike organically stratified societies in which persons are strongly connected with one another as a consequence of fixed obligations, duties, and responsibilities, equality implies an isolation of persons one from another – if only because the clear "sense of place" indigenous to the feudal society is now lacking. This isolation on the one hand allows every man to "concentrate [his] attention upon himself"

(vol. 2, p. 23) and on the other hand increases even more his awareness of and sensitivity to the opinions of others. To Tocqueville:

> Whereas the authority of a king is physical, and controls...actions
> without subduing [the] will...the majority possesses a power which
> is physical and moral at the same time, which acts upon the will as
> much as upon the actions, and represses not only all contest, but all
> controversy. (vol. 1, p. 273; see also pp. 276–78)

> The majority...exercise a prodigious actual authority, and a power
> of opinion which is nearly as great; no obstacles exist which can
> impede or even retain its progress, so as to make it heed the com-
> plaints of those whom it crushes upon its path. This state of things
> is harmful in itself and dangerous for the future. (vol. 1, p. 266)

Nonetheless, Tocqueville discovered an array of significant forces that
tend to counteract and hold in check this "tyranny." Taken together,
they moderate his fears regarding the dangerous consequences that
follow from the majority's "omnipotence."

He first calls attention to several secondary factors: a decentralized administration in the United States that refrains from "descend-
ing to the details" of governance (vol. 1, pp. 281–82); a strong legal
profession which, oriented to legality, regularity, and public order,
stands "above the masses" as a "natural aristocracy," opposing innovation, and "neutralizing the vices of popular government" (vol.
1, pp. 282–90); and the institution of trial by jury, which acquaints
citizens with laws and "invests the people with the direction of society," thereby cultivating responsibility and caution. Jury trials
as well "oblige [them] to turn their attention to other affairs than
their own [land and hence diminish] private selfishness" (vol. 1,
pp. 291–97).

Tocqueville also notes the importance of a free press (vol. 2, p. 343),
a widespread respect in the United States for laws, a strong court and
judicial system to uphold laws, "restrain the masses, and counteract
the imperfections of human nature" (vol. 2, p. 343; vol. 1, pp. 309–
10). Finally, he contends that township institutions "impart a taste for
freedom" (vol. 1, p. 310). However, Tocqueville focuses his analysis
upon two further safeguards that "mitigate the tyranny of the masses"
and "maintain democracy": religion and civil associations.

He repeatedly emphasizes the significance of religion. The sheer flux and perpetual change that reigns in those epochs characterized by an equality of conditions poses a great danger to democracies. Indeed, to Tocqueville, equality implies innovation and a continuous shifting of daily politics and morality. "Everything seems doubtful and indeterminate in the moral world" whenever equality reigns (vol. 1, p. 339). The "daily practice of men's lives" requires "constancy," he contends, and "happiness and greatness" can only appear if "a salutary restraint [is imposed] on the intellect" (vol. 2, p. 22).

Hence, as equality spreads, religions all the more become a necessity, for it "inspires diametrically contrary principles" (vol. 2, p. 23): "Fixed ideas about God and human nature" and "standards of truth and virtue...that then need not be sought in daily polities" (vol. 2, p. 22). By laying down absolute principles and hence relativizing greed, envy, and self-interests, religion safeguards morality "and morality [is] the best security of law and the surest pledge of the duration of freedom" (vol. 1, p. 46):

> Despotism may govern without faith, but liberty cannot. Religion is much more necessary in the republic...; it is more needed in democratic republics than in any others. How is it possible that society should escape destruction if the moral tie is not strengthened in proportion as the political tie is relaxed? And what can be done with a people who are their own masters if they are not submissive to the Deity? (vol. 1, p. 318; see also vol. 2, p. 27)

> I am inclined to think that if faith be wanting in him, he must be subject; and if h be free, he must be free, he must believe. (vol. 1, p. 23)

Civil associations also constitute a strong safeguard against the tyranny of the majority. They serve, Tocqueville argues, as obstacles against the unmediated opinion of the majority and hence insulate their members. On the other hand, civil associations counteract the psychological isolation that results from the equality of conditions, thereby offering boundaries and guidelines to individuals otherwise restless (vol. 2, p. 124). As well, they assist individuals "easily lost" and at risk of disappearing into the throng" (vol. 1, p. 339), far better than occurs when individuals either stand alone or join an "uncontrolled mob," to acquire practice in self-government, to engage in political activity, and to make their voices heard: "The greater the multiplicity of small affairs, the more do men...acquire facility in prosecuting great undertakings in common" (vol. 2, p. 123). Finally, civil associations introduce continuity and, when numerous, balance out contending groupings.

These safeguards might well be effective against the dangers – both isolation and conformity pressures – presented by the equality of conditions, for they prevent the extreme centralization of opinion prerequisite to a constitution of majorities and their unequivocal endorsement by public opinion. Rather than quickly rendered superfluous, political discussion could then continue, the rights of minorities would be preserved, opinions would be less circumscribed, and the "exercise of thought" and imagination would be less restricted.

Nonetheless, a deep doubt, even skepticism regarding the long-term stability of democratic governance under conditions of equality reappears in nearly every section throughout *Democracy in America*. This theme is explored from a vast variety of perspectives. Tocqueville sees a distinct narrowing of the parameters of debate and public opinion in the United States. Owing to the importance in this regard of religion and civil associations, he is especially unwilling to recommend the adoption of an American-style democracy in Europe, where civil associations and religions were weak (see vol. 2, p. 114). He remains wary to the end.

Max Weber's writings address the tyranny of the majority theme from a different perspective. They implicitly pose the question of whether Tocqueville's analysis accurately captures the central dimensions of the American political culture. Might Tocqueville have oversimplified the omnipotence of the majority and the tyranny danger? Did he adequately portray the character of American individualism?

Max Weber. As Tocqueville, Weber called attention to the unusually group-based nature of American society and the severity of the resulting conformity pressures (*Konformitaetsdrang*). However, he never saw a tyranny of the majority danger or a weak, "enfeebled" individual. Rather, he discovered a force at the very center of the American political culture – the "world-mastery" (*weltbeherrschende*) individualism called forth by ascetic Protestantism – that appeared effectively to counterbalance any tendency toward such a tyranny, indeed in a manner far more comprehensively than the safeguards identified by Tocqueville. Might American political culture, following *both* Tocqueville and Weber, be best captured by reference to a tension between the conformist pressures inherent to the "equality of conditions" on the one hand and the self-reliant individualism of the ascetic Protestant tradition on the other? If so, what lessons for an understanding of American democracy and the political culture of citizenship can be drawn?

Weber rejected the view that, dominant in Europe at the turn of the century, understood American democracy as founded in atomistic and solitary individuals ("Sects I," pp. 231–32; "Sects II," pp. 214–17). He argued instead, as Tocqueville, that ubiquitous associations characterized this society: churches, sects, social clubs, hobby organizations, and so on. Both theorists observed that Americans formulated groups in an exceedingly quick and nimble fashion.

Moreover, although membership surely provided to some extent a sense of belonging and a safe and secure locus for activity, Weber emphasized that it also constituted a "badge of respectability," or a mark of social honor. The orientation toward honor so central in feudal societies had not simply vanished; on the contrary, it remained strong in egalitarian societies yet assumed a different form: it now was "acquired" through admission to organizations widely respected in one's community rather than given by birth (see "Sects II," pp. 214–16; "Sects I," p. 229; *E&S*, p. 933). American democracy, he argued, could not be characterized as a "sandheap" of lonesome individuals; rather, the United States must be comprehended as a society of "joiners," massive associations, and exclusivities.

The genuine American society – and here we include especially the "middle" and "lower" strata of the population – was never such a sandpile. Nor was it a building where everyone who entered without exception found open doors. It was and is permeated with "exclusivities" of every kind. Where the old relationships still exist, the individual does not have firm footing, either at the university or in business life, when he has been unable to be accepted into or maintain his position in a *social organization* (earlier almost always religious, today of one kind or another). ("Sects I," pp. 231–32; original emphasis):

In the past...it has been a characteristic precisely of the specifically American democracy that it did *not* constitute a formless sandheap of individuals, but rather a buzzing complex of strictly exclusive, yet voluntary associations. ("Sects II," p. 310; original emphasis)

It is still true that American democracy is not a sandpile of unrelated individuals but a maze of highly exclusive, yet absolutely voluntary sects, associations, and clubs which provide the center of the individual's social life. (*E&S*, p. 1207)

Thus, Weber calls attention to an aspect of American life stressed in the strongest terms by Tocqueville: its multiple and multifarious "civil associations." Although he never explicitly notes the manner in which these associations restrict the "independence of mind" of the Americans, he was surely aware of this danger, as is apparent particularly in his discussions of the conformist pressures within the ascetic Protestant sects and their powers to expel and then socially ostracize the disobedient:

The [sect] member's reputation largely corresponds to his actual qualities, for the intensity of indoctrination and the impact of exclusion are much more effective than any authoritarian ecclesiastic discipline can be. (*E&S*, p. 1206; see also pp. 1205–07)

The extraordinarily strict moral discipline of the self-governing congregation...was unavoidable because of the interest in the purity of the sacramental community. ("Sects," II, p. 221; see *passim*; see also "Sects I," pp. 228–29)

These observations would seem to lead Weber to Tocqueville's conclusion: a great tyranny of the majority danger exists in the United States. In effect, the influence upon behavior of the ascetic Protestant sects and churches, according to Weber's rendering, could be understood as elucidating the sociological basis for such a tyranny. However, he never draws this conclusion; indeed, his attention turns strongly toward another aspect of American democracy: the *world-mastery individualism* called forth by ascetic Protestantism.

This focus led Weber to conclude that any potential danger would be mitigated in the United States by a counterbalancing force even more effective than the safeguards Tocqueville identified. At the foundation of this difference regarding the American political culture stand very different approaches to comparative-historical sociology: while one is rooted in the notion of *verstehen* and a strong acknowledgment of values, the other offers a more structural and interest-based methodology.

World-Mastery Individualism. Ascetic Protestants undoubtedly adhered to God's commandments as a consequence of the purely pragmatic possibility of expulsion from their religious communities and social ostracism. Weber's entire sociology, however, emphasizes as well another dimension to human experience: belief. He does not doubt that religious faith can be sincere, conscientious, and sociologically significant. As he notes frequently, it is, of course, difficult for "we moderns" to imagine the urgency of the central question to sixteenth and seventeenth century ascetic Protestants (see *PE,* pp. 123–24, 158–59, 178; 337–39, note 76; "Sects I," p. 230: "Am I among the saved"). However, this difficulty should not lead sociologists to conclude that Calvinists, Methodists, Baptists, Quakers, and Pietists could not be sincerely devout.

Central to Weber's sociology is the attempt to *understand* the subjective meaningfulness of social action by persons situated in sociologically significant groups (e.g., status groups and organizations such as churches, sects, and bureaucracies). If the subjective meaning of Calvinists, for example, is reconstructed, it will become apparent that conformity to the opinions of peers in the church indeed constituted only one aspect of their religious devoutness. Another component – their strong individualism or, in Weber's terms, their world-mastery asceticism – is equally significant *and* grounded directly in their beliefs. Neglected by Tocqueville, *this* individualism, Weber holds, *coexists* in American democracy with the social conformity that presents a tyranny of the majority danger. Indeed, it offers a powerful safeguard against this tyranny. How did it do so?

Unlike Catholics, Calvinist[5] believers stood alone before their Deity, unassisted by a Church of virtuoso believers with special access to God: priests, bishops, cardinals, and popes. Expected to read and interpret scripture on their own, Calvinists remained in a one-to-one relationship with God. Moreover, their Deity – the wrathful, vengeful, distant, and all-powerful God of the Old Testament – expected strict adherence to His Commandments, and human weaknesses could not be absolved through the Confession. Finally, the Calvinist devout were expected, as the Catholic monks before them, to be loyal alone

to God, and thus intimate relationships in particular – even those between spouses – must assume a tone of moderation and restraint, for
strong allegiances to others could only endanger the most important
Relationship. Such a doctrine could only have had the effect of calling
forth a sturdy and self-reliant individualism.

Yet, Weber sees Calvinism as doing so in perhaps an even more fundamental manner. According to the reforms undertaken above all by
Richard Baxter, an influential seventeenth-century English pastor and
writer on Puritan ethics, activity in the world – hard work, regular
competition, and a search for profit and even wealth – could provide
believers with the wealth that, *or so they could convince themselves*,
indeed derived from the favoring hand of an omnipotent and omniscient God. And, of course, it could be logically reasoned, God would
favor only those he had chosen – or *predestined* – to be saved. In this
manner, practical activity itself or *mastery* of the world on behalf of
the creation on earth of God's just and affluent Kingdom acquired a
"psychological premium," all the more owing to the distinctly ascetic
character of the believer's conduct (*PE*, pp. 87–137, 158–79). Methodical work, as well as the search for profit and wealth, now became *sanctified* or closely linked to the salvation hopes of the devout.

Hence, all activities undertaken on behalf of the accumulation
of wealth now became legitimated, even highly acclaimed: rugged
competition, innovation, upward mobility, and initiative-taking and
risk-taking. This new way of leading and directing one's energies and
even life itself (*Lebensfuehrung*) implied to Weber a new *ethos* or set
of values – not only unleashed a tremendous energy and injected a
massive dynamism into American economic development, but also
implied a strong, activity-oriented individualism.

While Puritanism mainly directed this individualism toward the as-
certainment of the believer's state of grace, it *also* required that the
devout hold others responsible for their conduct. All, in the new "City
on the Hill," must now demonstrate allegiance to God and uphold
His Commandments, for in His community "weakness" and "worldly
evil" must be mastered. A passive acceptance of evil was prohibited:
the faithful must "be strong" and act *against* evil (*PE*, pp. 87–137).
Moreover, with Puritanism believers now stood under *a religious* obligation, should rulers violate God's decrees, to protest against and
overthrow such "illegitimate" rulership (see "Sects I," pp. 229–30;

E&S, pp. 1208–09). In these ways, the devout became empowered to act decisively on behalf of a set of beliefs in both the political and economic arenas (see *PE*, pp. 158–72):

> The ascetic conventicles and sects formed one of the most important historical foundations of modern "individualism." Their radical break away from patriarchal and authoritarian bondage, as well as *their* way of interpreting the statement that one owes more obedience to God than to man was especially important. ("Sects II," pp. 225–28; emphasis original; see "Sects I," pp. 230–31)

This brief and incomplete overview (see Chapters 2–5; see also Kalberg, 2011, pp. 8–63) of Weber's argument in *PE* must suffice to indicate that Puritanism introduced a strong and self-reliant individualism into the American political and economic landscapes, as did ascetic Protestantism generally. A readiness to act and to reform the world on behalf of religious values arose out of the ascetic Protestant churches and sects. Neither cautious nor contemplative, nor accepting of the random daily life, the faithful were now, through their *ethical* action, motivated to transform society as a whole. The teaching and cultivation of this ascetic, world-mastery individualism occurred in the family and the self-governing congregation.

Weber emphasizes that the devout were encouraged by their beliefs to act not simply against unjust secular authority, but also, if necessary, against popular opinion (*E&S*, pp. 1208–09; "Sects I," p. 230). If the "practical-ethical" action that organized daily life contradicted the opinions of groups, whether constituted from majorities or otherwise, the faithful were *obligated* to stand against popular opinion. Their asceticism itself imbued their ethical action with a great intensity. Moreover, the overriding importance of the salvation (*certitudo salutis*) question insured that the herculean labors of believers to control daily activity would take God's abstract principles and rules as their fulcrum rather than the particular features of persons, emotional bonds with them, or popular and fashionable currents (see *PE*, pp. 127–28; *E&S*, pp. 424, 578).

As industrialization, urbanization, and secularization occurred in the eighteenth and nineteenth centuries, the extreme aspects of inner-worldly asceticism became routinized into utilitarian modes of action (see *PE*, pp. 76–82). Nonetheless, in many communities, a world-mastery individualism remained and assumed normative status. At times fully devoid of its religious tenor, it now became carried and cultivated by families, neighborhoods, and community leaders. This activity-oriented and self-reliant individualism was characterized by resoluteness and a robust optimism regarding the capacity of persons to challenge firm traditions and to confront social problems. As well, it motivated individuals to stand against popular opinion.

Tocqueville and Weber: A Tyranny of the Majority? Tocqueville's understanding of individualism varies dramatically from Weber's. He fails go attribute a particular influence upon its development in the United States to ascetic Protestantism. His examination of religion remains almost entirely limited to general discussions regarding the manner in which religious beliefs provide standards of behavior and virtue especially indispensable if a tyranny of the majority is to be avoided in egalitarian societies (see vol. 2, pp. 22–29).[6]

For Tocqueville, as noted, individualism arises with the decline of feudalism and the appearance of egalitarianism; for him, "individualism is of democratic origin, and it threatens to spread in the same ratio as the equality of condition" (vol. 2, p. 104). According to this purely structural argument, equality itself loses the fixed position and duties inherent to feudalism's organic stratification and allows persons to view themselves as separate from the past as well as all firm societal anchoring; the "bond of human affection is extended, but it is relaxed" (vol. 2, p. 104). Without firm social hierarchies, persons are no longer "linked in a chain."

They become disconnected from one another and even strangers: "...as social conditions become more equal, the number of persons increases... [who] owe nothing to any man: they acquire the habit of always considering themselves as standing alone, and they are apt to imagine that their whole destiny is in their own hands" (vol. 2, p. 105; see also pp. 104–07). Fundamentally, Tocqueville defines individualism as involving an isolation of persons – an "atomism" – and "concentration of attention upon oneself": "...democracy...throws him back forever upon himself alone, and threatens in the end to confine him entirely within the solitude of his own heart" (vol. 2, p. 106).[7]

Far from oriented to world-mastery or rooted in the ascetic's rigid adherence to abstract principles and rules, this individualism is "enfeebled" and devoid of a clear line of internal direction, for "equality sets men apart and weakens them" (vol. 2, p. 344).[8] Not surprisingly, in his discussions of the various safeguards against a tyranny of the majority, Tocqueville fails to mention individualism. The individual Weber sees in American democracy – anchored in the world-mastery orientations of ascetic Protestant *belief*[9] rather than a social leveling process – diverges dramatically from that of Tocqueville.

In sum, Tocqueville's tyranny of the majority thesis derives from a view of the individual as fundamentally passive. As reconstructed here, Weber's observations on the American political culture call attention to a very different individualism characterized by severe conformity, yet *also* anchored "from within" by orientations to values and principles. Capable of acting "in the world" on their behalf, this individualism may stand *against* even popular opinion bolstered by the "omnipotence of the majority."[10]

Weber's analysis reveals Tocqueville's "tyranny of the majority" danger as stemming from a portrait of American democracy that attends to only one of its two major axes. An enduring *tension* in the political culture of the United States between a world-mastery individualism on the one hand and strong pressures toward social conformity and group orientations on the other is at the center of his investigations. A *pendulum* movement across a spectrum ranging from "world-oriented" individualism to social conformity is typical. Both axes are deeply rotted in America's religious history and neither locates its source, according to Weber, in a purely structural transformation: the rise of conditions of equality and social equality. When utilized as an explanatory framework, egalitarianism, he argues, neglects the crucial question of its *cultural* context.

Both Tocqueville and Weber also address the central sociological significance of civil associations in the American political culture and both marvel at their ubiquitousness. However, once again their explanatory frameworks diverge distinctly: while Tocqueville sees civil associations as originating from political associations as well as a variety of interests, Weber argues that a set of conducive values – which together constitute a demarcated *civic sphere* – prove indispensable if civic associations are to appear on a broad scale.

7.2 The Critical Role of Civil Associations

Alexis de Tocqueville. As noted, as the social hierarchies of feudalism decline and "social conditions" become more equal, Tocqueville argues that a great danger arises: individuals will become more and more isolated. Cut off from all firm "sense of place" and hence without a defined connection to others or to the past, amidst this social leveling individuals increasingly stand on their own (vol. 2, pp. 109–10). This separation not only leads to individuality on the one hand and a massive conformism on the other; in addition, it implies "the danger of severe instability followed by a call for the authoritarianism of a strong leader." The omnipotence of the majority, Tocqueville holds, is "full of peril to the American republics" (vol. 1, p. 202; see also vol. 2, pp. 336–38).

"Democratic nations are menaced [by a new species of oppression]...unlike...ever before existed" (vol. 2, p. 336): anarchy and servitude threaten their long-term stability. As Tocqueville notes: "The principle of equality begets two tendencies: the one leads men straight to independence and may suddenly drive tendencies: the one leads men straight to independence and may suddenly drive them into anarchy; the other conducts...them to servitude" (vol. 2, p. 304):

> If ever the free institutions of America are destroyed, that even may be attributed to the omnipotence of the majority, which may at some future time urge the minorities to desperation and oblige them to have recourse to physical force. Anarchy will then be the result, but it will have been brought about by despotism. (vol. 1, p. 279)

> When there is no longer any principle of authority in religion any more than in politics, men are speedily frightened at the aspect of this unbounded independence. The constant agitation of all surrounding things alarm and exhausts them. As everything is at sea in the sphere of the mind, they determine at least that the mechanism of society shall be firm and fixed, and as they cannot resume their ancient belief, they assume a master. (vol. 2, p. 23)

This servitude also arises as a consequence of the "tendency of democracy to destroy all that stands between the individual and kings," thus leaving the individual alone and isolated "before the power of the state" (vol. 2, pp. 336–37).

All the safeguards noted above oppose anarchy and servitude (see vol. 2, pp. 202–03). Tocqueville pays special attention to civil associations. The tendency of egalitarian societies toward authoritarianism can be curtailed, he contends, if the formation of civil associations takes place to the same degree that social leveling occurs:

> If each citizen did not learn, in proportion as he individually becomes more feeble and consequently more incapable of preserving his freedom single-handed, to combine with his fellow citizens for the purpose of defending it, it is clear that tyranny would unavoidably increase together with equality. (vol. 2, p. 114; see also pp. 115–16, 118)

Whether more oriented to political, religious, occupational, hobby, or leisure activities, these associations stand firm against despotism. As organizations that empower otherwise weak citizens and offer tutelage in the fine arts of governance, civil associations prove indispensable under conditions of equality.

Fortunately, the Americans, he stresses, are remarkably adept at forming these associations. They do so "constantly" and in a natural and spontaneous fashion. He speaks of an "extreme skill" in founding civil associations "of a thousand kinds" (vol. 2, p. 114) and "for [even] the smallest undertakings" (vol. 2, p. 115): "The most democratic country on the face of the earth is that in which men have, in our time, carried to the highest perfection the art of pursuing in common the object of their common desires" (vol. 2, p. 115; see also p. 117). Whereas in America civil associations are quickly created to address civil ailments of all sorts, in England the upper class and in France the government undertake to do so (vol. 2, p. 114). In this respect, the Americans could teach the Europeans a great deal: "Nothing, in my opinion, is more deserving of our attention than the intellectual and moral associations of America" (vol. 2, p. 118).

The centrality of civil associations in Tocqueville's analysis poses an urgent question: how do the Americans manage to form them with such "extreme skill?" That civil associations did not simply appear of their own accord with conditions of equality is apparent from his comment on France. As feudalism declined and social leveling expanded throughout the seventeenth, eighteenth, and nineteenth centuries, this leveling brought forth on the one hand calls for a "more able and active government" (vol. 2, p. 116) and on the other a "group individualism": varieties of classes with firm boundaries developed, each asserting a claim to social honor and destructiveness (vol. 2, p. 96).

Tocqueville sees the first impulse toward civil associations in America as deriving from the realm of commerce. Common economic interests, he asserts, draw people together into associations. As such affairs multiply, persons acquire experience in coming together in consequence of common interests. A facility in doing so is born (see vol. 2, p. 123).

As it develops, this facility carries over into the political realm. In turn, political associations effectively give sustenance to civil associations. As the knowledge of public life increases, "the notion of associations and the wish to coalesce present themselves" and "political life makes the love and practice of association more general" (vol. 2, p. 123). Thus, from the political realm itself, there arises "a desire of union." Moreover, by teaching persons how to associate in groups, this realm repeatedly brings persons together and eventually for a variety of purposes:

> In politics men combine for great undertakings, and the use they make of the principle of association in important affairs practically teaches them that it is in their interest to help one another in those of less moment. A political association draws a number of individuals at the same time out of their own circle; however they may be naturally kept asunder by age, mind, and fortune, it places them nearer together and brings them into contact. Once met, they can always meet again. (vol. 2, p. 124)

Thus, the major impulse toward association, Tocqueville contends, comes from the political realm – not least because, unlike commercial undertakings, far fewer monetary risks are involved. But, as participants learn "how order is maintained among a large number of men" and how goals are realized in common, they acquire skills readily transferable to a variety of activities. Indeed, wherever freedom of political association is openly allowed, citizens come to view "public association as the universal...mean that men can employ to accomplish the different purposes they may have in view" (vol. 2, p. 125):

> In their political associations the Americans...daily acquire a general taste for association and grow accustomed to the use of it. There they meet together in large numbers, they converse, they listen to one another, and they are mutually stimulated to all sorts of undertakings. They afterwards transfer to civil live the notions they have thus acquired and make them subservient to a thousand purposes. (vol. 2, p. 127)

As Tocqueville notes, "a natural and perhaps necessary connection" (vol. 2, p. 123) exists between political and civil associations.

Yet he understands the unusual growth of civil associations in the United States in several further ways. Tocqueville maintains that citizens participate in public affairs merely because they readily become aware that in democracies, the successful pursuit of private interests is closely related to the prosperity of the public realm – and the public welfare requires joint activity (vol. 2, pp. 111–13). In addition, freedom itself and free institutions, Tocqueville contends, oppose the evils produced by equality and lead to civil associations: "Local freedom... perpetually brings men together, and forces them to help one another, in spite of the propensities which sever them" (vol. 2, p. 111). Freedom also calls forth a notion of service to the public:

> Free institutions...and political rights...remind every citizen...that he lives in society. They every instant impress upon his mind the notion that it is the duty, as well as the interest, of men to make themselves useful to their feline-creatures...Men attend to the interests of the public, first by necessity, afterwards by choice: what was intentional becomes an instinct: and by dint of working for the good of one's fellow-citizens, the habit and the taste for serving them is at length acquired. (vol. 2, p. 112)

Tocqueville also finds a well-developed sense of "public spirit" in the American political culture. In turn, the public spirit assists the growth of civil associations. He discovers its origin on the one hand in the belief of the Americans that their nation, owing to the opportunity it affords for open participation, is of their own making, and on the other, in their conviction that participation is beneficial to the realization of one's own interests:

> [Attachment to country]...springs from knowledge; it is nurtured by the laws; it grows by the exercise of civil rights; and, in the end, it is confounded with the personal interests of the citizen. A man comprehends the influence which the well-being of his country has upon his own; he is aware that the laws permit him to contribute to that prosperity, and he labors to promote it, at first because it benefits him, and secondly because it is in part his own work. (vol. 1, p. 251; see also vol. 2, pp. 109–10; note 13, p. 212)[11]

Tocqueville is convinced that the most effective means of awakening an interest in citizens in their country's welfare "is to make them partakers in the government" (vol. 1, p. 252). Where people "look upon the fortune of the public as their own," as in democracies, they will, he maintains, develop a zealous interest in the public welfare and become active participants (vol. 1, p. 252; see also vol. 2, p. 112). Accordingly, the public spirit as well as civil associations grow.[12]

Weber's analysis in respect to the rise of civil associations diverges distinctly from that of Tocqueville. If the unusual success of the Americans in formulating civil associations is to be explained, then a *civic sphere*, he suggests, comprised of specific and facilitating *values*, must be acknowledged. Wherever they appear on a broad scale, civil associations must be understood as having crystallized in reference to such a social context characterized by a distinct set of conducive, value-based *ideals*.

Max Weber: The Origin of the Civic Sphere and its Value-Based Nature. How did a civic sphere arise in the United States? Weber again calls attention to religious beliefs in the Colonial era. He examines the manner in which ascetic Protestant doctrine encouraged the devout to create the Kingdom of God on earth, the understanding of the congregation as an "ethical community," and the generalization of the congregation's values into secularized neighborhoods, schools, and communities. Together, these developments created a social context that assisted the birth of civil associations.

Creating and Expanding the Kingdom of God and Its Expansion. The world-mastery individualism of Puritanism, as noted,[13] implied a strong orientation to the *individual's* salvation, yet an equally strong orientation *to a community*: God's Will must be served by creating His Kingdom on earth. Rather than to be utilized for the believer's own enjoyment, riches serve, through their reinvestment, the community as a whole – for we are *all* God's children engaged in a grand mission to enhance His glory through the creation of prosperous communities. Thus, believers never viewed the improvement of their communities in purely utilitarian or cognitive terms but as part and parcel to their religious obligations. An orientation to the community's prosperity manifestly constituted a *service* to God.

However, Puritanism pushed the devout in an even more effective way further in this direction. As discussed above, this church left individual's alone to discover "signs" of their predestined status. Neither a church, nor its sacraments, nor holy intermediaries could assist in the alleviation of the extreme anxiety that accompanied uncertainty regarding one's salvation status. Yet, Puritanism offered several means of doing so.

For example, if worldly success were attained, the faithful could *convince* themselves that this wealth itself indicated the favor of their mighty God. Nothing in His universe occurred by chance, and of course He would assist *only* the foreordained (see *PE*, pp. 127–28; *E&S*, pp. 1198–200). In this manner, for the devout, unusually strong psychological premiums rewarded methodical work: great riches might be attained only through such systematic labor.[14]

Remarkably, a deepening of the believer's commitment *to a community* resulted from this intensification of work and its elevation to a central place in their lives. Although Puritan doctrine left the faithful alone to create "evidence" of their predestined status, the means of doing so – methodical work – never served the individual alone. Instead, as noted, labor on behalf of God's glory and the creation of the human earthly Kingdom constituted a firm obligation. Thus, work now served to *bind* believers to a community: labor in a vocation became both intensified and oriented to a task far broader than mere self-interested calculation regarding the accumulation of material goods.

Accordingly, community participation became a significant and important activity, one rendered all the more probable as a consequence of the congregation: this organization served as a natural training ground for the acquisition of group participation skills and practice in self-government (see *E&S*, p. 1208). The laity's involvement in the admission of new members proved central in this regard, as did its pivotal role in admonishing the "unworthy" to avoid communion and in selecting a righteous minister (see "Sects II," pp. 220–21), all in order strictly to insure "the purity of the sacramental community" ("Sects II," p. 221). As Weber notes: "The sect controlled and regulated the members' conduct *exclusively* in the sense of formal *righteousness* and methodical asceticism" ("Sects II," p. 221; emphasis original; see also p. 220; *E&S*, p. 1208).

In this way, Puritan churches and sects placed into motion a strong thrust toward the formulation of civil associations.[15] They did so in another manner as well. Weber's analysis at this point places the emphasis upon a set of further values called forth and cultivated by ascetic Protestantism. These values proved to be ones that created a specific tenor for social relationships in the congregation, and these in time came to set the tone for relationships in entire communities. They paved the way for, and assisted the widespread development of, civil associations.

The Ethical Community: The Congregation. In Weber's analysis, all Puritan congregations in Colonial America and the early United States called into being and cultivated candor and trust among persons unrelated by blood. Sect and church members understood their activity as involving a great Mission to create *communities of believers* in which *all* would be brothers ("Sects II," pp. 221–23).

New *family* relationships of trust, helpfulness, allegiance, and ethical conduct under the watchful eye of God were born among "the brethren." A quite practical mechanism ensured the purity of this ethical community: owing to rigid investigative procedures, only persons of "good moral character" could enter the community of believers.

Thus, membership implied a seal of righteous behavior as well as the member's commitment to trust God's children in strict accord with an ethos that stressed equality and fair play.[16] Good will and openness rather than fear, threat, insecurity, manipulation, and the sheer calculation of interests prevailed in the congregation. Indeed, sect and church membership established so securely a reputation for honesty and candor in business that nonbelievers preferred to conduct commercial dealings with the devout. Fair treatment, they were convinced, would be their reward ("Sects I," pp. 227–28; "Sects II," pp. 214, 222–23).

In this way, carried by ascetic Protestant congregations, trust, ethical conduct, and goodwill broke through their original locus in the particularist ties of the family and clan and became awarded to "unknown others" – as long as they were members of an ascetic Protestant church or sect. Trust now became, Weber argues, understood as an *impersonal and binding principle* – a firm *ideal* even for commercial relationships – rather than as constituted from a strong personal relationship alone (see "Sects II," pp. 210–13, 219–20; "Sects I," pp. 227–29). This transformation proved to be a crucial step toward the formation of a delimited civic sphere characterized by an ideal of trust.

However, the ethical community contributed to the development of a value-based civic sphere in a further significant manner: it set into motion a strong thrust toward civic activism. Because the faithful were expected to "master" worldly evil and to undertake the creation of the Kingdom of God on earth, a tolerance of or separation from evil remained unacceptable. Instead, a religious obligation of world-mastery constituted an imperative to the devout: to act *against* worldly evil, even if doing so involved challenges to secular authority or popular opinion.

As examined above, rather than a cautious and contemplative individualism, Puritan Protestantism called forth a world-mastery individualism that signified a *readiness* to reform the world on behalf of God's Will. This "practical-ethical" individualism endowed the devout with great confidence to participate in the alteration and improvement of their communities (*PE*, pp. 87–137; *E&S*, pp. 549, 578–79; "Sects I," p. 231). Activity would be assessed in terms of its *consistency* with God's abstract principle and rules. In this way, Puritanism again set into motion a strong thrust toward the formation of civil associations.

The Generalization of the Congregation's Values into Communities. Wherever ascetic Protestant congregations were influential, the values they carried became dominant throughout entire communities – and remained so, Weber insists, even as the sects and churches themselves eventually became, with secularization, weakened. Values originating in the religious domain lived on, now cultivated by families, schools, neighborhoods, and communities.

As this took place, "community standards" of "respectable" behavior became articulated. As social relationships based in trust, candor, honesty, fair play, norms of equality, and ethical conduct in general became widespread, ideals of public ethics – *civic* ideals – came into being. Public sphere activity could be evaluated against these ideal standards of conduct. Hence, Weber contends, discrete and random associations of citizens separate from the state, the family, and business-oriented organization never alone constituted the American civic sphere; rather, a specific constellation of *values* also characterized this arena. To the extent that social relationships were empirically influenced by these values, other relationships oriented to power, domination, the instrumental-rational calculation of interests, and conventions anchored in rigid social hierarchies were to the same degree called into question.[17]

By calling forth in the United States distinct, even ethical, ideals for public life, the values of Puritanism, Weber contends, assisted the creation of a civic realm. Such an arena of good will and trust proved agreeable and welcoming rather than harsh and authoritarian, and even capable of "pulling citizens into civic associations."[18] These ideals strongly facilitated their creation; once in place they also legitimated them.

A civic sphere crystallized in the manner of Colonial America and the early United States. Weber's analysis locates its source and substance in a specific religious tradition and its social carriers – Puritan churches and sects rather than in various civil associations arising largely from the realms of commerce and politics, as Tocqueville argues. This tradition provided the *social context* – civic activism and ideals – Weber views as indispensable if civil associations are to develop widely.[19]

Moreover, it established firm patterns, although civic activists in the more secularized America of the nineteenth century seldom viewed their participation as "doing God's work" or as an effort to acquire God's favor through a confrontation with evil and the creation of an ethical community. No longer a mark of devoutness but still one of trust and social honor, a secular "badge" of responsibility and a "status elevation" now accompanied membership in a civil association.[20] Indeed, because it alone certified persons as trustworthy and as "gentlemen," membership in an exclusive club proved decisive if one hoped to be fully accepted in one's community, let alone to be upwardly mobile (see "Sects II," pp. 216–17; "Sects I," pp. 227–29; E&S, p. 1207).[21]

As "community norms" of participation and "service" as well as ideals of public ethics, the legacies of ascetic Protestantism now strongly assisted the formation of diverse civil associations. Weber repeatedly calls attention to the significance of these legacies for an understanding of American society's proclivity to formulate such associations on a broad scale. For him, "the old 'sect spirit' holds sway with relentless effect in the intrinsic nature of the associations" ("Sects I," pp. 229–30). And:

> Today, large numbers of "orders" and clubs of all sorts have begun to assume in part the functions of the religious community. Almost every small businessman who thinks something of himself wears some kind of badge in his lapel. However, the archetype of this form, which *all* use to guarantee the "honorableness" of the individual, is indeed the ecclesiastical community. (Weber, 1985, p. 8; original emphasis)

> The modern position of the secular clubs and societies with recruitment by ballot is largely the product of a process of *secularization.* Their position is derived from the far more exclusive importance of the prototype of these voluntary associations, to wit, the sects. ("Sects II," p. 321; emphasis original)

> It is obvious that in all these points the modern functions of American sects and sectlike associations…are revealed as straight derivatives, rudiments, and survival of those conditions which once prevailed in all asceticist sects and conventicles. ("Sects II," p. 223)

Surely a political climate of openness can be understood as in part calling forth civil associations and social activism, as Tocqueville argues. In emphasizing the congealing in the American Colonies and early United States of a delineated *civic sphere* endowed with an array of conducive values, Weber quite differently addresses the same development. An explanation of the unusual "propensity" of the reference to commercial and political associations, freedom and free institutions, the idea that the nation's destiny lies in the hands of its citizens, and a realization that the furtherance of one's private interests is connected to the public prosperity, for these elements have existed in political cultures where civil associations have remained rare. Rather, these associations are formed on a broad scale, Weber maintains, only where facilitating civic values, complemented by the practical experience of self-governance in sects and churches,[22] have paved the way for their development (see Kalberg, 1993).[23]

7.3 Conclusion

Although far less well known than Alexis de Tocqueville's commentary upon the political culture of the United States, Max Weber's writings on America address the two major themes of *Democracy in America*: a tyranny of the majority danger and the central role of civil associations. In regard to both themes, however, he offers interpretations distinctly at variance with those of Tocqueville.

A fundamental point of departure anchors Tocqueville's entire analysis: he sees a structural transformation – the development from "aristocratic to democratic nations" and the rise of the "equality of conditions" – as the root cause of all that distinguishes the U.S. Egalitarianism not only calls forth an enfeebled individualism as well as the potential of tyranny, but also renders civil associations indispensable if democratic stability is to be maintained.

Weber's attention to different features of the American political culture leads him to different conclusion. Its distinctiveness can be best isolated, he maintains, by reference to a set of religious values rather than a structural transformation. The world-mastery individualism of Puritanism, which placed abstract principles at the core of the believer's life and obligated the devout to orient their action toward them, stands in direct opposition to all tyranny of the majority pressures. Instead of a dangerous potential for tyranny, at the center of Weber's analysis stands a permanent tension between strong pressure toward social conformity and group orientations on the one hand and this "world-oriented" individualism on the other.

Tocqueville and Weber diverge as well in respect to civil associations, even though both note the American capacity to formulate groups as unusually nimble and swift. Tocqueville understands the formation of civil associations as arising on the one hand from commercial and political associations and on the other from a combination of freedom and free institutions, the idea that the nation's destiny lies in the hands of its citizens and a realization that the furtherance of one's private interests is connected to public prosperity.

In opposing fundamentally Tocqueville's explanation, Weber again sees values and beliefs as pivotal. For him, an array of civic values constituted in a delineated *civic sphere* proved indispensable. They provided, in effect, a facilitating pathway – within which Tocqueville's explanatory forces could be located – for the development of civil associations.

In respect to both major themes, Weber's *verstehende* sociology points to a background factor neglected by Tocqueville's mode of analysis: a crucial cultural context influenced by ascetic Protestantism. Rather than the equality of conditions, values, and beliefs, and their "carrier organizations" – churches and sects – stand at the forefront of Weber's analysis. Moreover, while Tocqueville's approach attends primarily to a monumental macro transformation, Weber focuses upon particular groups, their values, and the manner in which the subjective meaning of persons in groups establishes firm patterns of action.

If "carried" by powerful organizations, these patterns cast their impact across the ages; they do so, as legacies, even as monumental changes – secularization, for example – lead to an alteration of their social carriers. Tocqueville's emphasis upon a global structural transformation on the one hand and the rational enlightened interests of individuals on the other renders his analysis, when compared to Weber's, ahistorical[24] and acontextual.

Weber identifies a world-mastery individualism and a demarcated civic sphere penetrated by a specific set of values as pivotal components in the American political culture, and locates their original source in ascetic Protestantism.[25] His analysis argues forcefully that this odd juxtaposition – self-reliant individuals yet also individuals oriented to civic activities – was founded neither upon chance occurrences nor minor or deviant currents in American history.[26] Rather than the equality of conditions, values and beliefs and their "carrier organizations" – churches and sects – stand at the forefront. Uniquely American in its intensity, this dualism remains obscured to all modes

of analysis that take global concepts – industrialization, modernization, and evolutionary progress, for example – as their focus as well as
to Tocqueville's master key concept: the equality of conditions.

Furthermore, as long as it endures, the juxtaposition of an accentuated, world-mastery with an accentuated orientation to civic sphere
ideals endows the American political landscape with an inherent
tension: although possessing a common origin and inextricably intertwined, the 'individual" and "civic" components of this dualism
strain in opposite directions and clash repeatedly.[27] However, far from
random, these conflicts occur across a firmly bounded spectrum. Pendulum movements too far in one direction are invariably pulled back
toward the center (see Chapter 8).

This dualism injects dynamism into the American political culture. On the one hand, if a prominent civic aspect had been lacking,
world-mastery individualism would long ago have become routinized
into an individualism focused alone upon the calculation of self-
interests. Ultimately, massive cynicism would stand at the end of such
a development – in respect to *both* the realm of politics and the realm
of ethical action generally.

On the other hand, if a world-mastery individualism had been lacking, a widespread and oppressive social conformism which, unlike
"the authority of a king, ...acts upon the will as much as the actions"
(Tocqueville, vol. 1, p. 273) and would long ago have called forth severe social, political, and economic crises.[28]

The very tension between these central and interwoven components
of the American political culture injects a vigorous capacity for rejuvenation. In doing so, this tension itself stands in opposition to tendencies toward a tyranny of the majority.

Notes

1 Interestingly, this study acquired little attention in the United States before 1950.
2 "The importance of customs is a common truth to which study and experience incessantly direct our attention. It may be regarded as a central
point in the range of observation, and the common termination of all
my inquiries. So seriously do insist upon this head that, if I have hitherto
failed in making the reader feel the important influence of the practical experience, the habits, the opinion, in short, if the customs of the Americans

upon the maintenance of their institutions, I have failed in the principal object of the work" (1945, vol. 1, p. 334). And "It is the influence of customs that produces the different degrees of order and prosperity which may be distinguished in the several Anglo-American democracies" (1945, vol. 1, p. 334; see also pp. 310, 331–34). (Hereafter the volume alone is given for *Democracy in America*.)

3 In a letter to J. P. Mayer, Marianne Weber states that Max Weber had "doubtlessly" read Tocqueville (see Mayer, 1972, p. 166, note 11). In discussing the broad reception of Tocqueville in Germany, Eschenburg (1976) notes that Dilthey (pp. 876, 923–24), Roscher (pp. 922–23), and Toennies (pp. 927–28) had all read Tocqueville. However, to my knowledge, Weber never comments upon or cites Tocqueville.

4 Tocqueville's ambivalence regarding democracy is apparent. He perceived the United States as offering not the ideal form of government, but the best possible: "The gradual growth of democratic manners and institutions should be regarded, not as the best, but as the only means of preserving freedom; and, without caring for the democratic form of government, it might be adopted as the most applicable, and the fairest remedy for the present ills of society" (vol. 1, p. 341).

However, Tocqueville unequivocally opposes a simple transposition of the American political culture onto France: "Those who, after having read this book, should imagine that my intention in writing it was to propose the laws and customs of the Anglo-Americans for the imitation of all democratic communities would make a great mistake: they must have paid more attention to the form than to the substance of my thought. My aim has been to show, by the example of America, that laws, and especially customs, may allow a democratic people to remain free. But I am very far from thinking that we ought to follow the example of the American democracy and copy the means that it has employed to attain this end" (vol. 1, p. 342). Rather, he wishes to demonstrate that if democratic institutions are not gradually introduced, "there will be no independence at all....but an equal tyranny over all, and...the unlimited authority of a single man" (vol. 1, p. 342; see also pp. 14–15).

5 I am here focusing, as did Weber, upon the "Reformed" churches and notably the churches deeply within this tradition, namely those indebted in the fifteenth century to Calvinism and those that led in the sixteenth and seventeenth centuries to Puritanism and the "Puritan Divines" (see *PE*, pp. 158–76). These terms, as well as "ascetic Protestantism," are used here synonymously.

6 While Tocqueville sees religion in Europe as weak (see vol. 1, p. 339), he finds it to be extremely strong in the US (see vol. 1, pp. 45, 314–16, 319–26).

7 "The principle of equality, which makes men independent of each other, gives them a habit and a taste for following in their private actions no other guide than their own will" (vol. 2, p. 304; see also p. 343).

8 Tocqueville's description of individualism is quite harsh. He equates it with selfishness and sees it as "[sapping] the virtues of public life" as well as "in the long run [destroying] all others." Moreover, individualism proceeds from erroneous judgment more than from depraved feelings; it originates as much in deficiencies of mind as in perversity of heart (vol. 2, pp. 104–05). It is very clear throughout his writings that he does not believe in *populism* or a trust in the good judgment and basic wisdom of the common man. On the contrary, he fears the common man, seeing him as liable to impulsive behavior, easy manipulation by charismatic figures, and – unless restrained – ruled by restless passions and "a love of material gratification" (vol. 2, p. 23). Hence, again the central importance for him, in democracies, of civil associations and religion: both set indispensable standards for behavior, truth, and virtue, without which mob rule and social chaos looms (see. vol. 2, pp. 22–23; see p. 211). In this regard, Tocqueville's (Counterrevolution) anthropology varies little from that of Durkheim.

9 If Weber's methodology had focused exclusively upon a charting of structural transformations, he would have noted the "equality of conditions" as leading to a specific outcome: "passive democratization" (see *E&S*, pp. 984–87, 1453). This term refers to the social leveling "of the governed" that follows whenever feudal hierarchies are weakened and even banished. New groups of persons formally equal appear. Typically, Weber's discussion of this development is distinguished by their reference to specific historical cases (rather than a putatively global uniformity) – and hence the possibility that this structural transformation could be inhibited and even counteracted under specific conditions (such as the broad growth and competition of sect organizations, multiple exclusive associations, and the presence of a world-mastery individualism). This new equality does not call forth, as for Tocqueville, an isolated, weak, and "atomized" individual; rather, it gives rise to bureaucratization within state administrations as well as political parties, and thus the domination by officials (although the extent to which this occurs also varies depending upon nation-specific constellations). As bureaucratization develops, Weber argues, it often calls forth atomization: "'Atomization'" is usually a consequence not of democracy but of bureaucratic rationalism" ("Sects I," p. 231).

10 Weber here discovers a strong sociological source for the notion of the "Rights of Man" (see *E&S*, pp. 1208–09).

11 Thus, in respect to the origin of both civil associations and the public spirit, Tocqueville prominently refers to the individual's own interests. In fact, this mode of explanation reoccurs with great frequency throughout *Democracy in America*. By reference to self-interests, Tocqueville explains, for example, the contribution of jury trials to social stability (vol. 1, pp. 291–97), the assistance one gives to others and support for the welfare of the state (vol. 2, p. 130), the "habits of regularity, temperance,

moderation, foresight, and self-command" (vol. 1, p. 131), the "means by which religions…govern men" (vol. 2, p. 134; see also pp. 133–35), patriotism (vol. 1, p. 250), the unwillingness to attack the rights of others (vol. 1, pp. 254–55), the enforcement of obedience to the law (vol. 1, p. 257), the necessity for religions to proselytize (vol. 1, p. 318), the correct manner of teaching individuals to exercise political rights (vol. I, p. 255), the cooperation of individuals engaged in public affairs (vol. 2, pp. 109–10), and the willingness of "the more opulent [to] take great care not to stand aloof from the people" (vol. 2, pp. 111). He is unequivocal in particular in regard to political rights: "If…you do not succeed in connecting the notion of [political rights] with that of private interest, which is the only immutable point in the human heart, what means will you have of governing the world except by fear" (vol. 1, p. 255; see also vol. 2, p. 112)? Tocqueville states directly the causal centrality for him of self-interests on a number of occasions; for example, "The Anglo-American relies upon personal interest to accomplish his ends" (vol. 1, p. 452). And "The principal of self-interest rightly understand appears to me the best suited of all philosophical theories to the wants of the men of our time…It must…be adopted as necessary" (vol. 2, p. 111; see also pp. 112, 129–32).

12 This mode of explanation – people will support that which they believe to be of their own making – also appears frequently in *Democracy in America*. Tocqueville refers to it not only in discussing the origins of a public spirit and civil associations, but also, for example, patriotism (vol. 1, p. 250), civic zeal (vol. 1, pp. 252–53), and the authority of the law (vol. 1, pp. 256–57).

13 Again, Baxter's Reform Calvinist doctrine best exemplifies Weber's argument (see *PE*, pp. 158–60).

14 Weber's argument was examined in detail in Chapters 2–4.

15 Weber speaks of a "community-forming energy" imparted by the ascetic Protestant sects "to an Anglo-Saxon world." See "Sects I" and "Sects II" *et passim*.

16 "For the individual, this basic nature of a congregation formed by selective admission has the practical significance of legitimating his personal qualities. Anyone admitted as a member can thereby demonstrate to the world that he has measured up to the congregation's religious and moral standards after a thorough examination" (*E&S*, p. 1205). See also Chapter 2.

17 Given the strength of these opposing forces, Weber is quite well aware that often these ideals had little actual impact. Nonetheless, the tension established against them as a consequence of a demarcated constellation of civic sphere values remained significant to him.

18 Surely, here can be seen as well as the trust cultivated among believers in the congregation one of the sociological sources for the widespread belief in America in populism or trust in the good judgment and basic wisdom of the common man. Tocqueville's entire study neglects this very central

aspect of the American political culture. He emphasizes, on the contrary, the great dangers of empowering the common person. Lipset sees populism as *the* distinguishing attribute of the American political culture (see 1963).

19 Industrialism's advance and the concomitant expansion of the public sphere will never alone establish, Weber is convinced, the civic ideal of public trust central for the formation of civil associations. As well, a "generalization" of the values of the family and clan (in-group solidarity, assistance in time of need, openness and trust, and so on), as a consequence alone of far greater contact among "unknown others," did not occur. Nor can social trust be understood as a result of an evolutionary development as such (see Parsons, 1966, 1971). Specific values, specific sources for them, and specific strong carriers, according to Weber, prove indispensable.

20 Thus, a formal parallel here exists to Weber's argument regarding the relationship between the Protestant ethic and the spirit of capitalism (see *PE*, pp. 176–78); in both cases, the religious roots had died out.

21 Just the extreme importance for one's social status of admission into a community's church and clubs led Weber to describe the US as a society of "benevolent feudalism" (see 1978, p. 281; see also Chapter 2).

22 Although Weber's analysis strongly emphasizes the importance of activities oriented to values in formulating a social context conducive to the formation of civil associations, he does not stop at this point. He pays particular attention, as noted in Chapter 2, to social carriers. Furthermore, he strongly acknowledges the significance of the state, the state's authority, and its law (as does Tocqueville). Because the importance of value constellations is frequently neglected in the citizenship literature and attention to the state, the state's authority, and laws is nearly universal, I have chosen to focus upon values and omit Weber's discussion of these factors. A more comprehensive – and accurate – Weberian analysis would address all of these factors and, in particular, their unique interweaving in the American political culture.

23 Had Tocqueville viewed the civic sphere as a discrete realm characterized by constellations of social action oriented to values, he would have surely noted it as capable of offering, as religions, a set of ideals that stood in opposition to – or safeguarded against – any tyranny of the majority.

24 Time and again, Tocqueville explains features of American society by reference to the equality of conditions rather than to the legacies of ascetic Protestantism. For example, the "willingness to work," the high honor attached to labor, the tendency of the wealthy to devote their leisure time to "public business" (vol. 2, p. 161), the inclination for persons in America to follow "commercial and industrial occupations" (vol. 2, p. 163; see also pp. 165, 168; vol. 1, pp. 442–44), the "taste for well-being" (vol. 2, p. 164, n. 2), the directing of all "energetic passions" to trade and commerce, "the immense progress [of the Americans] in productive industry" (vol. 2, p. 165), the "sober way of life" and "serious, deliberate, and

positive turn" of the minds of "all who live in democratic times" (vol. 2, p. 219; see also p. 131), the "purity of morals of the Americans (vol. 2, p. 220; see also pp. 216–18), their "love of riches" (see vol. 2, pp. 238–40; vol. 1, p. 30), the "transporting of the habits of public life into...[private] manners" (vol. 1, p. 330), their methodical and deliberate "zeal" (vol. 2, p. 134), and their "tendency to...look upon all authority with a jealous eye" (vol. 2, p. 304).

25 Tocqueville notes that "innumerable" sects are to be found in the US (vol. 1, p. 314; vol. 2, p. 28), yet he nowhere distinguishes them either by name or by doctrine. Rather, his discussion is remarkably generic. He asserts that "all Christian morality is everywhere the same" (vol. 1, p. 314) and that "all [Americans] look upon their religion in the same light" (vol. 2, p. 28; see also pp. 22–33 *passim*, 133–34). Only rarely does he note distinctions even between Protestants and Catholics (see vol. 1, p. 311; vol. 2, pp. 30–31). His focus in regard to religion remains, throughout *Democracy in America*, consistently upon its capacity to set standards and boundaries and thus its indispensability in periods of equality (see above and vol. 2, pp. 21–29).

26 One can see this tension from a different angle in those passages where Weber notes the peculiarly individual orientations even of group members:

> [In associations] the individual seeks to maintain *his own* position by becoming a member of the social group....The cool objectivity (*Sachlichkeit*) of sociation (*Vergesellschaftung*) promotes the precise placement of the individual in the purposive activity (*Zwecktaetigkeit*) of the group, be it a football team or a political party. However, this in no way means a lessening of the individual's need to constantly attend to his self-affirmation. On the contrary, this task of *"proving himself"* is present more than ever *within* the group, in the circle of his associations. And thus, the social association to which the individual belongs is for him never something "organic," never a mystical total essence which floats over him and envelops him. Rather, he is *always* completely conscious of it as a mechanism for his own material and ideal *ends* (*Zwecke*). ("Sects I," p. 230; original emphasis).

And:

> Only [the sects] gave...American democracy its own flexible structure and its individualistic stamp. On the one hand,... [they place] the individual absolutely on his own in the matter most important to him. On the other hand, this qualification through self-probation is viewed exclusively as the foundation for the social union of the congregation. Thus, the tremendous flood of social structures which penetrate every nook and cranny of American life is constituted in accordance with the schema of the "sect". ("Sect I," p. 230)

27 It remains an open question, and one at the center of a lively debate, whether this tension endures to this day. Weber himself saw the civic

sphere as drastically weakened and noted, on many occasions, the widespread corruption in American politics (see Kalberg, 2014). Many recent commentators have argued that "the civic" has declined dramatically (see Etzioni, 1998; Bellah, 1985; Putnam, 1995, 2015; Selznick, 1994). Albeit enduring, this "communitarian-libertarian" debate cannot be addressed here.

28 Egalitarianism without activity-oriented individualism would imply a massive conformity scarcely imaginable to Americans today (the old German Democratic Republic?), one accompanied by a *rigid* defense of the few remaining hierarchies untouched by egalitarianism.

8

THE ANALYSIS OF THE UNIQUE AMERICAN CIVIC SPHERE

More than 100 years ago, Max Weber insisted that any description of American society as a "sandpile" (*Sandhaufen*) of unconnected individuals must be rejected ("Sects I"; "Sects II," pp. 224–26; see Chapter 2). He sought to offer a more differentiated portrait of its political culture and vehemently opposed this view widespread among his European colleagues. Nearly all understood modernity as tantamount to atomization.

A thick civic sphere[1] was introduced in the American Colonies by ascetic Protestant sects and churches in the seventeenth and eighteenth centuries, Weber contends.[2] Often invisible to Europeans, its singular "political-ethical" action injected a decisive "community-building energy" into American society. Moreover, these religious groups, he maintains, called forth deep cultural strains that fostered the growth of innumerable solidary organizations in the nineteenth century: civic associations.

This chapter summarizes his major concepts and analytical framework, reconstructs a "Weberian model," and utilizes his rich set of ideal types to form complementary constructs. In doing so, it aims to define clearly the American civic sphere's unique features, origins, expansion, and ossifications across a demarcated spectrum. By both drawing upon Weber and extending his analysis in this manner, his distinct mode of analysis will be delineated. Above all, distinguishing features of his sociology – the systematic attention to subjective meaning,

DOI: 10.4324/9781032631813-12

the deep cultural contexts of social action, the perpetual influence of the past upon the present, and the formation of hypotheses – will become apparent. Weber's strict opposition to Tocqueville, as well as to all modernization, neo-functionalist, and neo-Marxian approaches, will again become evident.

His exploration of the civic realm's religious origins and growth must be first summarized. This section articulates concepts and an analytic framework that define this arena's parameters. Two themes remain important throughout: an unusual symbiotic dualism between this sphere and a *world-mastery* (*weltbeherrschende*) individualism and the antagonism between this value-grounded individualism and practical-rational individualism.

The great social transformations that accompanied the nineteenth and twentieth centuries severely challenged the civic realm's original parameters, Weber holds. A reconstructed Weberian model indicates the ensuing threat to the American civic arena's viability and to political-ethical action in general. Pivotal here are three sub-constructs that chart important developments occurring in this political culture: "the privatization of work," the circumscription of the civic sphere by "the power of goods," and "Europeanization." All map the magnitude of this social metamorphosis and demarcate central features of the American political culture.

Nonetheless, the Weberian model's overarching hypothesis, namely, that a severe weakening and even dissolution of the civic sphere takes place in the twentieth century, must be acknowledged as foreshortened; it depicts only one of several possible outcomes. Indeed, his own concepts point to further constructs and diverging hypotheses. This study then reconstructs three alternative, albeit highly Weber-indebted models. All prove indispensable for a more adequate comprehension of the American civic sphere's distinct contours, parameters, and long-term transformations: the "generalization," "professional associations," and "conflict" constructs.

These models, combined with the Weberian construct, offer a *Weberian analysis* that traces the oscillations of the civic sphere across a spectrum from more thick, expansive, and independent manifestations to more porous, circumscribed, and dependent forms. Taken together, these models provide a unique portrait of the *past and present multidimensionality* of the American political culture. This manner of summarizing, reconstructing, and utilizing Weber's heuristic concepts and framework enables his complex analysis of the civic sphere to offer a singular contribution to the ongoing quest to define American particularity. This chapter also seeks to fill in part a large gap in the Weber literature.[3]

8.1   Weber's Concepts and Analytic Framework: The Origin and Expansion of the Civic Sphere

The capacity of Protestant sects and churches in the seventeenth and eighteenth centuries to initiate and nourish the distinct type of action at the foundation of the American civic realm – political-ethical action – must be first addressed. Its growth in the nineteenth century was effectively cultivated by civic associations. World-mastery individualism became allied with and ultimately sustained the civic arena's values, Weber contends.

The Origins of the Civic Sphere: Ascetic Protestant Sects and Churches.[4] Weber's three-month journey throughout the United States in 1904 offered the opportunity for firsthand observation of the American civic realm's workings. Similar to Tocqueville, he viewed it as anchored in all-pervasive groups and organizations. Unlike his French predecessor, however, who attributed the origin of these "civic associations" to free institutions, a developed public spirit, and a pursuit of common economic interests (1945, vol. 2, pp. 109–13, 123–27; see Chapter 7). Weber discovered their sources in religious carrier groups, namely, the ascetic Protestant sects and churches (*PERW*, pp. 185–204).

These organizations required of believers a deep and comprehensive engagement in "the religious life." Even bonds to the family were loosened. Moreover, the faithful toiled together in order to fulfill their purpose on earth: to build an affluent kingdom of God that would, owing to its abundance and justice, serve to praise unequivocally His majesty and righteousness. The sources of political-ethical action and an American civic arena can be located in these groups, Weber holds.

Thrusts toward independent communities of believers were also set into motion, he holds, by the *asceticism* of the devout: an intensity of belief and a disciplined adherence in daily life despite temptations to religious values and God's commandments. The sincere faith of believers and the necessity for teamwork, if the large tasks commanded by this Divinity were to be accomplished, established strong ties among the devout, ones that oriented all toward both exemplary personal conduct and allegiance to His community. Should their place of residence change, members of these tightly knit congregations required only a certificate from a home pastor to be welcomed into a new sect or church – and, indeed, to acquire through membership the immediate trust of residents throughout the new region. Moving now radically beyond its traditional locus in the blood bond of the extended family and the tribe, trust extended into these congregations, Weber contends ("Sects I," pp. 227–28; *PERW*, pp. 186–90, 193–94, 198–89; see above, pp. 33–40.). It assisted the formation of communities.

All ascetic Protestant sects and churches cultivated this "brotherhood ethos" and community-building energy, and the "sect spirit" expanded diffusely. Hence, rather than a "sandpile" of unconnected individuals, the United States was constituted from innumerable exclusive organizations, Weber insists (see Chapter 7, pp. 146–53). Rooted firmly in constellations of values and the asceticism of the faithful, these groups imprinted American political culture comprehensively. They comprised the early social carriers of the extensive interpersonal bonds that pushed aside atomization, nourished social trust, and gave birth to political-ethical action and a civic sphere (*PERW*, pp. 185–99, 202–04; see Chapter 7).

Furthermore, amid nineteenth-century urbanization and industrialization, the frame of mind (*Gesinnung*) created by ascetic Protestant sects and churches proved amenable to the formation of associations. On the basis of membership procedures rooted in sect-like exclusion and inclusion practices and an emphasis upon high standards for conduct, these groups – the Lions, Rotary, and Kiwanis clubs, for example, and other secular social clubs and societies – perpetuated the cultivation of social trust, community service ideals, and high standards of personal conduct. As in the sect, members reciprocally monitored behavior and punished severely whenever an offense occurred. Expulsion involved a severe social stigma and banishment from an entire community often followed (*PERW*, pp. 187–91, 195, 200).

Whereas seventeenth and eighteenth century believers experienced a compelling obligation to *order* their lives systematically in accord with God's commandments, and did so in a "watchful," self-monitoring manner, members of civic associations in the nineteenth century rigorously organized their behavior to conform to norms now widespread in their communities, namely, those that, in routinized forms, approximated the expectations and practices characteristic in the sect. "Decency" and the "respectable demeanor" no longer indicated "God's presence within" and one's predestined salvation status; rather, they demonstrated a sincere and trustworthy moral character.

In this manner, quasi-religious values guided action and the earlier moral rigor endured to a significant degree. Manifest as political-ethical action, "service," and "civic ethics," social trust and a variety of community-building values beyond the private sphere – yet separate from the state and the worldviews of nineteenth-century European ideologies (socialism, communism) – became viable (*E&S*, pp. 1204–10; *PERW*, pp. 185–204).

Hence, ascetic Protestantism's legacies formed a fertile and conducive foundation and context, Weber maintains, for the growth of civic associations throughout American society in the nineteenth century. A *thick* civic sphere appeared. Uniquely located, its political-ethical action, he affirms in opposition to Tocqueville's stress upon free institutions, a widespread public spirit, and a pursuit of common economic interests, developed out of the sect spirit and its direct offspring: the civic association.

Thus, rejected fundamentally is all characterization of the American response to industrialization and urbanization as involving a sandpile atomization. The United States diverged unmistakably from the nineteenth-century European historical experience, Weber contends: lacking a sect and civic association heritage, societal integration, solidarity, and social trust were provided exclusively by the worldview ideologies of political parties and an extension of the state's "protection and care" services (*E&S*, pp. 1381–469).

Weber's investigations of the American civic sphere's religious origins stood almost alone in the scholarship of his generation in Europe.[5] He defined its contours and location in just this way, namely, by exploring the long-range influence of ascetic Protestant groups and their descendents: civic associations.[6] However, an explanation for this sphere's uniquely thick consistency requires attention to a further theme, he emphasizes. In unexpected ways, the particular form of individualism widespread in Colonial America and the United States reaffirmed and bolstered the civic sphere.

The Growth of the Civic Sphere: World-Mastery Individualism.[7] As noted in Chapter 7, the sect heritage gave rise not only to civic associations and a civic sphere but also to an unusual dualism, Weber insists. It linked the civic sphere's rigorous cultivation with its opposite: an initiative-taking, activity-oriented, and entrepreneurial "world-mastery" individualism relatively unrestricted by tradition. Important for the location of political-ethical action in the distinctly American civic sphere, this individualism could be traced back to the Colonial era's ascetic Protestantism (*PERW*, pp. 141–59, 185–204; *E&S*, 1204–10; see also Chapter 3).

Although convinced by 1900 that both the civic and world-mastery components of this dualism had become weakened, Weber viewed their capacity to interlock otherwise incompatible action-orientations as sociologically significant. This juxtaposition implied a steering of American individualism away from individualism's frequent empirical manifestation, he argues: a *practical rationality* characterized by interest-based utilitarianism and egocentric calculations (*PERW*, p. 88; see Kalberg, 2021, pp. 57–72). Instead, American individualism became focused in part upon civic activity. How did this occur?

Asceticism opposed worldly pleasures to an unusual degree. Hence, the faithful were required to maintain an especially vigilant watchfulness over all creaturely drives – yet this proved a difficult task. Moreover, lacking legitimacy to absolve sins through the Confession, the Protestant clergy could no longer offer assistance regarding salvation. Standing alone before a wrathful, omnipotent, and vengeful Old Testament God, and responsible solely to Him, the devout were forced to rely exclusively on themselves; they alone could create the "evidence" of their predestination. The excruciating anxiety that accompanied the most important question to every believer – "am I among the saved" – could be ameliorated only in this way (*E&S*, pp. 1198–200; *PERW*, pp. 106–07, 119–20).

Labor now linked the faithful *systematically* into a configuration of fixed religious goals. It did so on behalf of a goal separated from all self-interested accumulation of material goods. Indeed, methodical work not only nourished social trust and community-building, it also sustained a civic dimension. A clear dualism emerged: a world-mastery individualism focused upon believers' capacity to mold their salvation destinies through work and the search for profit became accentuated;

however, the same salvation quest pushed the devout toward participation in social reform activities on behalf of God's commandments and honor. Now no longer exclusively anchored in the blood bond, *ethical* action became oriented to civic activity – indeed, in a systematic manner. *Political-ethical* action was born and acquired a dynamic momentum.

Furthermore, a firm and enduring organization crystallized as the social carrier of the psychological rewards ascetic Protestantism bestowed upon both world-mastery individualism and community engagement: the congregation.[8] Because a tightly knit *family* of trust and helpfulness, this organization comprised of "God's children" offered effective training and encouraged behavior in conformity with this Deity's abstract principles and instructed the devout in group participation skills. The *rules* of self-government could be taught in this secure milieu of certified believers and honest "brethren," and service *to the group* could be cultivated.[9] Far removed from utilitarian concerns, this *religious life* oriented the devout toward civic activism, Weber insists.

Hence, Protestant asceticism exercised a broad influence upon the economic and political cultures of Colonial America and the early United States (*PERW*, pp. 185–204). Owing to its sanctification of trade, profit, and systematic labor, and the ascetic believer's strict respect for God's Commandments, a constellation of interpersonal values now assumed the form of *ideals* for interaction and even for commercial relationships: trust, truthful advice, honesty, and fair play. Once secure in the economy and religion domains, these integrating and solidary values extended into the political sphere and introduced strong ideals of truthfulness, social trust, good will, and fair play for public life generally.

To Weber, this expansion of the political-ethical action formulated in sects and churches into the economy and political arenas implied a continuous tension with the means-end rational action – even sheer instrumental calculation – that normally held sway in these realms. Nonetheless, wherever strong carrier organizations appeared, political-ethical action could permeate – *as an ideal* – even these spheres, he maintained. Indeed, long before industrialism's appearance in America in the mid-nineteenth century, these ideals began to infuse the economy and political domains. The demarcation of a *civic sphere of public ethics* placed elected officials and private businesspersons alike under an obligation to uphold *its* high standards. Weber maintained that this *sphere* proved indispensable for the origin and extension of civic associations. As a consequence of a common foundation in ascetic Protestantism's singular doctrine and organizations, civic values and an activist individualism became intertwined in Colonial America.

This interweaving took place in a manner that *intensified both* components. A thick civic realm empowered to direct even this strong individualism crystallized. Manifest as public ethics, a civic sphere now delineated – and defended – values, ideals, and a domain of activity antagonistic to all utilitarian action rooted in instrumental calculations. Conversely, a civic-oriented individualism,[10] characterized by a self-confidence capable of *acting* on behalf of values, principles, and rights even against great obstacles, perpetually rejuvenated the civic realm's autonomy. In turn, reinvigorated civic ideals placed high expectations upon persons to reform communities in accordance with ethical values – and thus an intensification of world-mastery individualism occurred.

However, *this* individualism remained locked within the civic arena's parameters and hence in opposition to all practical rationalism, utilitarianism's interest-based calculations, and egocentric striving, Weber insists. A mutually sustaining *dynamic* developed in this manner out of this strong individualism – civic sphere dualism (see Chapter 7, pp. 136–45). A symbiosis was apparent. Finally, the sheer pervasiveness of *innumerable* (and in part conflicting) civic associations, societies, and clubs itself created a continuous jostling that rejuvenated – because loyalties and commitments to specific groups had to be repeatedly justified – each organization's values.

The birth and expansion of an American civic sphere occurred in this way, Weber holds, rather than as a consequence of free institutions, a developed public spirit, or the pursuit of common economic interests, as Tocqueville maintains, or as an outgrowth of an evolutionary concomitant of industrialization and differentiation processes. This delimited realm implied to him constellations of cohesive groupings, a community formation element, and crosscutting conflicts.

Far from "unconnected atoms," Americans lived deeply within, although not subordinated to, a multitude of groups. A civic realm of activism and ideals, indebted to ascetic Protestant doctrine, the congregations of Protestant sects and churches, and civic associations, potentially oriented action. Moreover, this sphere cultivated social integration, fair play, and trust; rather than harsh and authoritarian, it was permeated by ideals of good will and ethical conduct. Its political-ethical action proved unique, Weber ascertains, and it followed a trajectory distinct from modernizing European political cultures. Lacking a broadly ranging ascetic Protestant heritage, political-ethical action was here located more narrowly, namely, in the working class unions of the late nineteenth century, worldview ideologies on the Left and Right, political parties, and the prestige and laws of the developing social welfare state.[11]

Weber depicts the classical manifestation of the American civic sphere in this manner. His identification of political-ethical action's unique location and pivotal dualism – world-mastery individualism's juxtaposition with a developed civic sphere – conveys major features of the American political culture. Weber emphasizes the mutually sustaining interaction between its central components, its community-building energy, and its particular modes of integration.[12]

The empirical fragility of this singular dualism also captures his attention. Its duration requires a delicate balancing of groups that are perpetually in flux. Significant and rapid social change endangers its intricate symmetry and harbingers its fragmentation, he is convinced. The separate axes of this dualism, wherever they become independent and lose their symbiotic character, lose their capacity efficiently to orient action. The civic sphere then becomes exposed and vulnerable, expanding or contracting depending upon domination constellations, the irregular flow of power, and multiple alignments. A routinization of political-ethical action to practical-rational orientations follows directly upon any weakening of this sphere.

Originating in the agrarian and religious landscapes of the seventeenth and eighteenth centuries, the American civic sphere confronted severe challenges in the nineteenth and twentieth centuries, Weber holds. Deeply anchored in ascetic Protestantism, would this thick civic sphere retain an independent influence? The frontier's "rugged individual," who survived against great odds and even conquered a vast landscape, became mythologized.

American society, rendered conducive by ascetic Protestantism to the values of an expanding bourgeois class, became permeated far and wide by the orientation of action to competition, achievement, hard work, self-reliance, upward mobility, an optimistic frame of mind in respect to the individual's ability, and an energetic approach to problems and tasks. By the 1870s, heroes in Horatio Alger's mold, severed from binding tradition and on the basis of their own talent, energy, and will, climbed "from rags to riches." Urbanization, industrialization, and modern capitalism implied a massive societal metamorphosis. Standing alone, the individual became in major circles legitimate, worthy of praise, and placed on a pedestal.[13]

Weber maintains that these developments reaffirmed a practical-rational individualism directly antagonistic to the civic realms. Would the dynamic reciprocity that strengthened the world-mastery individualism – civic sphere dualism – remain in place in the twentieth century? Or would a rejuvenated practical rationalism shatter this civic-oriented individualism? Would civic associations continue to permeate American society and sustain an integrating and community-building infrastructure that circumscribed atomization? Even though still substantially nourished at the end of the nineteenth century by churches and civic associations, the civic sphere, unceasingly challenged by practical rationalism, appeared significantly weakened.[14]

The *possible fates* of the thick civic sphere in the rapidly changing twentieth and twenty-first centuries must be now addressed. Our orientation thus shifts away from the distant past and toward the more immediate past and the present. However, we shall do so utilizing Weber's concepts and analytic framework; they once again guide the analysis, both directly through the reconstruction of "a Weberian model" and indirectly through the formation of three updated alternative models: the generalization, professional associations, and conflict constructs. Each model postulates a likely outcome for the American civic sphere.

Hence, the following discussion *extends* the Weberian conceptual framework. Now more wide-ranging, it maps out the broad spectrum within which *present-day* oscillations of the civic sphere take place. Significant changes of "location" occur over generations and at times, even within a decade. This spectrum demarcates the parameters and possible lines of development of today's civic sphere. We turn first to the Weberian model.

8.2 The Weberian Model: The Absence of the Civic Sphere

This model reconstructs the several ways in which Weber viewed the course of the American civic realm's weakening and dissolution. Three sub-models constitute this *Weberian* construct. Each formulates hypotheses regarding challenges to the civic arena.[15] Brief scrutiny of each must suffice.

The Privatization of Work and the Expansion of Practical Rationalism. According to this model, the *sanctification* of work in the eighteenth and nineteenth centuries faded and individualism became routinized back from its practical-ethical form to an interest-based, practical-rational form. This construct hypothesizes that a depletion and circumscription of the civic sphere followed. A vicious cycle ensued.

Although weakened with the waning of asceticism, the aim of building God's kingdom endured in secularized form, this model postulates: *citizens* sought in the eighteenth and nineteenth centuries to establish the *just and good civic society*. Unsurprisingly, in light of the major American religious heritage, work became viewed as the central means toward this end. Thus, a nurturing of the earlier symbiosis between the civic sphere and world-mastery individualism was sustained, this model maintains. However, as the nineteenth century drew to a close, the civic realm experienced a further pathway of decline. Its capacity *to direct* the activity of broad cross-sections of the American population weakened amid expanding practical-rational individualism.

In this new urban and industrialized milieu, neither Benjamin Franklin's spirit of capitalism nor the Protestant ethic's values endowed methodical work with subjective meaning (*PERW*, pp. 157–58). Labor became, as the historical journey distinguished by asceticism's prodigious sanctification of work drew to a close, simply a utilitarian activity. Now decoupled from the religion sphere and routinized back to its practical-rational form, labor more and more served the egoistic interests of individuals, this Weberian model hypothesizes.

This construct captures the full *privatization* dominant at the final stage of this monumental journey. It also depicts the social context that influenced this development, according to Weber: modern capitalism's coercive aspects and practical rationalism. Whether employees or entrepreneurs, those "born into this powerful cosmos" are forced – in order to survive – to adapt to market-based laws and the impersonal exchange of goods. Once "in the saddle," the workplace tempo of "victorious capitalism" imposes upon all within its reach an organized mode of life. Within this "grinding mechanism," characterized by an "inescapable network of pragmatic necessities," survival of businesses, as well as the individual's capacity to earn a livelihood, requires nothing less.

According to this construct, the modern era's grounding is not "spiritual" but "mechanical": "The idea of an 'obligation to search for and then accept a vocational calling' now wanders around in our lives as the ghost of beliefs no longer anchored in the substance of religion" (*PERW*, p. 157). In one of his most famous passages, Weber tersely captures this significant transformation at the level of subjective meaning and motives: "The Puritan *wanted* to be a person with a vocational calling; we *must* be" (*PERW*, p. 157; see pp. 157–58, 446–48).

Of central significance for the fate of the civic arena, work in this model is eviscerated of its prior religious and civic underpinnings, as well as all community-building and integrative capacities – even though it remained at the center of daily life. Hence, this construct hypothesizes a massive alteration of meaning away from the world-mastery individualism – civic sphere dualism and toward unsanctified labor and practical rationalism. Accordingly, the civic realm's political-ethical action was pushed to the margins. A sub-postulate follows: citizenship, in its broader sense as the *regular* orientation of persons to the civic arena's ideals and to engagement in communities, also reached a final stage. It becomes redefined as a hobby activity and relocated within the realm of leisure.

The Circumscription of the Civic Sphere by the "Power of Material Goods." A significant development in more recent decades – the expansion of the "power of material goods" – also affirms the untamed individual and stands in a relationship of antagonism to a vibrant civic realm. A further Weberian sub-model captures this transformation and its outcome: an expansion of practical rationalism.

This construct also focuses upon the social milieu surrounding this development. Under "victorious capitalism," it postulates, the power of goods acquires a firm grip over persons. Whereas seventeenth and eighteenth century American Protestants, living *in this world* but oriented to the *next* world, could resist the temptations presented by products like "a lightweight coat that one can throw off at any time," their power by the early twentieth century had "become a steel-hard casing" (*PERW,* pp. 153–54, 157–58).

Material goods now acquire, Weber's sub-model holds, "an increasing and, in the end, inescapable power over people – as never before in history" (*PERW,* p. 158). A ubiquitous and intense consumer culture develops parallel with the onset of prosperity. Alluring products *must* be possessed. Moreover, the striving for their possession has acquired a new intensity and become a vigorous "pursuit of gain in the United States," this construct hypothesizes, displacing the vocational calling's "spirit of asceticism" and all practical-ethical orientations. Reigning now are "purely competitive passions," and this quest in the twentieth century assumes the "character of a sports event" (*PERW,* p. 158; see Bell, 1996).

What consequences followed from this development for the American civic arena? According to this model, the ubiquitous consumerist ethos of this "new cosmos" invigorated practical rationalism further. To the same extent, an acceleration of the civic realm's porousness followed. Its independence waned, as did that of political-ethical action. Again, a vicious cycle ensued.

Circumscription of the Civic Sphere by "Europeanization." This Weberian construct postulates a gradual "Europeanization" – or bureaucratization – of American political culture. It views these large-scale organizations as indigenous to industrial societies and expects this development to whittle away and constrict the civic arena.

The constraints accompanying industrialization render this alteration likely, this sub-model indicates. Characteristic is a centralization of power and an increase in the prestige and authority of civil servants and managers. Their specialized knowledge of the workings of the state and the economy lead in these directions – and this aggrandizement is accompanied by a diminution in the authority of elected politicians over policy-making decisions. A civic realm dominated by contending political parties, open debate, pluralistic and competing values, and freedom of ideas loses viability with ever-widening bureaucratization, this model hypothesizes As substantive conflict becomes tame and then quiescent, civic ideals – no longer rejuvenated by the widespread controversies that appear wherever groups compete vigorously – fade as well (*E&S*, pp. 1396–405; Weber, 1978, pp. 281–82).

A "societal ossification" follows, according to this construct, intensified by ever greater class stratification and restricted occupational and social mobility. The survival of political-ethical action becomes questionable – all the more so as the prestige and authority of functionaries increases. A rigid, inward-looking, and stagnant society, dominated by risk-averse, security-seeking, and cautious managers, is postulated. The civic arena as well as all residuals of the sect spirit's community-building energy is circumscribed and pushed to the margins. Simultaneously, the bureaucracy's *formal* rationality, in light of its orientation to procedures, statutes, codes, and written regulations, confronts and weakens further any legacies of world-mastery individualism rooted in value-orientations, this sub-model holds. Survival of the older symbiosis – the strong individualism/civic sphere mutual affirmation – is threatened. Circumscription of the civic realm's independence and a weakening of its expansive thrust follows (*RCM*, pp. 255–71).[16]

These three sub-constructs have offered Weberian conceptualizations of the American civic sphere in the twentieth century. Each postulates its dissolution. Taken together, they constitute *the Weberian model*, namely, an updated construct that demarcates likely parameters of the American civic sphere, according to, on the one hand, the analytic framework and rich set of concepts summarized above and, on the other hand, to a variety of Weber's writings. Rather than intended as an accurate depiction of empirical reality, this model, as utilized here, has sought to formulate hypotheses and guidelines for empirical research today.

This investigation must pursue further its orientation toward model building rather than searching for a confirmation or rejection of the hypotheses formulated by each Weberian model (a task far beyond the scope of this study). It now formulates three complementary constructs, all of which are indebted to his concepts and analytic framework. They expand the conceptual grid provided by the Weberian model, and hence demarcate the civic arena's wider parameters. They bring Weber more up-to-date as concerns the American political culture.

8.3 Complementary Models: Updating and Extending the Weberian Analytic Framework

In combination, the Weberian, generalization, professional associations, and conflict models form an extended spectrum that allows us to conceptualize a broader range of the American civic realm's major features, tensions, dynamics, and developmental pathways. More thick, expansive, and independent manifestations stand at one end of this spectrum and more porous, circumscribed, and dependent forms stand at the other. This expanded analytic framework captures the major ossifications followed by political-ethical action.[17]

The Generalization Model: The Civic Sphere's Longevity. Compared to the Weberian model, the generalization construct anchors the extreme opposite end of the civic sphere spectrum. At its foundation stands an assumption at the core of Weber's sociology: the past never fades away simply as a consequence of structural changes, even monumental macro-level transformations. Rather, it endures into the present.

Thus, according to the generalization model, the world-mastery individualism of the seventeenth and eighteenth centuries retains over a longer term its civic orientation, the ascetic Protestant focus upon work sustains aggressively a community-building element, the sect legacy's long-term influence becomes generalized into various sectors of the American society, and the original symbiotic relationship between world-mastery individualism and the civic sphere remains vibrant. In this construct, the thick civic realm maintains its expansiveness and independence and moreover, defends its boundaries against practical rationalism, the power of goods, bureaucratization, the specialization of labor, and the functionary's cautious frame of mind. The policy-making arena continues to be rooted in a strong parliament and electoral politics.

In general, civic arena values, political-ethical action, and a strong individualism are transferred to a broad pluralism of socializing groups and independently cultivated. A notion of "service to a community" remains viable. Finally, the sheer number and wide dispersion of civic associations, by injecting a pluralistic dynamism, resist societal stagnation. Instead, these organizations support political-ethical action and form a bulwark against the value configuration carried by civil servants, functionaries, and managers.

As is the case for the Weberian model, the empirical appearance of all these aspects of the generalization model requires the presence of facilitating arrays of cohesive carrier groups. Wherever they acquire authority, status, and power vis-à-vis opposing groups, the civic realm retains its thick consistency and independence, this model postulates. Rather than expanding exclusively into the arenas of work and politics, it then spreads generally across the breadth of American society: its political-ethical action extends into families, neighborhoods, schools, civic-oriented charities and foundations, volunteer groups, universities, the military, and other mainstream organizations and institutions.

As discussed above, the Weberian model's secularization weakened both the civic sphere *and* world-mastery individualism; indeed, it postulated a dissolution of the civic realm. On the other hand, according to the generalization construct, work retains far longer its sanctified, or quasi-sanctioned, aspect. Hence, to a greater or lesser extent, all of these organizations and institutions transmit a community-building energy.

In sum, the generalization model hypothesizes, and despite nineteenth- and twentieth-century transformations, the civic sphere substantially maintains its earlier intensity and influence. In direct contrast to the Weberian construct, it sustains a thick, expansive, and independent civic sphere.[18]

The Professional Associations Model: The Relocation and Narrowing of the Sect Legacy. In contrast to the generalization model, the professional associations construct shares a pivotal hypothesis with the Weberian model: a twentieth-century social metamorphosis of American society has led to an expansion of practical rationalism. However, the generalization construct rejects the Weberian model's central presupposition: ascetic Protestantism's singular achievement in the postwar period – the sublimation and rationalization of work *across many strata* into a value-based activity – has been eviscerated. Instead, and even though acknowledging labor's longer-term decoupling from sanctifying value configurations, this model hypothesizes that the sect's legacies permeate into this era deeply. Nonetheless, their scope fails to rival the broad expanse achieved under the generalization model. The professional associations construct articulates their *circumscribed location* in the postwar United States and calls attention to their continuing influence.

A generalization of the ascetic Protestant heritage to the same magnitude as characteristic of the nineteenth century is no longer apparent in this era, according to this model. Moreover, sect legacies become significantly separated from civic associations – which become more porous and internally less rigorous, it maintains. A sector of American society becomes the home for these legacies: its upper-middle-class professional associations. Here, they are cultivated and sustained, this construct contends. As carried by these secular organizations, a methodical and value-based orientation to work and vocations compete directly with practical-rational and utilitarian orientations. How do postwar professional associations manifest sect legacies, according to this construct?[19]

Acceptable behavior and appropriate moral conduct for members are prescribed. An orientation to high standards must characterize behavior. The admission candidate's suitable conduct is testified to by certificates of educational attainment (rather than a minister's letter of recommendation); they provide the basis for membership. In turn, behavior is monitored formally and informally for its conformity to the organization's standards. To do so, the sect's external form is adopted: observational mechanisms and discipline are apparent.

Articulated in "codes of conduct," rules and statutes become enforced by designated committees empowered to punish violators. Penalties can be imposed, including the loss of membership, and severe sanctions may bring careers to a sudden conclusion. Finally, professionals measured their self-worth and dignity against a set of moral codes. Does the member "live up to" the association's standards? Has "professional integrity" been maintained throughout the career? A sincere "professionalism" and "the professional career," substantively bounded and separate from other realms, here acquire legitimacy and prestige. The professional association in this manner maintains its integrity and that of its members (Barber, 1978–1979; Abbott, 1983; Friedson, 1984; Abel and Lewis, 1989).

This model comprehends these associations as abundantly manifesting sect legacies.[20] A great variety of vocation-based associations have crystallized in the United States, many of which predate the postwar period: for example, the American Medical Association, the American Bar Association, the American Psychological Association, the American Association of Social Workers, and the American Sociological Association. Business corporations, large and small, define "business ethics," codes of conduct, and "mission statements" (see Barber, 1978–1979; Abbott, 1983; Friedson, 1984; Abel, 1985, 1986; Parsons, 2007).

This relocation of asceticism's legacies to professional associations implies significant consequences for the American civic sphere, according to this model. The sect spirit's relationship to American society generally has been transformed. Its legacies, instead of setting standards for *civic* endeavors in an expansive way, as did both the sect in the seventeenth and eighteenth centuries and the civic association in the nineteenth century, are now more narrowly located, this construct hypothesizes: they have become restricted to members of professional associations. And because a cultivation of ethical action now occurs outside the civic sphere, its rejuvenation in a manner parallel to previous centuries – as *political-ethical* action – is precluded.

Furthermore, as a consequence of the internal orientation of professional association members, these organizations, compared to civic associations, sects, and churches in earlier eras, demonstrate a weakened capacity to challenge practical rationalism, the power of goods, and bureaucratization. A vacuum appears in the civic realm. Indeed, this model maps a decoupling of the sect legacy from the civic arena and hypothesizes the end of ascetic Protestantism's capacity to nourish civic life.

This absence of a *linkage* between professional organizations and the civic sphere implies not only an exclusive orientation of members' behavior to standards and codes of conduct internal to these associations. In addition, a relationship of antagonism develops between these realms, this construct hypothesizes, wherever a methodical work ethos among professionals acquires a halo of "self-fulfillment" and "self-realization": itself a legacy of ascetic Protestantism, this legitimating aura bestows further autonomy upon "professional life." Other activities, such as civic engagement, are not only curtailed owing to scarce energy and time, according to this model, but also as a result of their loss of meaning to professionals.[21]

In sum,[22] this construct postulates that the growth in the nineteenth and twentieth centuries of practical rationalism, the power of goods and bureaucracies never eradicated ascetic Protestantism's legacies. However, their manifestation narrowly in the postwar era's professional associations failed to convey political-ethical action into the civic realm of sufficient intensity to counteract the spread of utilitarian and interest-oriented activity. In stark opposition to the generalization model, the professional associations construct hypothesizes a curtailment of the sect spirit's more far-reaching capacity to call forth a demarcated civic realm infused by political-ethical action. On the other hand, and in sharp opposition to the Weberian model, the professional associations model does not postulate an aggressive confrontation with this sphere and its subsequent dissolution.

The Conflict Model. This construct articulates further hypotheses designed to delineate the civic arena's magnitude and scope. It contributes the final construct to a uniquely American spectrum of possibilities.

Competition and relationships of tension across groupings of approximately equal weight are characteristic. Conflict appears on a regular basis. The rejuvenation that originates from crosscutting rivalries – allegiances of group members are strengthened – sustains a vibrant cultivation of pluralistic arrays of groups and a societal openness. This dynamism, rooted in the sect legacies and civic associations, confronts the privatization of work, the intensification of the power of goods, bureaucratization, and the restriction of sect legacies to professional associations. Although never dominant, political-ethical action and world-mastery individualism continue to be nourished amid regular confrontations and "culture wars." "Service to a community" and a community-building element remain of sufficient expanse to place significant restrictions around practical rationalism.

Hence, in strict opposition to the Weberian construct, the conflict model postulates that the civic sphere continues to exist, albeit to a less substantive extent than hypothesized by the generalization model and although perpetually beset by tensions. Powerful carrier organizations, whether families, schools, or volunteer groups, for example, sustain this arena. According to this construct, the civic realm permeates influential organizations.

Nonetheless, the conflict model hypothesizes also unceasing challenges and threats to the civic sphere. Its boundaries become less firm. Interest-oriented activity develops more intensively than postulated by the generalization construct and persons, unconstrained by political-ethical action, are more frequently oriented by utilitarian considerations. Furthermore, secularization has weakened world-mastery individualism, the halo of sanctity around work, and all God-oriented community-building, this model postulates. Thus, the civic arena's thick quality is depleted; accordingly, fewer hindrances obstruct the permeation of daily life by the power of goods. Bureaucratization proceeds and contests the civic realm's independence on a regular basis. In this context, a generalization of the ethical action cultivated in professional organizations is precluded; rather, it retained its exclusively internal focus.

The generalization, professional associations, and conflict models expand and update Weber's foreshortened analytic framework. This remains the case, even though these constructs are grounded in his rich set of concepts. All models have formulated arrays of operationalizable hypotheses capable of orienting even today the empirical investigation of the American civic sphere.

In combination, these constructs define a spectrum that conceptualizes this sphere's past and present oscillations. More thick, generalizing, and independent manifestations are apparent at one end of this heuristic tool and more porous, circumscribed, and dependent forms anchor the other. Moreover, as an orientational research mechanism, this conceptual framework can be utilized to identify directional movements, coalitions across groups, and conflicts across groups. Only arrays of causally effective groups, Weber insists, push movement across this spectrum (see Kalberg, 1994, pp. 52–78, 168–76). In concluding, several aspects of his analysis must be briefly highlighted.

Moreover, his models indicate that an independent civic sphere endures with greater likelihood if rooted in competing groups and regular, pluralistic tensions (*RCM*, pp. 168–72, 255–71). A societal openness derives from sustained, moderate-level conflict; ossification occurs, with a greater probability, wherever a single group or organization acquires hegemony, he holds.

In this respect, the bureaucracy's certified, risk-averse, and conformist functionaries constitute a central problem – yet not one of overwhelming magnitude. A society's stagnation looms more likely whenever *bureaucratization* proceeds to such an extent that few social, economic, political, or legal constraints stand effectively against this development – one that will eventually lead to the substitution of decision-making in reference to values by decision-making in reference to pragmatic, utilitarian, and instrumental considerations (*RCM*, pp. 255–71). The civic sphere will then be diminished in scope. Typically, while examining the adverse consequences of bureaucratization, Weber acknowledges a paradox: although they hold bureaucratization in check, dynamic and tension-filled societies today strengthen the power of goods and practical rationalism's unbounded individualism. As discussed, both will also lead to a circumscription of the civic sphere. In concluding, several aspects of his analysis must be briefly highlighted.

First, as evident from this entire study, Weber contends that investigations of the American civic sphere (or that of any other country) focused exclusively on the present fail to yield an adequate comprehension of its unique value contours, origin, expansion, parameters, and oscillations. An orientation to the rational choices of individuals, the economic interests of powerful actors in groups, structural factors, or this sphere's "functions" identifies only surface-level factors.

Influences from the past, when carried by cohesive and effective groups, must be acknowledged in a systematic manner in all sociological investigations of the present, Weber holds. Once anchored in firm carrier organizations, strata, and classes, pivotal values, traditions, and interests seldom entirely fade from a society's landscape. He embraces strongly the notion that cultural influences may endure despite broad structural transformations. For this reason, all global dichotomies (e.g., *Gemeinschaft–Gesellschaft* and tradition–modernity) are rejected entirely. This central tenet of Weber's sociology underpins all models above.

Fourth, Weber's writings on the American civic sphere stress that its viability will fade in the absence of an initiative-taking individualism. Persons must not only become oriented to the civic arena's values in a cognitive manner, he argues, but also possess capacities that allow *activity* consistent with them. How does the delicate balance indispensable for the unfolding of a thick civic sphere – between individualism and a civic orientation – congeal in certain groups and in certain societies?

Weber's analysis maintains that a practical-rational individualism, because lacking consistent *internal* guidance by values, must be rationalized and sublimated into a world-mastery individualism if a substantive civic sphere is to crystallize – for civic orientations are *inherent* to *this* asceticism-oriented individualism. However, according to his analysis, this value-based individualism proves rare and frequently undergoes routinization back to interest-oriented action. Practical rationalism, the privatization of work, the power of goods, and bureaucratization present significant challenges to world-mastery individualism and to practical-ethical action – as well as to the civic sphere itself.

Notes

1 This is my term.
2 That is, the Methodist, Presbyterian, Baptist, Quaker, Mennonite sects and churches. Weber distinguishes these Protestant groups sharply from Lutheranism. His generic term – "Puritanism" (see *PEWR*, pp. 141–59) – will be sparingly used synonymously.
3 His writings on the American civic arena have been examined only infrequently (see, above all, Kim, 2004; see also Loader and Alexander, 1985).
4 See Chapters 7 and 9.
5 Jellinek constitutes a clear exception (1895).
6 The origins and formation of the civic sphere are addressed here in a manner that opposes radically Alexander's position. An analysis grounded historically or in carrier groups is not to be found in his long study. Rather, for him (as for Parsons), the civic sphere emerges out of a macro differentiation process that gives rise to "different kinds of institutional spheres and discourses" – one of which is the civic sphere (see 2006, p. 195).
7 On this section, see also Chapter 9.
8 Weber saw *American* individualism (unlike the more inward-looking individualism of German elites) as fundamentally located in groups, even in those groups – especially sects – that expect strict adherence to firm norms. Rather than losing the capacity for decision-making when in groups, Americans "hold their own," he contends, on the basis of defined standards, values, and goals. To him, here ascetic Protestantism's influence is evident (see *RCM*, pp. 277–90).
9 One central source of American manners can be located here.
10 This is my term.
11 That these modes of solidarity were not viewed by sociologists in Europe as adequately giving rise to a community-building energy in part itself led to their conclusion that atomization inherently accompanied capitalism and urbanization. Their error must be seen as involving a false transposition onto the United States. This conclusion, because it viewed all societies

amid this transformation as fundamentally alike, occluded cognizance of American exceptionalism.

12 This depiction should be viewed as a Weberian ideal type. Many empirical examples from American history that vary distinctly from this model are apparent in Weber's writings. He is, for example, quite aware of widespread corruption in American cities (see 1968, pp. 1397–98; 2005, pp. 108–12).

13 On the *American* worldview, see, for example, Bellah *et al.* (1985); Hartz (1959); Hofstadter (1955); Konwitz and Kennedy (1960); Lipset (1963); Lynd (1976); Miller (1961); Parrington (1954); and White (1957).

14 The "communitarian" and "bowling alone" discussions can be seen as recent revisitations of the classic American world-mastery individualism – civic sphere dualism (see, e.g., Etzioni, 1997, 1998; Selznick, 1992; Bellah, 1985; Putnam, 2000; and Hall and Lindholm, 1999).

15 Thus, the *conceptual* yield of Weber's analysis is stressed rather than its empirical accuracy. In opposition to the position taken here, many may argue that the three models, all recognizable to readers of Weber, constitute for him actual depictions of reality. This complex question cannot be resolved in a study of limited length. Suffice it to say, the orientation in *this* investigation toward Weber is purely conceptual: utilizing his concepts and framework, it seeks to offer a purely *analytical* consideration that maps the full spectrum, in reference to which the civic sphere, according to Weber, oscillates across the American political culture. Such "clear conceptualization" and model building, according to Weber's methodology, must always constitute the *first* step in the research process, that is, a stage prior to commencement of the empirical investigation (see "Obj," pp. 90–104).

16 Again, the "Weberian sub-models" are constructed here as hypothesis-forming aids for research rather than as constructs designed to capture empirical reality. Interpreters have generally comprehended Weber's "Europeanization thesis" as an empirical development and offered trenchant criticisms (see Mommsen, 1974, 1989; Roth, 1985, 2005a, 2005b).

17 It is here maintained that these constructs, although not exhaustive, constitute the *most plausible* models to be derived from Weber's concepts and conceptual grid.

18 This model approximates the major presuppositions of the Parsonsian vision of American society. From the point of view of the "pluralistic models" mode of theorizing undertaken in this study, Parsonian theorizing on American society diverges distinctly: although it also sees pendular movements, it foreshortens the American spectrum's scope. Hence, compared to Weber, Parsons offers a far more monolithic vision of American society and American political culture (see Parsons, 1966, 1971, 2007).

19 Of course, such professional associations are also found in other countries. They have originated, however, either from the laws of a state or the leadership initiative of elite groups rather than from a broad-based sect heritage (see Rueschemeyer, 1973; Abel, 1985; Abel and Lewis 1989).

20 If Weber had lived to observe the full development and scope of the professional association, he would have viewed it also from another vantage point, namely as offering further support for his fundamental position: American society is not constituted from a sandpile of unconnected individuals.

21 Americans now work more hours per year than the people of any other nation. While not rejecting the role of external constraint and domination (see above), Weber's interpretive sociology of subjective meaning insists upon a recognition of the deep cultural meanings behind this quantitative indicator.

22 An empirical substantiation of this model would require a comparative investigation. Professional associations in other nations, it would postulate, assume a less activist posture in respect to monitoring and effective punishing than their American counterparts. Moreover, the power to impose penalties for "unprofessional conduct" usually lies in other nations with legal authorities and outside the association (see Rueschemeyer, 1973; Abel and Lewis, 1989; Savelsberg, 1994; Parsons, 2007).

9

THE MODERN WORLD AS A MONOLITHIC IRON CAGE? UTILIZING MAX WEBER TO DEFINE THE INTERNAL DYNAMICS OF THE AMERICAN POLITICAL CULTURE TODAY

Max Weber is well known for his depiction of the modern world as an "iron cage" (*stahlhartes Gehäuse*). Along with most of his German colleagues at the fin de siècle, he viewed the coming of modern capitalism with trepidation and foreboding. How does Weber define the iron cage and does this metaphor accurately capture his view of modernity? More generally, do Weber's distinguished sociological writings assist Americans *today*, at the dawn of the twenty-first century, to understand their own society and, in particular, its political culture?

9.1 The "Iron Cage"

In his most famous book, *The Protestant Ethic and the Spirit of Capitalism*, Weber argued that the "inner-worldly" asceticism of Reform Calvinism had given birth to the notion of a "vocational calling." This methodical orientation toward work, as it spread widely in the American Colonies, lost its religious foundations after several generations. Nonetheless, this *spirit* of capitalism, now simply a "practical-ethical" constellation of values or ethos had assisted in giving birth to an industrial and highly organized form of capitalism. However, we who are born into this "cosmos of the modern economic order" are no longer motivated to work systematically on the basis of a calling; rather, we do so simply because "this economy...bound to the technical and economic conditions of mechanized, machine-based production" coerces us to do so in order to survive (*PE*, p. 177).

DOI: 10.4324/9781032631813-13

A mighty structure founded in an "instrumental rationality" of technical, administrative, and market contingencies "determine our style of life" and a "mechanical foundation" now anchors capitalism, whereas "the Puritan *wanted* to work in a calling...we *must* do so" (*PE*, p. 177; emphasis in original). Once intrically linked to work, values are no longer crucial to or cultivated in "modern industrial labor," even though work has become elevated to the very center of our lives: "The idea of...a [vocational calling] now wanders around in our lives as the ghost of past religious belief" (*PE*, p. 177).

Moreover, the advance of modern capitalism in the West occurred parallel to the development of a specific organization supremely adapted to its functioning. It affirms an indispensable value: technically superior administration:

> The bureaucratic organization, with its specialization of trained skills, its delineation of competencies, its rules and hierarchical relations of obedience....is...in the process of erecting a cage of bondage which persons – lacking all powers of resistance – will perhaps one day be forced to inhabit, as the fellahs of ancient Egypt. This *might happen if a purely technical value – a rational civil service administration (Beamtenverwaltung) and distribution of welfare benefits – becomes viewed as the ultimate and single value in reference to which the organization of all affairs ought to be decided.* The bureaucracy achieves this result much better than any other structure of domination. (*E&S*, p. 1402; emphasis in original; translation altered)

In this iron cage model, the domination of bureaucracies calls forth a caste of functionaries and civil servants who monopolize power. To the extent that this takes place, "...a fettering [of] every individual to his job..., his class..., and maybe to his occupation" occurs as well as the imposition upon the ruled of a "status order" tied to the bureaucracy (*E&S*, p. 1402). Opportunities for the development of genuine entrepreneurs and political leaders vanish in this rigidly stratified society "as austerly rational as a machine" (*E&S*, p. 1402). If the "inescapable power" of the bureaucracy's functionaries reigns, a "pacifism of social impotence," a loss of all societal dynamism, and a thorough stagnation throughout the society will result (*E&S*, pp. 1402–03; see Weber, 1978, pp. 281–83).

Devoid of brotherhood, compassion, and heroic ethical action, this iron cage society becomes more and more dominated by the impersonal and cautious values of the functionary on the one hand – duty, punctuality, reliability, respect for hierarchy, etc. – and practical rationalism's instrumental calculations of interests and advantage on the other hand. A retreat into the private realm of intimacy where emotion and personal-oriented values are still pulsating – and the *cultivation* of this private realm – is viewed as the single means of survival with a measure of dignity intact.

"Home and hearth" become the refuge; here alone, warmth and deep bonds are found. In this portrait, all civic virtues and public ethics are absent and as well, most values overarching the private domain exist as mere moribund legacies from earlier – mainly religious – epochs. They are now threatened with extinction by the mighty, inexorable expansion of calculation, manipulation, and instrumental rationality (*PE*, pp. 177–78; "SV," p. 155; "PV," p. 128).

Innumerable interpreters to this day have taken this depiction as Weber's actual characterization of our times. He is then portrayed as a dour and haunted figure, fatalistic and despairing, yet also heroic and stoical – a brooding giant who carried the bleak burdens of the twentieth century upon his broad shoulders.

It must be acknowledged that his view of the modern era was a distant cry from the many *fin de siècle* Anglo-Saxon, Social Darwinist theorists who hailed the coming of the industrial age as "progress," a new advance of civilization, and a further stage in the triumphant evolution of mankind. Weber also clearly parted ways with all "theorists of democracy" who discovered in the industrialized world a broad and deep *civic* realm of open participation, public ideals and public ethics, and citizenship and personal liberties. Had he still been writing in the 1950s, he would have sharply disagreed with the "modernization" theorists, all of whom asserted (in one way or another) that capitalism itself calls forth democracy and that democracy's advance proceeds roughly parallel with the march of industrialism (see Parsons, 1966, 1971). To Weber:

It is utterly ridiculous to attribute an elective affinity between present-day advanced capitalism as it…exists in America… and "democracy," or indeed with "freedom" (in any sense of the word). The only question to be asked is: where it prevails, how are all these things, in general and in the long term, *possible*? (Weber, 1978, p. 282; translation altered; emphasis original; see also *E&S*, p. 1403)

Nonetheless, the iron cage metaphor fails to encapsulate Weber's complex view of the twentieth century. First, rather than a reality or even a short-term scenario, the iron cage constituted to him a nightmare vision that *might be* on our horizon. The subjunctive case, qualifying expressions (see the quotation at p. 180), and multiple preconditions are almost always attached to his usage of this phrase (*E&S*, pp. 960–61, 969–71, 991, 1403–04; see Mommsen, 1974, pp. 86–87).

Second, in central ways, Max Weber *welcomed* the modern world – in particular the freedoms and rights it bestowed upon individuals and the very notion of the autonomous individual – and scorned the past, as well as the naive romanticism of most of his colleagues: "After all, it is a gross deception to believe that without the achievements of the age of the 'Rights of Man' any one of us (including the most conservative) can go on living his life" (*E&S*, p. 1403). He spoke and wrote tirelessly in support of strong and contending political parties, the constitutional division of powers, an "ethic of responsibility" for politicians, constitutional guarantees of civil liberties, and an extension of suffrage (see *E&S*, p. 1462; "PV," pp. 115–27).

He argued vehemently that democracy would be possible only where strong parliaments existed, which he saw as a training ground for the political leaders of the "plebiscitary leadership democracy" he advocated (*E&S*, pp. 1409–14; Mommsen, 1974, pp. 72–94; 1974b, pp. 44–71). And he sought to erect various mechanisms that would sustain pluralistic, competing interest groupings in order to check the power of bureaucracies, for "we 'individualist' and party member partisans of 'democratic' institutions...are swimming 'against the tide' of material constellations" (Weber, 1978, p. 282; see pp. 281–82).

Rather than the fatalism and despair so prominent among his contemporaries in Germany, particularly Nietzsche and Georg Simmel, skepticism mixed with appreciation characterizes Weber's position. Indeed, he believed that, if dynamic, industrial societies offered an opportunity for the development of the autonomous individual guided by *ethical* values (Weber, "PV," pp. 115–27; *E&S*, pp. 960–61, 979–80, 1207–10; Weber, 1978, p. 282; see Löwith, 1970; Mommsen, 1974, pp. 86–87, 93–95; Kalberg, 2021).

Third, this common portrayal of Weber as a social theorist who saw the twentieth century as an iron cage is derived largely from his political and social-philosophical essays rather than his sociological writings. His comparative-historical sociology presents a far more differentiated portrait. If extracted from these writings, his posture regarding modern industrial and urban societies is both *more dynamic* and *more differentiated* than the iron cage metaphor suggests. *Cases* capture his attention – specific nation-states – rather than putatively global, irreversible, and monolithic developments.

9.2   More Dynamic and More Differentiated

Weber's understanding of "societies" as only loosely held together and as constituted from an array of competing, reciprocally interacting domains of action unfolding at varying speeds – the religion, economy, law, rulership (*Herrschaft*), status groups, and family domains (see *E&S*; Kalberg, 1994, pp. 104, 149–51; 2021) – persuades him that past developments were extremely important for any explanation of the present. It convinces him as well that customs, conventions, laws, relationships of domination, and values originating in the distinct past deeply permeate the present in multiple, though often obscure, ways. He rejects as far too global all modes of conceptualization that view societies as either *Gemeinschaften* or *Gesellschaften* ("traditional" or "modern").

Weber also opposes the view that past action, if influential in the present at all, remains circumscribed in its impact and endowed with little long-term, significant consequence. The past may live on for millennia within the interstices of the present, he asserts, and even within its central core. Even the abrupt appearance of "the new" – even the extraordinary power of charismatic leadership – never fully ruptures ties to the past: "That which has been handed down from the past becomes everywhere the immediate precursor of that taken in the present as valid" (*E&S*, p. 29; translation altered). Far from being banished, history interacts with the present to such an extent that, unless its influence is acknowledged, any attempt to explain the uniqueness of the present remains a hopeless undertaking (Kalberg, 1994, pp. 158–67, 187–89; 2021; see Chapter 7).

Weber calls attention, for example, to the many ways in which the values of ascetic Protestantism, originating in seventeenth-century Colonial America, endure in weakened and secularized forms in American daily life to this day: an unambivalent support of capitalism and a self-reliant individualism, a distrust of the state (especially the strong state), a basic orientation to the future and the "opportunities" it offers, an intolerance of perceived evil, a high rate of regular giving to charity organizations, a quick and nimble capacity to form civil associations, and a strong belief in the capacity of individuals to set goals, shape their own destinies, and even to be upwardly mobile. Despite vast structural transformations – bureaucratization, urbanization, and the rise of modern capitalism – such legacies from the past endure, he argues, today penetrating into and interweaving with the homogenizing "structural constraints" of industrialism (see *PE*, pp. 158–79; "IR"; "Sects I"; "Sects II").

Rather than to be understood as new and radically divorced from the past, modern societies are best conceptualized as mixtures – even *dynamic* mixtures – of past and present. Indeed, his mode of analysis advocates an examination of each particular country. The focus, he insists, must remain upon single cases and an assessment of each nation's *uniqueness* (see Kalberg, 1994, pp. 81–84; 2021). If we scrutinize civilizations, taking Weber's theoretical framework as our heuristic guide, we discover significant singularity rather than an expanse of bureaucratization to the same degree across all civilizations. Although both Germany and the United States, for example, were quite advanced industrial societies at the *fin de siècle*, they were separated by many significant differences.

Whereas in Germany a strong social welfare state, a powerful elite of state civil servants, an authoritarian centralization of power and a weak parliament, a passive citizenry "governed like sheep," a state church highly supportive of state authority, and a "formal-rational" – Continental – legal system anchored exclusively in a constitution prevailed as well as hierarchical social conventions and industrialization directed "from above" by the state (*E&S*, pp. 1381–1469; Mommsen, 1974, pp. 83–86; Kalberg, 2012, pp. 227–48), a quite different configuration became prominent in the United States: a decentralized and "weak state," a division of political powers, an activist citizenry and widespread civic associations, relatively egalitarian social customs, a separation of church and state, anti-authoritarian religious institutions, industrialization "from below," and a legal system (although based in a constitution) strongly indebted to the emphasis in English Common Law upon precedent (see "Sects I," "Sects II"; *E&S*, pp. 1197–1210; Mommsen, 1974, pp. 79–86, 92–95; Chapter 7).

Finally, the social prestige of civil servants, so high in Germany and so central to the iron cage model, is seen to be unusually low:

> Usually the social esteem of the officials is especially low where the demand for expert administration and the hold of status conventions are weak. This is often the case in new settlements by virtue of the great economic opportunities and the great instability of their social stratification: witness the United States. (*E&S*, p. 960)

Hence, again, the common depiction of Weber as upholding a monolithic "iron cage" vision of the modern West must be rejected. His sociological writings assert that the political culture of each industrial nation is distinct unto itself.[1] Weber insists upon case-specific contextualization even in respect to "bureaucratization."

> One must in every individual historical case analyze the special direction in which bureaucratization develops. For this reason, it must remain an open question whether the *power* of bureaucracy is, without exception, increasing in the modern states in which it is spreading....Whether the power of bureaucracy as such increases cannot be decided *a priori*... (*E&S*, p. 991; translation altered)

How, then, in his comparative-historical writings, did Weber portray the United States?[2] Can his analysis offer helpful insight even today into the internal workings of *fin de siècle* American society and, in particular, its political culture?

9.3   On the Political Culture of the United States

Weber saw an unusual dualism as specific to the American heritage. An initiative-taking, activity-oriented, and entrepreneurial "world-mastery" (*weltbeherrschende*) individualism relatively uncircumscribed by traditions was juxtaposed with its seeming opposite: a prominent *civic sphere* of ideals and values that pulled and guided individuals beyond self-interest calculations and toward the betterment of their communities. Although he recognized that both the civic and world-mastery components of the American configuration had become distinctly weakened at the dawn of the twentieth century, this intertwining of forces, otherwise so incompatible, fascinated Weber.[3] His investigations led to the conclusion that far from happenstance, *both* orientations – to self and to community – had planted deep roots in the American soil, particularly in its religious history (see *PE*, pp. 158–79; "Sects I"; "Sects II"; *E&S*, pp. 1204–11).

The Religious Origins of World-Mastery Individualism and Civic Sphere Ideals. American ascetic Protestantism – the Reform Calvinist, Congregationalist, Methodist, Baptist, Quaker, Presbyterian, and Mennonite churches – called forth an intense, task-oriented individualism. These believers were expected to keep an especially vigilant "watchfulness" over all creaturely impulses, for the corrupting enticements of worldly pleasure were abjured to an unusual degree; however, an exclusive reliance upon the believer's own inner resources was also expected. The Sacraments or other rituals could not assist the devout, even though "right" and "wrong" became understood in rigidly moral terms. Nor could a clergy provide assurance regarding salvation. Standing alone before a wrathful, omnipotent, and vengeful Old Testament God and responsible solely to Him, the devout had to rely exclusively upon themselves to create "evidence" of their predestined status and thereby to ameliorate anxiety regarding the most important question: "am I among the saved?" (*PE*, pp. 119–20, 133–34; *E&S*, pp. 1198–200).

However, the injunction of asceticism – to focus the individual's energies through heroic discipline on behalf of a taming of the creaturely impulses – was only one demand placed upon ascetic Protestants. In addition, the faithful were expected to "master" worldly evil by undertaking the creation on earth of the Kingdom of God. Because neither tolerance of nor separation from evil could be allowed, a religious obligation of world-mastery became an imperative to the devout: to act in accord with God's commandments and *against* worldly evil, even against secular authority and popular opinion if necessary.

Hence, these believers never practiced an individualism inclined toward compromise, caution, and contemplation. Instead, a steadfast, "world-oriented" individualism was cultivated that endowed early Americans with resoluteness and a robust optimism regarding their capacity to confront traditions. The alteration of society as a whole – the creation of the Kingdom of God – constituted its aim (*PE*, pp. 122–23; 327, note 34; "Sects II," pp. 224–25; "Sects," I, pp. 10–11; *E&S*, pp. 1207–09).[4] Thus, the improvement of the community became viewed by ascetic Protestants as part and parcel to one's religious obligation and as a service to God.

This occurred in another manner as well. As noted, the devout were alone responsible to seek alleviation of the excruciating anxiety that accompanied uncertainty regarding the central question for believers: their *personal* salvation status. Yet, Reform Calvinists in particular could convince themselves, through their actions (*Bewährung*), of their status among the saved. Weber emphasizes a particular mechanism for doing so: if worldly success – defined as material prosperity – is attained, the faithful can conclude that an omniscient and omnipotent God has bestowed his favor. And this Deity, of course, would offer such a "sign" *only* to the predestined. Unusually strong "psychological premiums" became awarded in this manner to methodical work: only through systematic labor might material prosperity be attained (*PE*, pp. 170–71; *E&S*, pp. 572–73, 1197–200, 1203–210).[5]

Remarkably, even though ultimately motivated by the search to clarify the *individual's* salvation status, precisely this intensification of work had the effect of accentuating the commitment of believers *to a community*. For although left alone by ascetic Protestant doctrine to create "evidence" of their membership among the saved, the methodical work of the devout in a calling (*Beruf*) – the means of doing so – never served only the individual. Instead, God's glory required the faithful to labor *on His behalf* and to create the humane earthly Kingdom in His honor. Hence, labor became methodical, yet also oriented in part away from the egocentric individual's interests and toward far broader tasks.

Moreover, this Mission constituted a *religious* obligation. In this way, work *tied* believers into a community and took place for a purpose larger than utilitarian calculations aimed to accumulate material goods. A clear dualism is apparent: a world-mastery individualism focused upon individual rights and the capacity of individuals to shape and reshape their personal destinies, yet an equally strong thrust toward engagement in a community and its improvement.

Furthermore, a delineated organization crystallized as the social carrier for the psychological premiums upon community participation introduced by ascetic, "inner-worldly" Protestantism: the congregation. Because a *family* of trust and helpfulness existed in this organization, it served as a viable and natural "training ground" for group participation skills. Here, in a secure milieu of fellow believers, the rules of "self-government" and a notion of service to the group could be taught. A push toward civic activism, yet also toward a goal-oriented individualism, crystallized from this religious experience and left a broad imprint upon Colonial America and the early United States (see "Sects I" and "Sects II").

Owing to the religious significance of successful trade and profit as well as the ascetic's strict vow to respect God's Commandments, trust, truthful advice, and the ethic of fair play became constituted as firm ideals even for commercial relationships. Once established in this domain, these ideals carried over – although to a varying extent *as a consequence of* regional differences – into the political sphere and erected strong *ideals* of truthfulness, social trust, good will, and fair play for public life generally. Occurring long before the onset of industrialism in the mid-nineteenth century, a strong penetration of the public realm by these ideals took place. A *civic sphere* of "public ethics" came into existence and elected officials were expected to abide by its high standards.[6]

Strong civic ideals appeared in the political cultures of nations, according to Weber, only rarely; they cannot be understood as simply evolutionary concomitants of industrialization (see Parsons, 1966; Kalberg, 1993; see also Chapter 7).[7] Moreover, their juxtaposition with a world-mastery individualism was extremely unusual, he believed. Indeed, on the basis of a common foundation in ascetic Protestantism, civic values were reciprocally intertwined with this activist individualism. As it became substantial and broad in scope, the civic realm became empowered to direct individualism, pulling it away, as asceticism became weaker and failed to do so, from an exclusive focus upon an egocentric striving for material prosperity and toward the improvement of community standards.

Civic ideals also prevented this individualism from readily following a course of decline into merely instrumental, self-oriented calculations of interests and advantage. Conversely, because it endowed persons with the strength and self-confidence to act "in the world" and to defend, in moral terms if necessary, values, principles, and rights, even against great obstacles, activist individualism in the Colonial era and early United States repeatedly rejuvenated public ethics. Indeed, this world-oriented individualism might be said to be a social-cultural necessity if a viable notion of the individual's right to oppose authority and power is to exist in a sociologically significant manner

(*E&S*, pp. 1204–11; 1988, pp. 438–49).[8] In turn, owing to the high demands civic ideals placed upon persons to reform communities – to *act* – on behalf of ethical values, world-mastery individualism was perpetually invigorated. A mutually sustaining dynamic congealed (see Chapter 7).

Weber saw that a quite unusual dualism, when viewed from a comparative perspective, characterized *this* political culture. Moreover, it broke asunder the iron cage dichotomy in which a public sphere pervaded by technical, administrative, and market constraints, devoid of civic ideals and dominated by raw power and calculations of interests unbounded by values, called forth its polar opposite: an apolitical, deeply private refuge in which intimate relations of warmth and compassion were cultivated (see "SV," p. 155). Instead, *civic ideals* of honesty, fair play, social trust, good will, and equality of treatment – an *ethos* – penetrated the public domain in the Colonial era and early United States. It directed an activist individualism away from sheer interest-oriented pursuits, power-seeking machinations, egocentrism, and indulgence in the unlimited temptations of daily life.

Of course, Weber knew well that corruption and a "spoils system" remained widespread in the America of the late nineteenth and early twentieth centuries, and that power and crass calculation frequently prevailed over public ethics. Indeed, he sees ethical action in reference to a public ethos as the exception and the corrupt politics of city machines as unusually widespread ("PV," pp. 108–10; *E&S*, p. 1401; Weber, 1978, pp. 281–82). Nonetheless, because deeply rooted in American religious history, the civic sphere remained to him of significant sociological impact – even if now mainly as a legacy.

Quite different parameters and dichotomies characterized the iron cage model as well as those political cultures in which civil servant functionaries, the state's laws, and closed political parties largely encompass – even monopolize – *all* understandings of the civic domain.[9] The unusual pendulum movement placed into motion by the uniquely American dualism – a broadened civic sphere penetrated by ethical values interweaving intimately with an accentuated practical-rational individualism – in large part accounted for the dynamism and restlessness characteristic of the American political culture, Weber surely would have argued (see Chapters 7 and 8).

9.4   Applying the Analysis: The American Political Culture Today

Although Weber adequately charted the American political culture's classic dualism, he failed to identify the manner in which it would become weakened. It appeared likely to him that large-scale bureaucratization would eventually accompany industrialization in the United States, as it had in Europe, and thus an enhancement of the power and prestige of civil servants and managers would likely occur. As functionaries in possession of specialized knowledge, and capable of concentrating power in large organizations, intruded into domains of policy-making appropriately ones of open political debate and conflict between parties, the few remaining legacies of public sphere ideals would, Weber feared, disappear.

Massive "ossification" would then proceed and a closed, rigid, and inward-looking society devoid of noble ideals as well as pluralistic and competing values would come into being. A civic sphere would vanish and the civil servant "type of person" (*Menschentyp*) – risk averse, cautious, and in possession of an exaggerated sense of importance – would acquire prestige and become a dominant figure ("PV," 88; *E&S*, pp. 971, 1398, 1400–51; Weber, 1978, pp. 281–82; Mommsen, 1974, pp. 86–89, 92; Roth, 1985). As social commentators in the United States in recent years have repeatedly lamented, a "loss of the civic" and a weakening of public ethics appear evident.

Yet American political history has repeatedly been marked by waves of protest and varieties of social movements in opposition to bureaucratization. A cohesive caste of prestigeful functionaries has not crystallized.[10]

American world-mastery individualism now appears less and less directed to *both* self-oriented material prosperity and a constellation of civic values, and more and more directed to *both* self-oriented material prosperity and the consumer-entertainment cultures. Originally thoroughly interwoven with and invigorated by the civic realm, activist individualism has become severed from this guiding value configuration to a significant degree and is now systematically courted and cultivated by Madison Avenue executives with social science degrees. As a consequence, civic ideals have become yet more narrow in scope and more easily permeated by the consumer and entertainment industries. Both offer friendliness, comfort, excitation, images of romance, and hope for the individual's prosperity.

The new political culture differs from the old in a further way. While the earlier dualism implied a strong civic component that held in check a decline of task-oriented individualism into egocentrism, the recent dualism places weakened barriers against all self-orientation: a contribution to civic improvement, let alone an overcoming of evil that indicates God's greater glory, now seems eviscerated as a force capable of pulling and directing activist individualism. Rather, both subtle and overt pressures to conform to "the fashionable," "the hot," and "the trendy" do so.

Furthermore, whereas the earlier individualism/civic dualism invoked a mutually sustaining *dynamism* that invigorated *both* individualism and civic values across a societal-wide spectrum (see above, pp. 183–89), the individualism/consumer-entertainment dualism pursues a different agenda: rather than in the end erecting obstacles against the individual's exclusive orientation to material prosperity, the consumer-entertainment cultures are closely aligned with this orientation. The long-term outcome is clear: a weakened activist individualism and civic sphere will become apparent as well as a decline of societal dynamism and a drifting unequivocally toward greater social conformism.

Although Weber only vaguely foresaw this metamorphosis (*PE*, pp. 176–78), he would not have been fully surprised at this paradoxical turn in which a single factor originating from an orientation of groups to transcendent commandments and religious values – a self-reliant and world-mastery individualism – in a later historical epoch subverted its indispensable sustaining counterpart: substantial and demarcated civic sphere ideals. He had discovered such ironic twists and unforeseen consequences of this order of historical magnitude throughout the histories of the East and West.[11] They stand at the very foundation of his comparative-historical sociology.

However, this depiction of the new American political culture, which assumes the near disappearance of civic ideals, stands opposed to a further basic axiom at the center of Weber's empirical sociology – one that casts a different light upon the monumental transformation noted above. He argued repeatedly and vehemently that significant developments, once firmly anchored sociologically, do not precipitously fade from a nation's social landscape, and surely not as a result of short-term challenges. Firmly rooted legacies from the past remain viable, especially if a societal shift occurs that calls to the fore new groups and organizations to serve as the social carriers of these action-orientations rooted in the past.[12] Even if dormant for longer periods, legacies live on, awaiting only alterations of groups and group dynamics to become strongly influential once again. Past and present are, to Weber, intimately intertwined.[13]

Cognizance of this major tenet in Weber's sociology forces revision of the above analysis; the individualism/consumer entertainment dualism must now be acknowledged as incompletely capturing the new American political culture of the twenty-first century. Rather, a *triumvirate* of forces now prevails: world-mastery individualism, the consumer-entertainment industries, *and* civic sphere ideals. Though threatened, these ideals live on owing to their deep rootedness in long-term, religion-based patterns of action.[14] At times, amid the cascading fluctuations of the present, these *three* realms retain delimited boundaries and, in varying degrees, oppose one another; at other times, each becomes, in varying degrees, interpenetrated by and interwoven with the others. At times, these domains ceaselessly compete with one another; at other times, they fall into firm alignments; at still other times, a single domain appears dominant.[15] The American political culture oscillates across these combinations.

Hence, a tripolar constellation now defines and pushes the American political culture's pendulum movements. Although thoroughly severed from the old dualism, this new configuration is unique and unlike that of any other postindustrial nation. It continues to stand as well in stark contrast to the iron cage model. Nearly 100 years later, fundamental aspects of Max Weber's sociology have assisted the identification of its content, parameters, tensions, and internal dynamics.

Notes

1 See, for example, *PE*; "PV"; "Sects I"; *E&S*, pp. 889–92, 1059–69, 1204–10, 1381–469; Weber, 1978, 1994; see also the overview discussion at "PV," pp. 87–114.

2 On the United States, see further *PE*; "Sects II"; *E&S*, pp. 1198–210; "Sects I"; see also Mommsen, 1974; Roth, 1985, 1987.

3 Roth (1985; 1987, pp. 165–200; 1997) and Mommsen (1974, pp. 72–96) offer summary portrayals of the significant ways in which Weber's generally positive views on the United States varied from those of his German colleagues. He admired in particular the self-reliant individualism of the Americans and their unwillingness to attribute exaggerated

authority to the state. He found Germans sorely lacking on both counts (see Mommsen, 1974, pp. 83–86; Roth, 1993; 1997, pp. 665–70).

4 On the elective affinity of this set of values even today – now fully secularized – with an American foreign policy in part anchored in a missionary consciousness, see Kalberg, 1991, 2014.

5 Weber's extremely complex analysis can be noted here only briefly (see Chapter 4 and Kalberg, 2011, 2014).

6 Wherever such a civic sphere becomes well developed, the violation of its values by elected officials will be noted.

7 Hence, the position taken here is fully analogous to Weber's argument in *PE*: the origin of an "economic ethic" (the spirit of capitalism) cannot be explained by reference to an "economic form" (a modern capitalist economy) (see *PE*, pp. 88–91, 95–96). The particular context of each case must be attended to.

8 Thus, Weber found this aspect of the American political culture to have specific religious roots. He found all to be lacking in Germany. The work of Jellinek stimulated his early interest in this theme (see Jellinek, 1901; Roth, 1971, pp. 308–11; Mommsen, 1974, p. 76).

9 As in the case of Germany (see "PV," pp. 103, 111–14; *E&S*, pp. 1381–469; 1994, pp. 80–129).

10 Both Roth and Mommsen have argued that Weber's prediction – the United States would follow the European path toward ever greater bureaucratization – has been proven erroneous. Roth offers an extended analysis (Roth, 1985, pp. 224–28; 1987, pp. 15–57; Mommsen, 1974, p. 89).

11 The most prominent example is from *PE*: anchored in religious values, the Puritan's methodical manner of organizing life (*Lebensführung*) created riches that ultimately undermined just these religious values (see *PE*, pp. 172–73). One way in which Weber documents unforeseen consequences is by reference to the "routinization" of charisma (see *E&S*, pp. 1121–48).

12 The successful shift from churches and sects ("the Protestant ethic") as carrier organizations to civic and voluntary associations ("the spirit of capitalism") as carriers stands as a central component in Weber's "Protestant ethic thesis." On social carriers, see Kalberg, 1994, pp. 58–62.

13 I have repeatedly discussed the manner in which this occurs in Weber's sociology (see Kalberg, 1994, pp. 158–68, 187–89).

14 Indeed, the classic American dualism is, in those more religion-oriented regions of the nation (e.g., the Midwest), overtly sustained to this day.

15 The endurance of civic ideals is evident in a variety of ways, from, for example, the comparatively high levels of participation by Americans in volunteer and charitable activities to the continuing discussion of communitarianism. Further evidence can be found in the continuing attempts by politicians to assert the viability of American civic ideals into American foreign policy – and hence to endow them with a universal validity.

PART IV

The Sociology of Civilizations

10

ECONOMY AND SOCIETY AND THE SOCIOLOGY OF CIVILIZATIONS

Built upon a vast knowledge of the ancient, medieval, and modern epochs in China, India, and the West, *E&S* conveys *both* the powerful conceptual component and the strong empirical orientation characteristic throughout Weber's sociology of civilizations. In addition, *E&S* defines and applies the rigorous research strategies and procedures that assist identification of a civilization's "particular rationalism." This systematic treatise also isolates the multiple causes that explain, according to Weber, a civilization's historical "direction," or developmental trajectory.

E&S constructs and utilizes mainly two distinct types of models: (1) those of more limited scope that take a specific organization as their object of inquiry and (2) others that range broadly across eras and formulate numerous hypotheses. Finally, stage-based "developmental" models (*Entwicklungsformen*) chart, in several *E&S* chapters, patterned social action of people in groups as it becomes manifest in reference to singular societal spheres, namely, the religion, economy, rulership, and law realms.

In sum, this three-volume *magnum opus* maps the terrain of Weber's cause-based, interpretive sociology of civilizations. It outlines distinct procedures and strategies empowered to demarcate a civilization's uniqueness and to offer a partial causal analysis of its origins and development.

DOI: 10.4324/9781032631813-15

Written over a period of nine years (1909–1918), *E&S* constitutes a highly impressive project. Nonetheless, it has proven a difficult – even tortuous – work owing to its tight interweaving of empirical detail with model-building. Unfortunately, Weber never provides a full-scale summary of *E&S*'s aims, themes, and procedures (see Roth, 1968).

Once formed, the *E&S* concepts can be utilized by researchers as helpful "yardsticks" and "means of orientation" vis-à-vis diffuse and amorphous realities. In this manner, they assist researchers seeking to define empirical cases and developments clearly, he hopes, and to facilitate the explanation of causes ("Obj," pp. 123–37). While the constructs of *E&S*'s Part I (pp. 3–307) often appear to provide an inventory of terms only, the hypothesis-forming and multilayered models of Part II (pp. 311–1462) capture constellations of patterned action and delineate complex hypotheses regarding their development and sources. Even the most dedicated reader is repeatedly challenged by the dryness of Part I's definitions and Part II's abrupt shifts between descriptions of empirical regularities and the creation of models.

American commentators have largely discussed those *E&S* chapters that outline detailed definitions. Institutionalized in the social sciences as classical constructs, they are frequently viewed as required reading alike for theory-oriented students and sociologists of all stripes engaged in specialized research. Here, the famous paragraphs and chapters on status groups, power, charismatic rulership, the bureaucracy, and the city come to mind. Indeed, this orientation to Weber's constructs long ago called forth a "concepts reception" in the United States. The consequence is now evident: while *E&S* model-formation strategies are employed by American researchers even today, discussions of *E&S*'s "big questions" oriented to the singular features and causal origins of the West vis-à-vis China and India have been largely neglected (see Nelson, 1981).

Thus, *E&S* is viewed rarely today as a foundational pillar of Weber's *sociology of civilizations*. Yet the underlying queries and themes that dominate this labyrinthine *tour de force* must be explored in this regard. In the process, major features of the strategies and procedures distinct to Weber's sociology of civilizations will be defined. We must first succinctly examine the intellectual milieu that stimulated the writing of *E&S*.

10.1   Economy and Society and Its Task[1]

The voluminous *Der moderne Kapitalismus* (1902) by the economic historian Werner Sombart (1863–1941) challenged Weber early in his career to develop a mode of conceptualizing patterned and meaningful action as "located" in a number of bounded societal spheres. He contested Sombart's view as early as the first version of *PE* (1904–1905; see pp. 62–98). The development of the fundamental feature of the modern economy – "economic rationalism" – could be causally explained, Sombart argued, as a consequence of a *general* advance of "rationality" that encompassed all major societal domains to an equal degree and in an overarching manner (*PE*, pp. 96–98; see Chapter 3 on Sombart).

According to this position, Weber's query in *PE* – whether a "spirit of capitalism" possessed in part religious origins – could be best comprehended as the vanguard manifestation of this general development. However, Weber here discovered a nonparallel unfolding of rationalism across pivotal societal spheres. The rationalization, for example, of law – in the sense of increasing conceptual clarity and a differentiation of law's content – reached its highest point in the Roman Law of later Antiquity, yet remained "least rationalized" in a number of those countries where a rationalization of the economy advanced farthest, most obviously in England where a less rationalized form of law – Common Law – prevailed (*PE*, pp. 96–98).

Similarly, the secular philosophy of the modern age, as embodied in the Enlightenment, did not originate in England or Holland where modern capitalism arose earliest, but in France – and long before the onset of industrialization in this nation. Likewise, Weber sees the "practical-rational" organization of life – the calculation of one's worldly interests as a central operating assumption and the judging action in terms of its potential for utilitarian gain (see below) – as expanding most prominently in nations surrounding the Mediterranean rather than in those regions that industrialized earliest (see *PE*, pp. 90–98).

This orientation to societal domains, as well as to a comparative framework, becomes overt in *E&S*. It systematized, as discussed, the knowledge Weber had acquired from his "case studies," such as *PE* and the EEWR volumes on China, India, and ancient Israel. Societal realms have here become central rather than a parallel unfolding of rationality and serve as organizing mechanisms: the religion, law, rulership, economy, universal organizations (family and clans), and status group domains are now pivotal.

Moreover, sphere-specific, ideal-typical models are ubiquitous: the paths to salvation in the realm of religion (through a savior, an institution, ritual, good works, mysticism, and asceticism), the types of law (primitive, traditional, natural, and logical-formal), the stages of economic development (the agricultural and industrial modes of organizing work; the natural, money, planned, market and capitalist types of economies), the types of authority (charismatic, patriarchal, feudal, patrimonial, and bureaucratic), and status groups (intellectuals, peasants, civil servants, and feudal nobles; see Kalberg, 2021, pp. 73–130), if to become influential, requires the presence of carrier groups.

Nor does *E&S* maintain that, as frequently alleged, *diverse* groups are all unilaterally influenced by the economy. Instead, Weber discovers a great pluralism of cross-domain relationships; for example, those between the clan and religious groups, types of law-oriented groups and types of rulership groups, religion and law groups, and religion and rulership groups. He then charts the *multiple* directions of these relationships (see *E&S*, p. 341; see also pp. 468–517, *et passim*).

More specifically, Weber discusses in *E&S* an array of *ideal-typical relationships* between logical-formal law, bureaucratic rulership, patriarchal rulership, and the clan, for example. He investigates as well the "ethics" of various status groups in relation to major salvation paths on the one hand (see *RCM*, pp. 151–62; *E&S*, pp. 941–1212) and to various types of economies, law, and rulership on the other (see *E&S*, pp. 311–85). Throughout *E&S* these *models* demarcate the *essential* features of groups *and* the extent to which – *at the analytical level* – "relations of tension" (*Spannungsverhaeltnisse*) and "relations of affinity" (*Wahlverhaeltnisse*) across groups can be constructed, Weber pursues this task even while explicitly – at the empirical level – leaving open the causal direction of all cross-domain relationships.

This emphasis in *E&S* upon numerous models itself opposes any elevation of a *particular* group to a position of causal priority. Nonetheless, Weber insists that domain-specific groups, taken together, constitute a complex *analytic* that serves as an indispensable heuristic device, namely, as a "standard" that facilitates the formation of clear models. Furthermore, this *conceptual tool* can be utilized as a point of reference for researchers seeking to construct testable hypotheses aimed at the exploration of the causal capacities of specific groups (see "Obj," pp. 123–37). How did Weber select the spheres and the sphere-specific ideal types?

He drew a firm conclusion from the vantage point of his wide-ranging empirical comparisons across the histories of various civilizations from Antiquity to the present and from East to West: meaningful and patterned – or causally significant – social action in carrier groups have very often appeared in reference to *these* realms and *their* respective ideal types. As a sociologist, he attends to regular action that has been *repeatedly* significant *empirically*. In addition, Weber does not attempt to capture *all* patterned action ("Obj," 125–33; see above, pp. 5–24). Rather than seeking to be "complete" or eternally valid on the one hand or to establish hierocracies of domains and domain-specific groups on the other hand, *E&S* aims to expand the research-er's conceptualization skills (see Kalberg, 1994, pp. 81–102, 143–52; 2021, pp. 33–54).

Furthermore, a *particular milieu* may be characterized by the prom-inence of a societal domain *not* included among those Weber assesses in *E&S* as sociologically significant for his theme and his explanation of causes. In addition, *E&S* constructs, as noted, an "open-ended" model, whether domain-specific groups coalesce into alliances – even multiple alliances that call forth "social order" and even *societal unity* – or exist in relations of tension and shifting conflicts where fragmentation prevails, can be evaluated only through investigations on a case-by-case basis. To Weber, the patterned action of people in groups *may* – in each group – flow in opposite directions. In some eras and in some civilizations, this may occur to such a degree that antagonisms across groups not amenable to negotiation and compro-mise crystallize and are sustained.

For Weber, the wide spectrum of potentially causal groups extends across multiple groups. *E&S* must not be perceived as charting out a linear empirical expansion of instrumental action or values-oriented action, *nor* as offering models putatively capturing a *general* course of evolution that portrays, for example, the triumph of universalist over particularist values or "modern" over "traditional" constella-tions of groups. *E&S*'s basic presuppositions instead maintain that domains develop at times in parallel and at other times in nonparallel ways – and to varying degrees. Here, Weber's research procedures and strategies must be once again distinguished forcefully from Marxism on the one hand and from all schools anchored in organic holism, evolutionary presuppositions, and the "question of social order."

Instead, each ideal type implies simply a *likelihood* of patterned and empirical orientations of social action by people in groups. As well, all societal domains are conceived in *E&S* as firmly bounded and viewed as articulating a specific set of questions. Nonetheless, Weber's emphasis in *E&S* upon *multiple* domains and ideal types itself opposes the notion that a *particular* sphere or ideal type can acquire an empirical position of enduring priority (see *E&S*, p. 341; also Roth, 1968).

The clan in China, for example, stood effectively against the rise of modern capitalism. This was the case in part as a result of its strengthening by compatible action regularities: patrimonialism, Confucianism, and ancestor worship. The clan failed in the ancient West, however, in part as a result of its weakening by Christianity's monotheism, Christianity's congregational form of worship, the development of urban guilds, and the appearance of a particularly independent type of city (*E&S*, pp. 1226–65; Kalberg, 2021, pp. 176–84) that remained strong against the rationalization of action in the economy domain, as occurred with modern capitalism's expansion. In this manner the domain-specific organization of *E&S* and its construction of innumerable ideal types that hypothesize patterns of empirical social action render starkly visible the causal capacities of multiple factors. By doing so, they assist researchers to isolate and define – through assessments of empirical deviation from the construct – action regularities located in groups.

In sum, the analytic framework of *E&S* must be understood as an ideal types-based mechanism that facilitates significantly the conceptualization of otherwise diffuse action. A continuous back-and-forth movement between the empirical action regularities that constitute the particular case or development under investigation and the constructs provided by the *E&S* matrix lies at the foundation of Weber's sociology of civilizations. Indeed, by *precluding* an exclusive focus upon empirical narrative or a *single* domain or ideal type, the *E&S* heuristic grid – anchored in ideal types and societal domains – incorporates firmly a theoretical component into Weber's sociology of civilizations.

10.2 The Sociology of Civilizations

In Weber's sociology of civilizations, values become viable when cultivated by individuals in groups and defended against interest-oriented calculations on the one hand and enduring conventions and customs on the other hand. They then guide meaningful action and formulate, as ideals, notions of dignity, honor, and ethical action. When anchored securely, values also provide a firm grounding for leadership. However, their impact diminishes rapidly, Weber holds, whenever they lose their sustaining support mechanisms: strong social carrier groups and vigorous competition with other values.

Hence, particular constellations of groups cultivate values to the point where they become binding upon persons, even at times despite opposing material interests, namely, *dynamic and open* arrays of groups, each of which nourishes frequent values-based struggles (*Wertkaempfe*) across several societal domains. The social action of persons becomes "responsible" in these civilizations in reference to sets of values that serve as carriers of values-based conduct.

Owing to wide-scale bureaucratization in the economy, rulership, and law spheres in industrial and postindustrial civilizations, Weber feared that contending constellations of groups oriented to values would eventually lose their distinct boundaries and collapse. A loss of societal dynamism would follow, he held, as well as an enduring loss of leaders capable of defending values.

Driven by a managerial orientation to technical efficiency, stagnation more and more appeared to be on the horizon. Weber saw an ominous "passion for bureaucratization" that would lead among citizens only to a broad-scale passivity. People will be "led like sheep," he worries (1978, p. 282). If this trend endures, how will it be possible "to save *any remnants* of 'individual' freedom of movement," he queries (*E&S*, p. 1403; original emphasis)? Such questions stood at the origin of Weber's interpretive sociology of civilizations. Only an outline of its elaborate themes and procedures can be offered here (see Kalberg, 2021).

The *E&S* and EEWR volumes attempt to distinguish, as contrast cases, the singularity of "Chinese rationalism," "Indian rationalism," the "rationalism of ancient Israel," "Western rationalism," and "modern Western rationalism." Weber offers comparisons and contrasts across these civilizations in order to isolate differences and form multi-causal explanations for particular historical "directions" of development.

In doing so, his investigations define a number of ways in which the West proved unique. It called forth, for example, a systematic science based rigorously upon the experimental method and carried out by trained and specialized personnel and a state based upon an "enacted 'constitution' and...enacted laws and administered by civil servants possessing *specialized* arenas of competence and oriented to rules and 'laws'" ("PR," p. 236; see pp. 233–46).

Furthermore, Weber acquired, through EEWR and *E&S*, essential insight, clarity, and knowledge regarding the overarching "tracks" – or directions – along which each major civilization developed (see "PR," pp. 241–42). The tracks in the West, for example, formulated in Antiquity and the cities of the Middle Ages were then cultivated by subsequent "world and religion" developments (see Chapter 6). Western civilizations eventually gave birth to the dominance of a rule-oriented and impersonal *formal rationality* in the domains of law, rulership, and the economy as well as to a theoretical rationality in the domain of knowledge.

Profound ramifications followed regarding the *type of human being* (*Menschentyp*) who *could* live under "modern Western rationalism," Weber insisted repeatedly. What were its particular features vis-à-vis the "rationalisms" of China, India, the Middle East, and the Western ancient and medieval worlds?

The EEWR volumes address further broad questions. How do persons in different social contexts, whether small in scale or encompassing entire civilizations, formulate meaning in their lives? What regularities of social action, he further asks, became meaningful in the rationalisms of Asian, Middle Eastern, and Eastern civilizations? Similarly, what patterns of action became meaningful, he questions, in the West's ancient, medieval, and modern eras? Moreover, what configurations of social action – means-end rational, value-rational, and traditional – became enduring and meaningful, he queries, in significant carrier groups in each of the major civilizations? What plausible causal explanations can be offered for each historical trajectory?

Answers to these quandaries became urgent for him because he viewed compassion, ethical action, and the "autonomous individual" as endangered in the modern West by the domination of formal and theoretical rationalization processes (see Kalberg, 2017, pp. 70–83). They stand at the core of his rigorous, comparative-historical sociology of civilizations.

Many interpreters of Weber, casting their focus exclusively on *PE* and specific concepts in *E&S* (see above), have failed to note this major orientation to civilizations and its ambitious agenda. Here, his sociology emphasizes that, for example, any scrutiny of the West's singularity must *also* acknowledge the unique extent of its "structural heterogeneity" (see Kalberg, 2021, pp. 404–15).

In comparison to China, India, the Middle East, and the ancient West, a greater intensity of pluralistic conflict between the economy, religion, law, rulership, universal organizations, and social honor domains distinguished the Western trajectory, Weber holds. The resulting tensions across relatively independent spheres called forth, over centuries, a comparative openness and societal flexibility that *facilitated* further cross-domain, intermediate-range conflict. Indeed, competing spheres introduced a sustaining middle-level dynamism that Weber sees as both specific to the West and as calling forth a social context conducive – eventually – to *modern* capitalism's unfolding (see *E&S*, pp. 1192–93; see Chapter 6).

Throughout his sweeping analysis, Weber never loses sight of his large-scale conundrum. Repeatedly, whenever the "civilizational rationalisms" indigenous to China, India, and the West appeared to acquire cohesion to such a degree that stagnation loomed, he recasts his central question: would *values*, he queried, continue to orient patterned action? If so, the random push and pull characteristic of the utilitarian flow of raw interests would then be counterbalanced to such an extent that action might become *directed* on behalf of compassion and ethical ideals.

Persons in groups would then become accountable to values and practice an "ethic of responsibility" (*Verantwortungsethik*) – and perhaps even an "ethic of conviction" (*Gesinnungsethik*). Of pivotal significance to Weber, the ethical ideal itself – to the extent that "the individual places himself under the common norm" – places a thrust toward community into motion ("IR," p. 342).

In sum, Weber seeks to investigate a variety of civilizations through both model-building *and* empirical, context-sensitive research procedures. He attempts also to chart the unique developmental paths each followed, particularly in the economy, rulership, law, and religion domains. In doing so, he wishes not only to understand the West's singular origins and particular developmental pathways, but also to comprehend the multiple ways in which persons in diverse epochs and innumerable groups create subjectively meaningful lives.

However, Weber sought to fulfill as well a further task, as we have seen, namely to define the heuristic tools and research procedures indispensable to an interpretive sociology of civilizations. Only comparative-historical investigations can support, he maintains, his quest to delineate rigorously the ways in which configurations of groups in the economy, law, rulership, religion, universal organizations, and status honor domains of each civilization give rise to unique "rationalisms" and "meaning complexes." To Weber, they may tie meaningful action not only to conventions, customs, and interests, but also to ethical values.

As evident now, Weber created research strategies and procedures that combined empirical description with theoretical generalization anchored in ideal types and societal domains. Distinguished by its comparative and historical range as well as its interpretive understanding focus, his sociology explored the patterned social action of persons in groups far and wide. It sought to offer causal analyses of the origins and development of unique cases by reference to ideal types, societal domains, empirical social contexts, and subjective meaning.

Weber's research procedures and strategies further stressed, as discussed, the past's ineluctable intertwining with the present and forcefully contended that the orientation of social action to the religion, economy, status honor, rulership, law, family, and clan societal spheres must be acknowledged as viable. In addition, cognizance must be taken of geographical forces, power, social carriers, historical events, competition, conflict, and technology innovations as further causes of patterned action (see Kalberg, 1994, pp. 52–78). While Weber recognizes that *some* societies *may* become, in certain epochs and because of multiple regularities of action by persons in groups, more closed or even ossified, he scorns organic holism and perceives conflict across groups as highly pluralistic and lacking "a resting point" (see Weber, 1988, p. 456; see also "PR," p. 246). However, he also sees that continuities of social action arise ubiquitously on the basis of values and traditions – and even on the basis of interests and emotions.

Moreover, Weber's interpretive sociology of civilizations maintains that a variety of conditions may congeal repeatedly and predispose people to view rulership as legitimate. If so, obedience is voluntarily rendered. Nonetheless, powerful groups regularly overthrow established ruling groups, he insists, only to erect further authorities. Social change, although never following an evolutionary or lawful pathway, is inevitable to Weber. It cannot be comprehended, for example, by reference *exclusively* to "material" or "ideal" interests (see *PE*, pp. 178–79; see Chapter 6).

By studying empirical groups and configurations of groups, as well as by constructing models incessantly, Weberian sociologists of civilizations seek to understand how persons in groups formulate singular "meaning clusters" and orient their action accordingly. Far from unidimensional, meaningful action to Weber assumes a vast variety of manifestations.

Finally, he stresses that internally consistent *sets of values* at times coalesce across groups. Some address ultimate questions. *Worldviews* then appear once charismatic figures and carrier groups congeal and some become capable of setting "tracks" that guide a civilization's "direction" over centuries and even millennia. A new realm of meaningful action now becomes outlined and visible, especially if powerful carrier groups crystallize to provide support. Practitioners of Weber's research procedures and strategies seek to understand group dynamics *also* in reference to a civilization's worldview (see Kalberg, 2012, pp. 73–91).

The five major themes of Weber's sociology of civilizations must now be addressed. This is the subject of Chapter 11.

Note

1 Roth's lengthy introduction to *E&S* offers discussions regarding both the content of *E&S* and the intellectual context within which it was written (1968). It remains indispensable for an understanding of *E&S*.

11

THE FIVE MAJOR CIVILIZATIONS THEMES

Five major themes characterize Weber's sociology of civilizations. They lay the groundwork and set the stage for innumerable discussions throughout this volume. Again, by articulating these themes, we seek to recognize Weber not only as an unusual practitioner of concept formation but also as an analyst of the West's modern capitalism and particular developmental pathway. Moreover, scrutiny of these themes will reveal this classical Founder as a rigorous sociologist of civilizations.

11.1   The Formation of Subjective Meaning and the Causes Behind Its Variation

As discussed in the Introduction, rather than referring "to an objectively 'correct' meaning or one which is 'true' in some metaphysical sense" (*E&S*, p. 4), Weber's sociology concerns the investigation of "subjective meaning complexes." Through interpretive understanding (*verstehen*), he seeks to "recapture" the manner in which subjective meaning motivates persons in demarcated groups in patterned ways. He does so by reconstructing, to the greatest degree possible, the variety of wider *contexts* of action in reference to which these patterns of action occur. Weberian researchers then seek *to understand* the ways in which actors, within their groups-based milieu, bestow subjective meaning upon their situations and act accordingly. On the basis of

DOI: 10.4324/9781032631813-16

in-depth empirical research, motives *can* be comprehended by social scientists, indeed even patterns of meaning in distant civilizations, Weber contends.

He attempts, in his best-known example, to clarify in the ways in which the seventeenth-century Puritan endowed particular action with subjective meaning. To a certain extent, the belief and conduct of the "inner-worldly ascetic" depicted in *The Protestant Ethic and the Spirit of Capitalism* baffled Weber.[1] From the standpoint of a "natural" attitude toward life that takes delight in diverse worldly pleasures, the Puritan's strict asceticism could only be seen as strange. The enjoyment of eating, drinking, and relaxation was denied to the faithful. In addition, the single activity deserving of their energies – regular and systematic labor in a calling – connoted sheer drudgery and pain to most people. Even the cultivation of friendship and intimacy was prohibited to this believer; both constitute threats to the exclusive allegiance owed by the devout to God.

Hence, the actions of the ascetic faithful must be judged as "irrational" and "odd" if examined from the perspective of all "enjoyment of life" (*PE*, pp. 80, 92–94, 98, 130–31). However, a mode of analysis rooted in interpretive understanding can never uphold this conclusion. Weber insists that even the actions of Puritans, if their *meaning complex* is reconstructed through rigorous research, can be recognized as subjectively meaningful.

PE sought to comprehend why seventeenth-century Puritan believers in England, Holland, and Colonial America attributed meaning to systematic work and a concerted search for wealth and profit – even to the point of placing labor and material success at the very core of their lives. Through the careful study of diaries, sermons, autobiographies, and other documents, Weber aimed to reconstruct the meaning behind the intense faith of the devout and to understand the ways in which their search for salvation placed "psychological premiums" upon certain endeavors. Although seemingly strange, the meaningfulness of the faithful's action would then become plausible and comprehensible to the social scientist. *PE* constitutes Weber's most powerful demonstration of how a variety of motives held by sincere Puritan, Catholic, and Lutheran believers can influence activity in different ways.

This orientation to subjective meaning guided his empirical investigations. In EEWR, for example, he explored the origins of the beliefs and actions typical, among others, of Confucians, Daoists, Hindus, Buddhists, and Jews. Even the extreme withdrawal from the world of Buddhist mystics can be understood as meaningful if placed contextually within the framework of *their* perception of the transcendental realm (as dominated by an immanent and impersonal Being rather than an anthropomorphic and omnipotent Deity), definition of the goal of salvation (escape from the endless wheel of reincarnation), and view of the appropriate means toward its attainment (contemplation and the "silencing of the soul" that alone allows immersion into the All-One). Why, Weber queried further, for example, was scholarship meaningful to the Confucian Gentleman? And why were the commandments of an anthropomorphic God meaningful to the Old Testament prophets?

Weber emphasized that such cross-cultural and cross-epochal explorations must be acknowledged as complex and even precarious. "We moderns" can scarcely imagine the intensity of the Puritan's devotion and focus upon the question of personal salvation, nor *"how* large a significance those components of our consciousness rooted in religious beliefs have actually had upon culture,…and the organization of life" (*PE*, p. 178).

This dual emphasis upon subjective meaning and its social context implies the rejection of a major axiom central to Marxism, neo-Marxism, organicism, and all structuralisms: external structures should constitute the major subject of sociological investigation. For Weber, a principled disjunction always remains between the influence upon action of "external forms" – classes, status groups, and organizations, for example – and the motivations of individuals. It *may* exist to such an extent that an entire range of motives can be found among persons who otherwise orient their action to a single class, status group, or organization (see *E&S*, pp. 29–38).

For example, the search for and legitimation of authority can be anchored in affectual motives (an emotional surrender to the ruler), traditional orientations (to customs and conventions), means-end rational calculations (conformity to conventions or obedience to laws for reasons of expediency and self-interest), and orientations to values (the belief in loyalty and duty, and in the rulership as just) – or a combination of all of these motives (see *E&S*, p. 31).[2] As is obvious if the functioning of structurally identical bureaucracies is compared across cultures, a "bureaucratic ethos" motivates functionaries and managers to varying degrees. Similarly, whether a civil servant within a bureaucracy fulfills tasks motivated by values or means-end rational calculations, or a respect for an accustomed way of doing things remains a question for empirical investigation, according to Weber (*E&S*, pp. 30–31) – one answered in different ways despite the formally similar features of this organization. He contends that even the extremely firm organizational structure of the religious sect will not entirely determine the subjective meaning of the devout.[3]

The assessment of the subjective meaning of persons in groups stands at the foundation of Weber's sociology of civilizations as well as his sociology generally. The motives behind observed action vary widely across groups and civilizations, Weber is convinced. Hence, a methodology anchored in subjective meaning (and the interpretive understanding of it) proves indispensable. The particular action that is *meaningful to persons in specific groups* must now be investigated – and on its *own* terms. Weber's abandonment of a fixed point implied to him that empirical explorations, which seek to define subjective meaning past and present in the civilizations of the East and West, must be conducted.

In essence, his sociology of civilizations defines and utilizes procedures that push aside Western-centric assumptions and allow an understanding *from within* – once the relevant research has been conducted in depth – *even* of patterns of action in groups radically different from groups familiar in the modern West. Weber's empirically rooted sociology of subjective meaning opposed the set of "universal" concepts commonly utilized in his era by social scientists to evaluate other cultures.

Indeed, his mode of analysis had the effect of delegitimizing Western-centric value configurations and triumphalism. Albeit odd at first glance, the subjective meaning of persons in groups, however distant, must be investigated in terms of its *own* dynamics, he maintains. Let us turn to the second major theme in Weber's sociology of civilizations.

11.2   The Uniqueness of Western Rationalism and Modern Western Rationalism

Weber wishes also to comprehend the ways in which *the modern West* can be appropriately understood as constituted from unique configurations of meaningful, patterned, and group-based actions. Only rigorous comparisons to China, India, the ancient Middle East, and the ancient and medieval West will enable a precise demarcation of this singularity, he insists. Here can be found a major focus of his sociology of civilizations. A further goal closely accompanied this orientation, as will become evident: Weber sought to explore the *causal origins* of the modern West's uniqueness.

He embarked around 1910 upon his comparative-historical research. Now evident was an expanded post-*PE* agenda. Weber's introduction to the EEWR series, "Prefatory Remarks," placed at its core a broad-ranging discussion of groups prominent only in the modern West. Central passages throughout *E&S* and EEWR turn to "a specifically formed 'rationalism' of Western civilization" ("PR," p. 245).[4]

Its major aspects include, for example, a legal system characterized by procedures formulated in reference to abstract, universally applicable prescriptions and executed as well as interpreted by specially trained jurists (see *E&S*, p. 883; *GEH*, p. 313). Typical of large-scale organizations in the West was bureaucratic rulership, as carried by officials and managers oriented to rules and laws who administered specialized tasks in an organized manner (*E&S*, p. 998; "PR," p. 236). Parliaments, which involve regularly elected representatives, also possess Western roots, Weber contends ("PR," p. 236).

Similarly, in the modern West, traditional forms of rulership (patriarchalism, feudalism, patrimonialism) have been replaced as the major "political organizations" by a constitutional state anchored in a "rationally enacted 'constitution' and rationally enacted laws" ("PR," p. 236). Modern science, characterized by the dominance of highly trained and specialized personnel, called forth systematic procedures based upon the rigorous application of the experimental method (see "PR," pp. 233–34).[5] "Modern capitalism," grounded in a systematic organization of free labor, businesses with fixed capital, certainty of calculation, and a unique "economic rationalism" rooted in a methodical economic ethic, came to dominate the West since the seventeenth century "as part of the rationalization of life in the public sphere which has become familiar in this part of the world" ("I," p. 293; see also "PR," pp. 236–37; *E&S*, p. 505).[6]

"Again and again," Weber remarks, "[we] discover in the West, and *only* in the West, specific *types* of rationalism" (*PR*, p. 250; see *GEH*, pp. 311–12). He queries in general: "How did it happen that scientific, artistic, and economic development, as well as state-building, were not directed in China and India into those tracks of *rationalization* specific to the West" ("PR," p. 245; emphasis original)? Although he remained convinced that modern capitalism, for example, could be *adopted* by and would flourish in a number of Eastern civilizations,[7] he insisted that his concern was different: the *origin* in a specific region of a *new* economic ethos and a *new* type of economy.[8]

However, Weber seeks not only to define the West's "particularity"; he aims also to offer causal explanations of its origins ("PR," p. 246). One of his latest methodological writings expresses succinctly the focal importance to him of the causal question: "Our European and American social and economic life is 'rationalized' in a specific way and in a specific sense. Consequently, it is one of the main tasks of our disciplines to explain this rationalization and to construct the concepts appropriate to it" ("Obj," p. 325).

Weber's quest to define the modern West's origins, contours, and trajectory – its particular rationalism – endured across nearly two decades as an overarching concern. This theme combines with his attempt to provide, through multiple comparative studies designed to isolate significant patterns of action as constituted in groups, causal explanations for this uniqueness.

Nonetheless, any description of Weber's project as one oriented exclusively toward a precise definition of the modern West and an exploration of *its* origins must be seen as a dramatic foreshortening. The full scope of his endeavor is scaled back too far by a focus upon a *particular* civilization. On the basis of rigorous comparative procedures, fine-grained and innumerable models, a multi-causal framework, a tight interweaving of past and present, and an orientation to subjective meanings, above all *E&S* and EEWR, he seeks to investigate an even larger theme: how *civilizations in general* establish unique patterned actions among groups of people, assume particular contours, and then follow pathways in specific directions.

This ambitious goal requires attention not only to the formation of subjective meaning and a definition of the modern West's singularity and causal origins, but also to three further themes central in Weber's sociology of civilizations: (a) the "rationalization of action" as it became anchored in constellations of value-oriented action, (b) the "particular rationalisms" of a variety of civilizations,[9] and (c) the manner in which civilizations may be conceptualized as existing along a spectrum anchored on one side by stagnation and on the other side by openness and even dynamism.

11.3 The Causal Impact of Values and the Rationalization of Action: The Variation Across Civilizations

Throughout history, values have influenced the orientation of action and the formation of groups. They *may* contest, and even constrict, economic interests, power calculations, established authority, and enduring conventions, Weber insists.

Feudalism, for example, can be examined by reference to the ways in which it orients conduct in a utilitarian manner toward economic interests and power. However, these patterns of action never capture fully this form of rulership, Weber is convinced. A feudal *ethos* is equally constitutive: a constellation of values that demarcates the rights, obligations, and life outlooks of vassals, princes, and peasants. In certain cases, values may *intensify* action oriented to economic interests. The Protestant ethic as well as the spirit of capitalism, for example, did so (see Chapters 2 and 3).

Weber's sociology at this point poses fundamental questions. How do *values* become salient to the extent that they significantly guide the conduct of people in groups and endow it with meaning and even continuity? How is subjective meaning formulated by reference to values and clusters of values rather than by reference to means-end calculations, tradition-oriented action, and affectual action?[10] And how do orientations of action to *ethical* values endure over longer periods despite their repeated contestation and violation by the orientation of action by people in groups to economic interests and power calculations? Is ethical action, especially if sanctified by a religious doctrine, capable of opposing action oriented to economic and political interests? Such queries enter into Weber's comparative-historical studies on a regular basis.

The social, economic, and political transformations of his time indicated to Weber the end of a 2,000-year trajectory in the West. He pondered throughout his life whether binding values would continue to offer continuity and dignity to the activities of people living in the new era of modern capitalism, widespread secularization, and rapid urbanization. If meaning is to be created and sustained by reference to values rather than to traditions on the one hand or the flow of economic interests and political power on the other hand, how might this occur?

The interpretive dimension of Weber's sociology now becomes especially apparent. As a sociologist concerned with the subjective meaning of people in demarcated groups, he wishes to *understand* the ways in which *certain* orientations of action to the "universal groups" (above all the family and clan) and to groups in the rulership, religion, economy, law, and social honor (status) arenas erect *contexts* of patterned action. How do these contexts, with some likelihood, he queries, give rise to values, especially ethical values? Or do they at all? How does the action of persons in groups become oriented to values? How do they then create further constellations of groups that cultivate orientations to values on a wider scale?

Although their impact may frequently be limited and circumscribed by conventions and customs, material interests and power, values remain resilient, Weber holds. They *may* have wide-ranging and long-lasting consequences and must not be *conceptualized* as fleeting or as perpetually of secondary or tertiary causal efficacy. Indeed, as noted, if supportive configurations of patterned action in groups congeal, values are empowered in Weber's sociology even to place obstacles against traditions and the flux and flow of material interests and power striving. He insists that researchers *must* take cognizance of values as potential causes of action.

However, Weber takes a further step in regard to the possible impact of values. In his terminology, when *carried* by supportive groups, value-anchored regularities of action *may rationalize* – or order under values – power-oriented, interest-based, and tradition-oriented patterns of action. And whenever values become aligned into an internally consistent configuration, a wide-ranging organization of life in reference to them *can* take place (*E&S*, p. 30; *RofC*, p. 248). Action then becomes "rationalized" – or organized and systematized – and acquires a "directional" character, Weber asserts.

This "value-rationalization" *may* influence subjective meaning to such an extreme extent that *all* pragmatic and traditional action in a group becomes transformed and oriented to values. In this unusual case, a *methodical-rational* organization of life and "ethic of conviction" (*Gesinnungsethik*), as found among monks, Puritans, prophets, mystics, and revolutionaries, suppresses orientations to traditions, material interests, and power-striving of all sorts *as well as the practical-rational* – or utilitarian – mode of organizing life. Among these elite "virtuosi," a *personality* – a unification of the person around a set of core values – then crystallizes. Emanating from *within the person* rather than as a utilitarian response to external occurrences and pressures, action becomes *comprehensively* directed by values.[11]

Weber often explores this value-rationalization theme by reference to variations in action's *intensity*. For example, with Puritanism, as discussed, a psychological premium was placed upon heretofore utilitarian activity oriented to work, profit, and material success. The effect is significant, he argues, because this premium connected mundane economic activity directly to the urgent need of anxious believers to clarify their "salvation status." Hence, it heightened the intensity of orientations to work, profit, and material success. Now *sanctified*, these orientations became value-based.

This rationalization of action proved crucial to Weber's Protestant ethic thesis: *only* the systematic and disciplined economic activity anchored in Puritan asceticism, he holds, is capable of uprooting and pushing aside the age-old and entrenched "traditional economic ethos" (see *PE*, pp. 78–85, 160–76). Concerted, interest-based, and power-based orientations lacked the requisite sustained intensity to do so, he insists. Sociologists of civilizations, seeking to comprehend social contours and transformations in various milieus, must formulate and practice methodologies capable of evaluating the *varying* intensity of social action, Weber maintains.

He examines throughout his inter-civilizational studies whether groups in different settings effectively cultivate and carry values to such an extent that a broad-ranging rationalization of action takes place. This important point must not be misunderstood: neither a mono-causal driving force nor a linear rationalization of action is implied. Indeed, Weber emphasizes also that the opposite line of development – a "routinization" – may occur in different empirical contexts (see Chapter 15). Here, the influence of values upon action is weakened and becomes manifest in its utilitarian, tradition-based, and affectual forms. And this path may also be comprehended as uneven, namely, this routinization, which occurs only as a consequence of the concatenation of multiple interacting causes, may proceed at varying speeds and may include numerous tangents. The pathways of history and the present cannot be conceptualized, Weber holds, as driven by a single cause or as following "evolution," "progress," and "decline" routes. Nor do they pursue unvarying rise and fall cycles.[12]

A *civilization's* development should never be understood in a linear fashion, Weber admonishes, as a long-term weakening of age-old traditions and values followed by a concomitant expansion – now unbounded – of conduct oriented to economic and political interests. Far from banished with industrialization and urbanization, values securely anchored in group often endure and influence action despite these vast structural transformations, he contends – at times, in sociologically significant ways. Lives organized in a methodical-rational manner around values, such as those of Puritans and their secular descendants, often possess an epoch-transcending influence, Weber argues.

He investigates continuously the group contexts in multiple group settings that give birth to – and cultivate – specific configurations of values capable of organizing and directing the "flow of life" (see "VF," p. 315). Civilizations are never constituted alone from utilitarian calculations, orientations to dominant groups, and the raw flux of power, Weber is convinced. All contain significant – perhaps even autonomous – groups oriented to values.

As will be examined, his four "types of rationality" – practical, theoretical, formal, and substantive – offer a heuristic framework that assists the formation of rigorous definitions of the major values in empirical groups. These models serve as yardsticks and points of orientation throughout Weber's sociology of civilizations. At its core stand explorations of both value-oriented action's causal capacity and the rationalization of action by values. These two pivotal themes, in terms of scope and analytic range, surpass far more familiar themes in his writings: bureaucratization, the disenchantment of the world, and the rise of a spirit of capitalism. Hence, they more adequately ground Weber's sociology of civilization.

11.4 Civilizational Rationalisms and World Views

The precise contours of his comparative-historical scholarship became apparent to Weber around 1908 or 1909. A variety of studies ranging across the entire histories of India, China, and the West, as well as the ancient Near East and Mediterranean areas, followed over the next decade. Albeit more circumscribed, short explorations of the Middle East also were written. Each civilization possesses distinguishing configurations of subjective meanings, he maintained. However daunting the task, rigorous research will enable the isolation, definition, and explanation of this uniqueness, Weber insists.

Utilizing comparative and experimental research procedures, sociologists can isolate and define patterns of action, the causes behind their origin and development, and their manifestations in groups possessing delineated boundaries. A civilization's particular rationalism – cohesive groups juxtaposed into multiple arrays of groups substantively connected one with another – can be delineated, Weber contends.[13] He discovers a "Chinese rationalism," an "Indian rationalism," a "rationalism of the Middle East," an "ancient rationalism," a "Western medieval rationalism," and a "modern Western rationalism."[14]

In each case, Weber aims to understand a civilization's broad spectrum of subjective meanings "from within." They become significantly (though not entirely) apparent to him from the empirically discovered patterns of action of persons in constellations of groups in the major spheres of life: again, the economy, religion, rulership, law, status honor, and universal organizations (the family and the clan) arenas. His research seeks to identify the *multiplicity* of groups in each civilization that interact, form specific configurations, and embed patterns of action deeply in complex arrays of action and new meaning complexes. The formulation of causal hypotheses regarding their origins, contours, and trajectories can then take place.

In pursuit of this research agenda, Weber's investigations span a broad horizon and at times replicate in rigor the controlled experiment. He maintains that, for example, economic interests assisted the development of a highly formal type of law in the West, yet failed to do so in China or India (see "PR," p. 245). And why did "this-worldly" asceticism appear forcefully in the West instead of "otherworldly" mysticism? Why did the latter arise prominently in India but not in China? And how did juxtapositions of multiple groups give birth to monotheism in ancient Israel, the caste system in India, and Confucianism in China (see Kalberg, 2012, pp. 145–91)?

Whereas intellectual strata tended to play important roles in the formation of the world religions in China and India, they proved less central in the Middle East and in the West. What constellations of groups, Weber queries, account for this difference and what consequences follow for the conduct of believers? How did it occur that the question of salvation became linked to systematic work almost exclusively in the West – and there only in a few religious groups?[15] How did firm classes, as common in Europe, become transformed only in India into rigid castes and an enduring caste system? Weber's questions turn also to the comparative strength of the sib group or clan: whereas it assumed an extended, long-term, and unusually influential form in China, its impact gradually waned in the West. Further comparative studies led him to investigate, for example, the *varying* strength, endurance, and impact in China, India, and the West of magic and ritual.

In Weber's writings, multi-causal investigations chart the crystallization of action-orientations into patterns of action and then bounded groups, configurations of groups, and arrays of large-scale groups. Central to a civilization's rationalism are constellations of groups on the one hand that embed deeply patterned action in further groups and, on the other hand, formulate deep contexts for epochal-range developments.

In these diverse ways, each civilization's distinguishing continuity and dynamic is shaped, as is its capacity to influence the action of persons in groups in a singular fashion through embedding processes.[16] Again, civilizations *do* possess indigenous configurations of subjective meaning, Weber maintains. The dominance of a class of highly literate administrators, in combination with an expansive patrimonial bureaucracy and the centralization of power around a strong emperor, constructed a "rationalism" that directed China's pathway for 2,000 years. The history of India unfolded along a different route as a consequence of the alliance of a caste of Hindu priests (Brahmins) with secular rulers (the Kshatriya) and a firm caste system interwoven with – and legitimized by – Hinduism (*RofI*, pp. 63–76, 123–33). Distinct also was the grounding of the West's salvation religions in ancient Judaism's monotheism. And singular as well was the extent to which politically independent cities, a formal-rational type of law, and Christianity developed in the Western medieval period. The long-term past of every civilization has an enduring impact.

However, arrays of groups, their dynamic interaction, and the manner in which they embed action never fully capture the long-range pathway of a civilization's rationalism, Weber holds. It becomes endowed with continuity *also* as a consequence of a further element: *worldviews* (*Weltbilder*). As "tracks" they chart outer boundaries and a direction of development, thereby further anchoring a civilization's uniqueness and rationalism (see "I," p. 280).

Worldviews always imply a coherent set of values, Weber argues. Although they vary in terms of their internal cohesiveness, these values assume comprehensiveness. They offer answers to ultimate questions. What is the meaning of life? What purpose does our existence serve? How do we best live our lives? Why do suffering, injustice, and misery persist?

Hence, a civilization's worldview, rooted in shared cultural presuppositions as carried effectively by identifiable and powerful groups, demarcates a moral universe and a cosmological vision that offers instructions regarding the meaningfulness – or lack thereof – of mundane activity. Even meaning constellations in strict opposition to the practical-rational, utilitarian flow of life are articulated. Weber especially attends to whether worldviews direct believers to "adapt to" the world (China) or to orient their search for salvation "toward" (the West) or "away from" the world (India). And does a worldview, he queries, imply modes of action that can be realistically pursued and fulfilled by the laity as well as by elites?

The *worldly* realm may also ground a worldview's coherent and expansive value constellation. Secularized intellectual, social, and political groups may offer broad-ranging sets of values and an "ordered meaningfulness," Weber maintains. However, this worldview's "correctness" or "superiority" also can never be definitively proven. The subjective meaningfulness of adherents' beliefs alone establishes its legitimacy.

Worldviews contribute to a civilization's rationalism in a further manner. By articulating coherent values and pronounced ideals, they formulate an "ethical order," whether rooted in "religion or world." A disjunction is apparent: although of varying intensity depending upon the worldview's values and the forcefulness of their articulation by prophets and carrier groups, this ethical order always sets standards against which pragmatic action is evaluated.[17] Given strong carriers, the *discrepancy* between an "ordered totality" and "irrational" earthly events itself places an *ideal, autonomous thrust* into motion. For example:

> To the [missionary] prophet, both life and the world, both social and cosmic events, have a certain systematic and coherent "meaning" to which man's conduct must be oriented if it is to bring salvation and after which it must be patterned in an integrally meaningful

manner....[This meaning] always contains the important religious conception of the "world" as a "cosmos" which is challenged to produce somehow a "meaningful," ordered totality, the particular manifestations of which are to be measured and evaluated according to this postulate. (*E&S*, pp. 450–51)

Weber emphasizes that worldviews provide a deep culture legitimation for the formation of consistent action and groups. Group formation, history's events and occurrences, and a civilization's rationalism arise not only from the economic, legal, political, and status interests of daily life, nor alone from traditions, mundane values, power considerations, and rational choices. The transformation, for example, of Christian religious doctrine from medieval Catholicism to Lutheranism and then to the ascetic Protestant sects and churches cannot be comprehended by reference to worldly action oriented alone to the rulership, law, economy, family, clan, and social status domains (see Kalberg, 2012, pp. 43–72). Hence, because they formulate the tracks along which each civilization develops, worldviews play a prominent role in defining a civilization's rationalism. In some civilizations, they cast a broad influence across millennia:

Not ideas, but (material and ideal) interests directly impact the action of people. Yet very frequently the "world views" that have been created by "ideas" have, like switchmen, determined the tracks within which action has been pushed by the dynamic of interest. "From what" and "for what" one wished to be "redeemed" and, let us not forget, could be "redeemed," were defined in accord with one's world view. ("I," p. 280; transl. alt.)

In this manner, worldviews stand "behind" historical developments as moral universes. They may, under conducive arrays of conditions, offer background justifications for particular patterns of social action by people in groups. They contribute coherence as well as uniqueness to each civilization's rationalism and a degree of continuity to its development – indeed, to an extent that barriers are erected against external influences. Here as well as elsewhere, Weber's sociology of civilizations distinctly diverges from all schools rooted predominantly in utilitarian axioms.[18]

In sum, "particular rationalisms" can be found in China, India, Israel, the Middle East, and the ancient, medieval, and the West, according to Weber. Each demarcates presuppositions for conduct and a developmental pathway endowed with a distinct direction. What diverse constellations of subjective meaning and patterned action, as aligned in groups, explain the unique origins, contours, and direction, Weber queries, of *each* civilization's rationalism? This query leads to the fifth major theme in his sociology of civilizations.

11.5 Conflict and Social Change: Stagnation and Dynamism

Weber's sociology of civilizations identifies the arrays of social groups dominant in a given civilization. Highly cognizant of paradoxical turns and unforeseen consequences, he rejects, as argued, all "meaning of history" theories that discover universal laws and chart evolutionary advances. The "faith in progress" schools widespread in the Anglo-Saxon world during his time, all of which pronounced the modern West's general superiority, as well failed to impress Weber. As now evident, his works also fundamentally oppose all schools of thought that view history as a random and unending flow of interests, power, class-based struggles, and status-based conflicts.

Rather than seeking either to demonstrate the existence of overarching developmental laws *or* history's ebb and flow, Weber aims to evaluate whether values, traditions, interests, emotions, and charismatic leaders (or combinations thereof) effectively orient the subjective meaning of persons to such an extent that delineated groups crystallize. How are their patterns of action distinct and what "directions" of action are manifest? Do *powerful* groups arise and *impose* a degree of cross-group continuity and uniformity? In addition, his sociology of civilizations constantly inquires whether – in light of the contexts and directions established by configurations of groups – groups carrying new regularities of action rooted in values, material and political interests, and emotional loyalties *can* arise and influence action. *Some* contexts render certain groups "available" as agents of change.

Hence, Weber's emphasis on the *diverse* origins of patterned action grounds his understanding of social transformations. Discrete historical events, technological innovations, geographical changes, and charismatic leaders may also give rise to social change. New sets of values articulated by noncharismatic actors may also call forth change. Moreover, conflict and competition regularly call forth new regularities of action (see *E&S*, pp. 38–40) as do the tendencies for groups in possession of prestige and power to define through the formulation of ideas and values their positive status as "legitimate."

Likewise, "negatively privileged groups" tend to form ideas and values that "compensate" for their lowly position (see *E&S*, pp. 490–92). And the defense of interests of all sorts, often occurring on the basis of sheer power, is all-pervasive, Weber contends. Finally, ideas and values that give rise to new patterns of actions and groups may emanate from the domain of religion. Indeed, as noted, they may even become ordered into a worldview that forms an overarching track for a civilization's development.

Acknowledgment of these pivotal elements in Weber's sociology of civilizations – its orientation to arrays of bounded groups and thus its broad multi-causality, its emphasis upon the multiple ways in which action regularities become situated in contexts of patterned action, and its conceptualization of civilizations as each in possession of a "characteristic individuality" or "rationalism" – lead to a clear conclusion: his understanding of long-range change and continuity cannot be captured by reference alone to charisma's transformative capacity and its subsequent routinization, as is often argued in commentaries on Weber. History's pathways follow far more complex processes, he contends. As discussed, their development must never be viewed as following a linear line, whether one of evolution, differentiation, or "value generalization" (see Parsons, 1966, 1971). Instead, multiple groups are perpetually involved in the most dissimilar fissions and fusions.

Whether alliances of groups cause entire civilizations to congeal and then to develop in a clear direction remains to Weber a question for empirical investigation. Even concerted social change may involve "progress" exclusively in respect to a specific societal domain. Similarly, whether "rationalization" and "bureaucratization" occur, and whether an "iron cage" society of cold and impersonal relationships appears, depends upon singular concatenations of multiple groups (see Chapter 9). Empirical investigations must explore the influence of each.

All such general phrases fail to depict adequately, for example, Western rationalism and its trajectory. In *E&S* in particular, Weber insists that the various nations of the West, due to intense and enduring competition, distinct indigenous constellations, and perpetual internal struggles between relatively autonomous societal spheres and their respective groups, followed unique pathways. These distinctions held even as each nation entered into the twentieth century, he argues – despite the often uniform constraints associated with the broad-scale impact of industrialization and urbanization.

Weber's focus upon domains and domain-specific ideal types (such as the types of rulership – patriarchal, feudal, patrimonial, and bureaucratic – and the multiple salvation paths in the religion realm), his proclivity to compare unceasingly, and his awareness of the sociological significance of historical occurrences and contingencies precludes an understanding of the "rationalization of action" as a *general* process in the West, one homogeneous across all industrializing states and nations (see, e.g., *PE*, pp. 96–98). As he repeatedly emphasizes, "fateful events" play a significant part and unrepeatable configurations abound as polychromatic tapestries repeatedly shift and kaleidoscopic interweavings take place. These same foundational features of his sociology led Weber to reject cross-epochal and cross-civilizational analogies and parallels (see *AG*, pp. 39, 341, 385; Kalberg, 1994, p. 83). They also place his sociology of civilizations, as noted, firmly in opposition to all cyclical views of history (*AG*, p. 357).

Weber stresses that a distinction between more closed and more open civilizations must not be understood as implying consecutive historical stages or pendulum movements. As discussed, "inevitable developments" remain foreign to his empirical investigations. What identifiable causes stand behind a particular civilization's relative stagnation or openness? Over the last millennium in the West, Weber discovers "less unity," a greater "structural heterogeneity," and a more accelerated tempo of change than appeared in India, China, and Egypt (*E&S*, pp. 1192–93).

Capitalism's transformation into modern capitalism in the West's High Middle Ages was opposed by multiple powerful groups. They took the form of competing patrimonial empires, their struggle against politically independent and wealthy cities, feudalism's scorn for the systematic pursuit of wealth, Catholicism's "traditional" economic ethic and Canon law, and English mercantilism's opposition supported by the monarchy to the methodical economic ethic of Puritans. Long-lasting conflicts created enduring competition, namely, a situation that sustained a relative openness and adaptation to the new: "Rulership was set against rulership, legitimacy against legitimacy, one office charisma against the other" (*E&S*, p. 1193). Thus, the rise of modern capitalism in the West must be comprehended not only by reference to a Protestant ethic and spirit of capitalism, Weber maintains, but also as a consequence of massive internal tensions and perpetual struggles.

In conclusion, this chapter has argued that five themes constitute the thematic foundation for a largely neglected aspect of Weber's works: his sociology of civilizations. This discussion has sought to identify these themes as pivotal and to demonstrate the ways in which they form the major axes for his analysis of civilizations. It has also attempted to convey a preliminary impression of their complexity and the *civilizational* range of Weber's works, in particular of EEWR and *E&S*. Taken in combination, these themes outline a series of steps that comparative researchers even today – if they wish to undertake a *Weberian* analysis of civilizations – must acknowledge and utilize as orienting guideposts.

Notes

1 Inner-worldly implies to Weber that the action *this* believer perceives as relevant and meaningful to personal salvation is action *in* the world rather than separate from the world (as is the action of the monk secluded in a monastery).

2 Weber's conviction that the diverse sources of legitimation constitute the central issue in respect to rulership (*Herrschaft*) rather than the sheer "external form" of a rulership organization stands at the foundation of his interest in rulership (see, e.g., *E&S*, pp. 952–54, 1068–69, 1104–09).

3 "Viewed externally, numerous Hinduist religious communities appear to be 'sects' just as do many religious communities in the West. The sacred values, however, and the manner in which values were mediated, pointed in radically opposed directions" ("I," p. 292; transl. alt.).

4 Weber further notes: "...important here above all are the special *characteristic features* of Western rationalism and, within this particular type of rationalism, the characteristic features of modern Western rationalism. Our concern is to identify this uniqueness and to explain its origin" ("PR," p. 246; see also pp. 233–34).

5 On the uniqueness of Western art, see "PR," pp. 234–35; *E&S*, pp. 602–10; "IR," pp. 340–43.

6 *Today*, these major aspects of Western civilization do not seem unique to it. It must be stressed that Weber's project aims to explain why these features developed *earliest* in the West. His position does not imply that the development of these and other major elements of Western civilization remain impossible outside the West, nor does his isolation of features specific to the West and modern West indicate either a personal preference for such civilizations nor a belief (as held by many of his colleagues in Germany) that Western civilization is superior to other civilizations (see note 8).

7 Indeed, Weber identified the forces that would allow this to occur; on Japan, see *RofI*, p. 275.

8 The notion that Weber, because he wishes to define the West's uniqueness vis-à-vis the ancient and medieval West, as well as China and India, *itself* indicates Eurocentrism and Western triumphalism is here rejected (see Goody, 2007). His harsh criticisms of the West (including the notion of its superiority; see "SV," p. 331) remained simply too profound throughout his last 15 years for this interpretation to be plausible. In addition, his methodology oriented to the interpretive understanding of subjective meaning, as noted, equipped him well to investigate the *internal* workings of non-Western and non-modern civilizations on their *own* terms. This point is addressed throughout this study.

9 Readers of *PE* may object that the "Western rationalism" theme is to be found even in this early volume. This is, in fact, the case. However, the major translations today (as well as the most frequently used German version) by Parsons and the author are based upon the slightly revised version Weber published in 1920 (see *PE*). He added references to this theme for this edition (see Kalberg 2011).

10 The point of reference, of course, for this sentence is Weber's "four types of social action" (see *E&S*, pp. 3–31; see below, pp. xxx).

11 Again, Weber contends that only a sociology grounded in subjective meaning (rather than, for example, networks, interaction, group dynamics, communicative action, and economic and political interests) is capable of capturing *these* distinctions at the level of motivations.

12 "...the long and continuous history of Mediterranean-European civilization does not show either closed 'cycles' or linear progress" (*AG*, p. 366).

13 Weber never offers a precise definition of a civilization's rationalism.

14 In calling attention to this "civilizational rationalism" theme, I am here opposing the prevalent interpretation among scholars of the EEWR series. They contend that these volumes on China, India, and ancient Israel offer "contrast cases" to the West only (see Bendix, 1962; Nelson, 1973; Tenbruck, 1980; Schluchter, 1996, pp. 17–21; Ertman, 2017).

15 Weber discovered a certain connection in Jainism in India (see *RofI*, pp. 193–203).

16 However, this conclusion – that civilizations for Weber possess a "characteristic individuality" or "particular rationalism" – should never lead to their conceptualization as "organic unities" – if only as a consequence of his sociology's rootedness in life-spheres and ideal types (rather than "society") and its general emphasis upon conflict. Unlike for structural-functionalists, the question of a culture's unity remains for Weber an *empirical* one and always one of degree (see, e.g., *E&S*, p. 1193).

17 Again, the severity of this tension varies. See Kalberg (2021) on China (Confucianism's predominant "adaptation to the world" ethos) and on India. Here, it relates mainly to Hindu and Buddhist elites.

18 For a more detailed discussion of worldviews, see Kalberg (2012, pp. 73–92).

12

THE NATURE OF WORK IN OLD AND NEW CIVILIZATIONS

12.1   An Introduction: Contrasting Rural Social Structures in Germany and the United States

Open, or "free," markets, Weber is convinced, did not appear simply as a consequence of a "'goal-oriented,' rational calculation with the technically most adequate available means." To him, conducive substantive rationalities had to be in place before "correct calculation" and the free market's formal rationality could develop.

The "spirit of capitalism" must be noted as a central "substantive condition" along the winding path toward widespread free markets. Weber insists that additional complex patterns of social action also came into play. They further demarcate his general position on economic development: the causal regularities of action behind it – constellations of cultural, political, economic, status, legal, urban, and familial orientations – must be acknowledged. To him, "the formal rationality of money calculation is dependent on certain quite specific substantive conditions" (*E&S*, p. 107).

How did it occur that in certain eras and regions traditional action and traditional economic ethics, which had existed unchanged from time immemorial, were altered and indeed destroyed? Modernity, and in particular its "calculating attitude," rests upon a wide-ranging constellation of "value postulates."

Weber argues this general point also by comparing the market economy to the planned economy. Economic action in the latter is

DOI: 10.4324/9781032631813-17

oriented "heteronomously," that is, to a set of nonmarket rules or ideals. When held to comprehensively, such altruistic ideals inevitably lead to a "reduction in formal, calculating rationality" and to lower standards of living in the end. In an ideal-typical formulation, he then succinctly charts out "the conditions of maximum formal rationality of capital accounting" (E&S, p. 85).

In his essay "Socialism,"[1] Weber contends that the "separation of the worker from the tools of his trade" should not be seen, following Marx, as unique to the situation of the working class in privately owned industries. Rather, ownership today remains in organizations rather than in a class. State ownership will not alter this concentration of "the tools" (machines, laboratories, etc.) in, for example, factories, corporations, universities, and hospitals, Weber is convinced.

Moreover, to him nonrandom forces stood behind this development toward the organization of economic activity in large-scale firms and factories. It occurred, on the one hand, as a consequence of the technologically more complex character of the tools and, on the other, as a result of the greater efficiency that follows wherever complex tasks are coordinated.

A further central feature of the modern economy is emphasized by Weber in a number of texts, namely the *specialization* of tasks. The modern economy requires specialists; it "cannot be run in any other way." Yet this precondition also leads in the direction of large-scale organizations, for the discrete tasks carried out by specialists must be ordered and coordinated.

The administrators, managers, clerks, and officials who do so acquire a central place in the modern economy – regardless of whether the bourgeoisie or the state owns the means of production. A "dictatorship of the official, not of the worker [is] on the advance," and industrialism's large-scale organization of production will alter "the spiritual face of mankind almost to the point of unrecognizability" in this way.

Attentive always to background cultural forces, Weber addresses also the manner in which discipline – "the consistently rationalized, methodically prepared and exact execution of the received order" – constitutes a central cornerstone underpinning bureaucratization. The impersonal and "unfailingly neutral" character of discipline "places [it] at the disposal of every power that claims its service" – and hence it stands in the most strict opposition to all personal devotion to charismatic figures. The feudal knight's strong orientation to a code of personal honor also contrasts clearly to the rational calculation and "orientation toward a purpose [and] a common cause" typical of discipline.

The suitability of discipline, which "puts the drill for the sake of habitual routinized skill" at the forefront, for the factory workplace is evident. Indeed, Weber identifies the rigorous discipline practiced in the military as the "ideal model for the modern capitalist factory." When disciplined, the "optimal profitability" of workers can be calculated, for the "psychophysical apparatus of man is [in the factory] completely adjusted to the …machines."[2] As rationalization occurs, especially in the factory and the administration of the state, discipline expands inexorably.

Weber explores the ramifications of these significant transformations of the workplace. The replacement of "the cultivated man" by "the specialist" is first examined. Weber renders these ideal types in stark terms. He characterizes their struggle, and its ultimate outcome, as arising out of bureaucratization and the increasing importance of specialized knowledge in the modern epoch. The unequivocal expansion of certificates and examinations in higher education institutions is a manifestation of this importance. Whereas in earlier epochs "proof of ancestry" opened doors and established privileges, today "full bureaucratization" brings the examination irresistibly to the fore as the "universal instrument" leading the way to the "patent of education."

Scientific research, Weber emphasizes in his classical essay "Science as a Vocation," is also undergoing massive specialization. This transformation is both inevitable and appropriate, he contends. The "definitive and good accomplishment" requires narrow training in demarcated subareas and an orientation to theoretical and empirical problems posed within them.

Although scientific work is consequently quite tedious, the scientist must have an enthusiasm for and commitment to his or her endeavor. A true "calling" for science is possessed only by scholars, even as they pursue their specialized research tasks and extremely narrow conjectures, who are awakened by a "strange intoxication"; "without this you have no calling for science." Moreover, however specialized and bureaucratized, science exists in the end, Weber is convinced, only on the basis of new ideas and inspiration. Scientists must have ideas, yet they occur "when they please" and "cannot be forced." How, he wonders, do they arise at all in highly bureaucratized and specialized settings?

Weber sees these features – the separation of the worker from the means of production, the specialist character of scientific research and labor in general, and the centrality of examinations, certificates, and discipline – as indigenous to the modern economy and workplace. Nonetheless, he typically is convinced that even seemingly universal and standard features of modern capitalism must be acknowledged as varying in weight and scope in the various modern economies, depending on arrays of background historical and deep cultural action patterns.

For example, Weber undertook to compare German and American capitalism by reference to underlying economic and political constellations in a lecture given in St Louis in 1904 at the World's Fair.[3] These "new" and "old" civilizations varied distinctly along many axes, and these differences shaped dramatically the particular contours of modern capitalism in each country. Weber's lecture stresses that any attempt to transpose understandings of American capitalism onto Germany or vice versa would only lead, owing to significant underlying historical divergence, to "entirely wrong conclusions." What differences did he have in mind?

His discussion focuses on the many forces in Germany that stand opposed to "moneymaking and its representatives." Written at the same time as *The Protestant Ethic and the Spirit of Capitalism*, this lecture emphasizes the "much more complicated social organization" in Germany. Here, over many centuries, a large stratum of state officials became powerful, together with a conservative, anti-capitalist Church and an "aristocracy" which dominated educational institutions. All opposed "the power of money-makers" and, in a "settled" Germany "less adventurous" than the United States, circumscribed dramatically any free space for the pursuit of profit.

Americans find these developments "difficult to understand," he concedes. Capitalism in Europe assumes an "authoritarian stamp," Weber contends, in contrast to the "citizens' equality of rights" widespread in America. Hence, the entrepreneurial economic culture called forth by the spirit of capitalism could more easily expand in the United States, Weber holds, which remained unburdened by any of these old civilization formations. Cognizance must be taken of the different milieu, he contends here and throughout his comparative-historical studies. When moving toward modern capitalism, countries do not stand on a level playing field, as little as they do when moving toward modern democracy. Nor are the different historical contexts shattered and banished by the wheels of modern capitalism to the same extent or in the same manner.

12.2 Selections from Weber's Texts

From "Socialism." 1972. Pp. 200–02, in *Max Weber*, edited by J. E. T. Eldridge. Translated by D. Hÿtch and revised slightly by Stephen Kalberg (London: Nelson).

What characterizes our current situation is this: the private economy, bound up with private bureaucratic organizations and hence with the separation of the worker from the tools of his trade, dominates the sphere of industrial production. History has never before seen these two characteristics together on such a scale. Moreover, this development coincides with the establishment of mechanical production within the factory – and thus with a local accumulation of labor on the same premises, the enslavement to the machine, and work-oriented discipline within the machine shop or pit. This discipline lends the contemporary mode of "separation" of workers from their materials its particular stamp.

This subjection to a workplace discipline is so extraordinarily marked for the industrial worker because, in contrast to, say, a slave plantation or a socage farm, modern industry functions on the basis of a highly efficient process of selection. A modern factory proprietor does not employ just any worker just because he might work for a low wage. Rather, he puts the man at the machine on piece wages and pronounces: "All right, now work, I shall see how much you earn." If the man does not prove himself capable of earning a certain minimum wage, he is told: "We are sorry but you are not suited to this occupation and we cannot use you." He is dismissed because the machine is not working to capacity unless the man in front of it knows how to utilize it fully.

Everywhere, it is the same, or similar. Every modern concern, in contrast to those of antiquity which employed slave labor, where the lord was bound to the slaves he owned – the death of one constituted for him a capital loss – rests on the principle of selection. On the other hand this selection, intensified to the extreme by competition between employers, constrains the individual employer to certain maximum wages. The inherent necessity of the worker's earnings corresponds to the inherent necessity of the discipline.

If the worker goes to the employer today and says: "We cannot live on these wages and you could pay us more," in nine out of ten cases – I mean in peacetime and in those branches where there is really fierce competition – the employer is in a position to show the workers from his books that it is impossible; my competitor pays such and such wages; if I pay you even only so much more, all the profit I could pay to the shareholders disappears from my books. I could not then carry on the business, for I would receive no credit from the bank. Indeed, he is very often just stating the naked truth.

There is the additional point that profits, under the pressure of competition, depend on the elimination of as much human labor as possible by labor-saving machines – and especially those highest-paid employees who cost the business most. Hence, skilled workers must be replaced by unskilled workers or by workers trained directly at the machine. This process is inevitable and is continually occurring.

Socialism terms all this the "domination of men by material forces," which means the domination of the end (supply meeting demand) by the means. It recognizes that although there were individuals in the past who could be held responsible for the fate of the client, bondsman, or slave, this is impossible today. Therefore, it attacks the organization of production as such rather than individuals. Any educated socialist will absolutely decline to hold an individual employer responsible for the worker's destined fate; rather, he will say it is inherent in the system and in the plight into which all parties find themselves driven – employer and employed alike.

From "Socialism." 1972. Pp. 203–04, in *Max Weber*, edited by J. E. T. Eldridge. Translated by D. Hÿtch and slightly revised by Stephen Kalberg (London: Nelson).

[Under socialism] the workers would very soon discover that the lot of a miner is not affected in the slightest by whether the pit is owned privately or by the state. The life of a worker in the coal mines of the Saar is just the same as in a private mining company: if the pit is badly run, that is, not very profitable, then things are bad for the workers too. The difference, however, is that to strike against the state is impossible; hence, under this kind of state socialism, the dependence of the worker is quite substantially increased. This is one of the reasons why social democracy generally rejects the form of socialism that involves a nationalization of the economy. It is a consortium of syndicates.

As before, profit is the decisive factor; the question of what is earned by the individual industrialists who have joined forces in the syndicate and of whom one is now the treasurer continues to determine the lines along which the economy runs. And the distressing thing would be that, while at present the political and private industrial administrations (of syndicates, banks, and giant concerns) stand side by side as separate bodies, and therefore industrial power can still be curbed by political power, the two administrations would then be one body with common interests and could no longer be checked.

From "Socialism." 1972. P. 209, in *Max Weber*, edited by J. E. T. Eldridge. Translated by D. Hÿtch and revised slightly by Stephen Kalberg (London: Nelson).

Above all, however, [socialism] means on the one hand the spread of officialdom, of specialist, commercially or technically trained clerks, but on the other hand the propagation of men of private means. That is, a class that just draws dividends and interest without performing the requisite mental work for it, as the employer does, but who, with all their financial interests, are committed to the capitalist system. Public and trust concerns, however, are strongly and quite exclusively dominated by the official, not the worker, who has more difficulty in achieving anything by strike action here than against private employers. It is the dictatorship of the official, not that of the worker, which, for the present at any rate, is on the advance.

From "A Research Strategy for the Study of Occupational Careers and Mobility Patterns." 1972. Pp. 154–55, in *Max Weber*, edited by J. E. T. Eldridge. Translated by D. Hÿtch and revised slightly by Stephen Kalberg (London: Nelson).

Only all these investigations combined could furnish a picture of the cultural significance of the development occurring before our eyes in major industries. The cultural problems, which it ultimately introduces, are of enormous extent.

In a memorandum for the subcommittee [Alfred] Weber stressed – in agreement with the views of many of us – that the structure of that peculiar "system" thrust upon the population by the organization of large-scale industrial production transcends, in its significance for their fate, the scope of the question of a "capitalist" or "socialist" organization of production. This results from the fact that the existence of this "equipment" as such is independent of this alternative.

Indeed, the modern workshop with its official hierarchy, its discipline, its chaining of the worker to the machine, its agglomeration, and yet – at the same time (compared, say, with the spinning-rooms of the past) – its isolation of workers,[4] its huge calculating machinery stretching right down to the direct manipulation of the worker, *is* – conceptually – independent of it. It possesses far-reaching specific effects on people and their "style of living" entirely unique to itself. …[The] present survey… may content itself, for its vindication, with the fact that the "system" as it is today, with [its] effects … has changed and will go on changing the spiritual face of mankind almost to the point of unrecognizability.

From "Organizational Discipline in the Factory." 1968. Pp. 1149–50, in *Economy and Society*. Translated by H. H. Gerth and C. Wright Mills; revised by Guenther Roth, Claus Wittich, and Stephen Kalberg.

[R]ational discipline … eradicates not only personal charisma but also stratification by status groups, or at least transforms them in a rationalizing direction.

The content of discipline is nothing but the consistently rationalized, methodically prepared, and exact execution of the received order, in which all personal criticism is unconditionally suspended and the actor is unswervingly and exclusively set for carrying out the command. In addition, this conduct under orders is uniform. The effects of this uniformity derive from its quality as social action within a mass structure. Those who obey are not necessarily a simultaneously obedient or an especially large mass, nor are they necessarily united in a specific locality. What is decisive for discipline is that the obedience of a plurality of men is rationally uniform.

Discipline in general, like its most rational offspring, bureaucracy, is impersonal. Unfailingly neutral, it places itself at the disposal of every power that claims its service and knows how to promote it. This does not prevent it from being intrinsically alien to charisma as well as status honor, especially of a feudal sort. The berserk with manic seizures of frenzy and the feudal knight who measures swords with an equal adversary in order to gain personal honor are equally alien to discipline, the former because of the irrationality of his action, the latter because his attitude lacks matter-of-factness. Discipline puts the drill for the sake of habitual routinized skill in place of heroic ecstasy, loyalty, spirited enthusiasm for a leader and personal devotion to him, the cult of honor, or the cultivation of personal fitness as an art. Insofar as discipline appeals to firm ethical motives, it presupposes a sense of duty and conscience – "men of conscience" versus "men of honor" in Cromwell's terms.

The sociologically decisive points... are first that everything is rationally calculated, especially those seemingly imponderable and irrational emotional factors – in principle, at least, calculable in the same manner as the yields of coal and iron deposits. Second, devotion is normally impersonal, oriented toward a purpose, a common cause, a rationally intended goal, not a person as such, however personally tinged devotion may be in the case of a fascinating leader....

From "The Economy and the Nature of Work." 1968. P. 1156, in *Economy and Society*. Translated by H. H. Gerth and C. Wright Mills, revised by Guenther Roth, Claus Wittich, and Stephen Kalberg.

No special proof is necessary to show that military discipline is the ideal model for the modern capitalist factory as it was for the ancient plantation. However, organizational discipline in the factory has a completely rational basis.

With the help of suitable methods of measurement, the optimum profitability of the individual worker is calculated like that of any material means of production. On this basis, the American system of "scientific management" triumphantly proceeds with its rational conditioning and training of work performances, thus drawing the ultimate conclusions from the mechanization and discipline of the organization. The psychophysical apparatus of man is completely adjusted to the demands of the outer world, the tools, the machines – in short, it is functionalized – and the individual is shorn of his natural rhythm as determined by his organism. In line with the demands of the work procedure, he is attuned to a new rhythm through the functional specialization of muscles and through the creation of an optimal economy of physical effort.

In the factory as elsewhere, and especially in the bureaucratic state machine, this whole process of rationalization parallels the centralization of the material implements of organization in the hands of the ruler. Thus, discipline inexorably takes over ever larger areas as the satisfaction of political and economic needs is increasingly rationalized.

This universal phenomenon more and more restricts the importance of charisma and of individually differentiated conduct.

From The "Specialist" and the "Cultivated Man." 1968. Pp. 998–1002, in *Economy and Society*. Translation by H. H. Gerth and C. Wright Mills; revised by Guenther Roth, Claus Wittich, and Stephen Kalberg.

[T]he bureaucratization of all domination very strongly furthers the development of "rational matter-of-factness" and the personality type of the professional expert. This has far-reaching ramifications, but only one important element of the process can be briefly indicated here: its effect upon the nature of education and personal culture (*Erziehung und Bildung*).

Educational institutions on the European continent, especially the institutions of higher learning – the universities, as well as technical academics, business colleges, gymnasia, and other secondary schools – are dominated and influenced by the need for the kind of "education" which is bred by the system of specialized examinations or tests of expertise (*Fachprüfungswesen*) increasingly indispensable for modern bureaucracies.

The "examination for expertise" in the modern sense was and is found also outside the strictly bureaucratic structures: today, for instance, in the so-called "free" professions of medicine and law, and in the guild organized trades....

Only the modern development of full bureaucratization brings the system of rational examinations for expertise irresistibly to the fore. The American Civil-Service Reform movement gradually imports expert training and specialized examinations into the United States; the examination system also advances into all other countries from its main (European) breeding ground, Germany. The increasing bureaucratization of administration enhances the importance of the specialized examination. In China, the attempt to replace the old semi-patrimonial bureaucracy by a modern bureaucracy brought the expert examination; it took the place of the former and quite differently structured system of examinations. The bureaucratization of capitalism, with its demand for expertly trained technicians, clerks, etc., carries such examinations all over the world.

This development is, above all, greatly furthered by the social prestige of the "patent of education" acquired through such specialized examinations, the more so since this prestige can again be turned to economic advantage. The role played in former days by the "proof of ancestry," as prerequisite for equality of birth, access to noble prebends and endowments and, wherever the nobility retained social power, for the qualification to state offices, is nowadays taken by the patent of education.

The elaboration of the diplomas from universities, business and engineering colleges, and the universal clamor for the creation of further educational certificates in all fields serve the formation of a privileged stratum in bureaus and in offices. Such certificates support their holders' claims for connubium with the notables (in business offices, too, they raise hope for preferment with the boss's daughter), claims to be admitted into the circles that adhere to "codes of honor," claims for a "status-appropriate" salary instead of a wage according to performance, claims for assured advancement and old-age insurance, and, above all, claims to the monopolization of socially and economically advantageous positions.

If we hear from all sides demands for the introduction of regulated curricula culminating in specialized examinations, the reason behind this is, of course, not a suddenly awakened "thirst for education," but the desire to limit the supply of candidates for these positions and to monopolize them for the holders of educational patents.

For such monopolization, the "examination" is today the universal instrument – hence its irresistible advance. As the curriculum required for the acquisition of the patent of education requires considerable expenses and a long period of gestation, this striving implies a repression of talent (of the "charisma") in favor of property, for the intellectual costs of the educational patent are always low and decrease, rather than increase, with increasing volume....

Social prestige based upon the advantage of schooling and education as such is by no means specific to bureaucracy. On the contrary. But educational prestige in other structures of domination rests upon substantially different foundations with respect to content. Expressed in slogans, the "cultivated man," rather than the "specialist," was the end sought by education and the basis of social esteem in the feudal, theocratic, and patrimonial structures of domination, in the English administration by notables, in the old Chinese patrimonial bureaucracy, as well as under the rule of demagogues in the Greek states during the so-called Democracy.

The term "cultivated man" is used here in a completely value-neutral sense; it is understood to mean solely that a quality of life conduct which was held to be "cultivated" was the goal of education rather than specialized training in some expertise. Such education may have been aimed at a knightly or at an ascetic type, at a literary type (as in China) or at a gymnastic-humanist type (as in Hellas), or at a conventional "gentleman" type of the Anglo-Saxon variety.

A personality "cultivated" in this sense formed the educational ideal stamped by the structure of domination and the conditions of membership in the ruling stratum of the society in question. The qualification of this ruling stratum rested upon the possession of a "plus" of such cultural quality (in the quite variable and value-neutral sense of the term as used here) rather than upon a "plus" of expert knowledge. Military, theological, and legal expertise was, of course, intensely cultivated at the same time. But the point of gravity in the Hellenic, in the medieval as well as in the Chinese educational curriculum was formed by elements entirely different from those which were "useful" in a technical sense.

Behind all the present discussions about the basic questions of the educational system, there lurks decisively the struggle of the "specialist" type of man against the older type of the "cultivated man," a struggle conditioned by the irresistibly expanding bureaucratization of all public and private relations of authority and by the ever-increasing importance of experts and specialized knowledge. This struggle affects the most intimate aspects of personal culture....

From "Capitalism and Rural Society in Germany." 1946. Pp. 364–65, in *From Max Weber: Essays in Sociology*, edited and translated by Hans H. Gerth and C. Wright Mills (New York: Oxford University Press).

The power of tradition inevitably predominates in agriculture; it creates and maintains types of rural population on the European Continent which do not exist in a new country, such as the United States; to these types belongs, first of all, the European peasant.

The European peasant is totally different from the farmer of England or of America. The English farmer today is sometimes quite a remarkable entrepreneur and producer for the market; almost always he has rented his estate. The American farmer is an agriculturist who has usually acquired, by purchase or by being the first settler, the land as his own property; but sometimes he rents it. In America, the farmer produces for the market. The market is older than the producer in America. The European peasant of the old type was a man who, in most instances, inherited the land and who produced primarily for his own wants. In Europe, the market is younger than the producer.

From "Capitalism and Rural Society in Germany." 1946. Pp. 369–72, in *From Max Weber: Essays in Sociology*, edited and translated by Hans H. Gerth and C. Wright Mills; slightly revised by Stephen Kalberg.

Even in America, with its democratic traditions handed down by Puritanism as an everlasting heirloom, the [Civil War] victory over the planters' aristocracy was difficult and was gained with great political and social sacrifices. But in countries with old civilizations, matters are much more complicated [than in America]. For there the struggle between the power of historical notions and the pressure of capitalist interests summon certain social forces to battle as adversaries of bourgeois capitalism. In the United States such forces were partly unknown or stood partly on the side of the North. A few remarks concerning this may be made here.

In the countries of old civilization and limited possibilities for economic expansion, moneymaking and its representatives necessarily play a considerably smaller social role than in a country that is still new. The importance of the stratum of state officials is and must be much greater in Europe than in the United States. The much more complicated social organization makes a host of specially trained officials, employed for life, indispensable in Europe. In the United States, only a much smaller number of them will exist, even after the movement of civil service reform shall have attained all its aims (1900–1910).

The jurist and administrative official in Germany, in spite of his shorter and more intensive education in preparation for the university, is about 35 years old when his time of preparation and his unsalaried activity is completed and he obtains a salaried office. Therefore, he can come only from wealthy circles; he is trained to unsalaried or low-salaried service and can find his reward for service only in the high social standing of his vocation. A character is thus stamped on him which is far from the interests of moneymakers and which places him on the side of the adversaries of their dominion.

The church belongs to the conservative forces in European countries; first, the Roman Catholic Church, which, in Europe, even on account of the multitude of its followers, is a power of quite different importance and character than it possesses in Anglo-Saxon countries, but also the Lutheran Church. Both of these churches support the peasant with his conservative way of life against the dominion of urban rationalist culture. The rural cooperative movement stands to a great extent under the guidance of clergymen, who are the only ones capable of leadership in the rural districts. Ecclesiastic, political, and economic points of view are here intermingled. In Belgium, the rural cooperatives are a means of the clerical party in their conflict against the socialists; the latter are supported by the consumers' unions and trade unions. In Italy, almost nobody finds credit with certain cooperatives unless he presents his confessional certificate.

Likewise, a landed aristocracy finds strong backing in the church, although the Catholic Church is, in social regards, more democratic nowadays than formerly. The church is pleased with patriarchal labor relations, because contrary to the purely commercial relations which capitalism creates, they are of a personal human character. The church holds the sentiment that the relation between a lord and a serf rather than the bare commercial conditions created by the labor market can be developed and penetrated ethically. Deep, historically conditioned contrasts, which have always separated Catholicism and Lutheranism from Calvinism, strengthen this anti-capitalistic attitude of the European churches.

Finally, in an old civilized country, the "aristocracy of education," as it likes to be called, is a definite stratum of the population without personal interests in economics. Hence, it views the triumphal procession of capitalism more skeptically and criticizes more sharply than can naturally and justly be the case in a country such as the United States.

As soon as intellectual and esthetic education has become a profession, its representatives are bound by an inner affinity to all the carriers of ancient social culture, because for them, as for their prototypes, their profession cannot and must not be a source of heedless gain. They look distrustfully upon the abolition of traditional conditions of the community and upon the annihilation of all the innumerable ethical and esthetic values which cling to these traditions. They doubt that the dominion of capital would give better, more lasting guaranties to personal liberty and to the development of intellectual, esthetic, and social culture which they represent than the aristocracy of the past has given. They want to be ruled only by persons whose social culture they consider equivalent to their own; therefore, they prefer the rule of the economically independent aristocracy to the rule of the professional politician.

Thus, it happens nowadays in the civilized countries – a peculiar and, in more than one respect, a serious fact – that the representatives of the highest interests of culture turn their eyes back, and with deep antipathy standing opposed to the inevitable development of capitalism, refuse to cooperate in rearing the structure of the future. Moreover, the disciplined masses of workingmen created by capitalism are naturally inclined to unite in a class party, if new districts for settlement are no longer available and if the workingman is conscious of being forced to remain inevitably a proletarian as long as he lives, which is bound to come about sooner or later also in [the United States], or has already come about.

The progress of capitalism is not hemmed in by this; the workingman's chances to gain political power are insignificant. Yet they weaken the political power of the bourgeoisie and strengthen the power of the bourgeois' aristocratic adversaries. The downfall of German bourgeois liberalism is based upon the joint effectiveness of these motives.

Thus, in [European] countries, where a rural community, aristocratically differentiated, exists, a complex of social and political problems arises. An American finds it difficult to understand the importance of agrarian questions on the European continent, especially in Germany, even in German politics. He will arrive at entirely wrong conclusions if he does not keep before his eyes these great complexes. A peculiar combination of motives is effective in these old countries and explains the deviation of European from American conditions. Besides the necessity for strong military preparedness, there are essentially two factors: first, something which never existed in the greater part of America, which may be designated as "backwardness," that is, the influence of a gradually disappearing older form of rural society.

The second set of circumstances which have not yet become effective in America but to which this country – so elated by every million of increased population and by every rise of the valuation of the land – will unavoidably be exposed exactly as Europe has been, is the density of population, the high value of the land, the stronger differentiation of occupations, and the peculiar conditions resulting therefrom.

Under all these conditions, the rural community of old civilized countries faces capitalism which is joined with the influence of great political and social powers only known to old countries. Even to-day under these circumstances, capitalism produces effects in Europe which can be produced in America only in the future. In consequence of all those influences, European capitalism, at least on the Continent, has a peculiar authoritarian stamp, which contrasts with the citizen's equality of rights and which is usually distinctly felt by Americans.

From "Capitalism and Rural Society in Germany." 1946. P. 383, in *From Max Weber: Essays in Sociology*, edited and translated by Hans H. Gerth and C. Wright Mills.

... For while it is correct to say that the burden of historical tradition does not overwhelm the United States and that the problems originating from the power of tradition do not exist here, yet the effects of the power of capitalism are the stronger and will, sooner or later, further the development of land monopolies. When the land has become costly enough to secure a certain rent; when the accumulation of large fortunes has reached a still higher point than today; when, at the same time, the possibility of gaining proportionate profits by constant new investments in trade and industry has been diminished so that the "captains of industry," as has occurred everywhere in the world, begin to strive for hereditary preservation of their possessions instead of new investments bringing both profit and risk – then, indeed, the desire of the capitalist families to form a "nobility" will arise, probably not in form though in fact.

The representatives of capitalism will not content themselves any longer with such harmless play as pedigree studies and the numerous pranks of social exclusiveness which are so startling to the foreigner. Only when capital has arrived at this course and begins to monopolize the land to a great extent will a great rural social question arise in the United States, a question which cannot be cut with the sword, as was the slave question....

From "Capitalism and Rural Society in Germany." 1946. P. 385, in *From Max Weber: Essays in Sociology*, edited and translated by Hans H. Gerth and C. Wright Mills; slightly revised by Stephen Kalberg.

The United States ... has no old aristocracy. Hence, the tensions caused by the contrast between authoritarian tradition and the purely commercial character of modern economic conditions do not exist.

...But...the greater part of the problems for whose solution we [Europeans] are now working will approach America within only a few generations. The way in which they will be solved will determine the character of the future culture of this continent. It was perhaps never before in history made so easy for any nation to become a great civilized power as for the American people. Yet, according to human calculation, it is also the last time, as long as the history of mankind shall last, that such conditions for a free and great development will be given; the areas of free soil are now vanishing everywhere in the world.

Notes

1 This text is from a lecture Weber gave in 1918 at a convention of Austrian army officers. Hence, its more informal tone.
2 This theme is treated in depth by Weber (see 1995).
3 Weber was invited to this "Universal Exposition" by his former colleague at Freiburg University, Hugo Münsterberg, then teaching in the Psychology Department at Harvard University. Owing to illness, this was Weber's first lecture in more than six years.
4 The question of how far conversation is or is not possible at work and why, the question of what qualities (professional and otherwise) acquire respect among fellow workers, and the question of the direction of ethical value-judgments among the workers – all these and similar questions need to be studied as concerns the ways in which they are determined by the workshop "community" (which, basically, is not a community) and by reference to the predominance (to be examined in terms of its degree) of a purely pecuniary involvement with work [Max Weber].

13

ON RACISM AND ITS SOCIAL CONTEXTS

13.1   An Introduction: On "Race," the Complexity of the Concept of Ethnicity, and Heredity

This chapter demonstrates Weber's strong aversion to the explanatory power of race, ethnicity, and "common descent."[1] The question of whether biological races exist or not never attracts his attention; rather, he focuses upon the extent to which "race membership" – or "common inherited and inheritable traits that actually derive from common descent" (*RCM*, p. 297) and consciousness of race – calls forth social action in a regular manner, indeed, to such an extent that it forms the foundation for a group. Is "race" influential enough to be group-forming?

Of course, race can be "subjectively perceived as [the] common trait" of a specific group and hence lead to group formation. Weber emphasizes, however, that highly complex issues are involved and counsels caution and circumspection. He is convinced in particular that any antipathy toward a racial group cannot be understood simply as a consequence of a dislike of inherited traits. Rather than a "natural" racial aversion, "visible differences" – such as variation in respect to power and social honor, and the extent to which political and status groups become closed – may just as likely provide an explanation for antipathy. Social forces, including general socialization differences, must be acknowledged.

DOI: 10.4324/9781032631813-18

Moreover, Weber stresses throughout this chapter that a variety of "historically accidental habits" have been just as important for the formation of groups as "inherited racial characteristics." Different hairstyles, beards, eating habits, and clothes, for example, may split people off one from another and serve as catalysts for a "consciousness of kind"; they do so as effectively as shared customs in political and religious communities. And shared customs, conventions, and memories may ground tendencies toward monopolistic closure, which then may be transmitted across generations.

A belief in membership in an "ethnic group" may arise from such similarities, and this belief *may* "facilitate group formation... particularly in the political sphere." Yet, Weber sees the reverse line of causation as equally plausible: a sense of membership in a political association may give rise to beliefs in a common ethnicity. And these beliefs, and even a sense of "ethnic honor" specific to the group, may endure even if the political association disintegrates.

A common language and a memory of emigration or peaceful secession may intensify the belief in a common ethnicity. A distinct physical appearance and perceptible uniqueness in the "conduct of everyday life" must be noted as further factors conducive to ethnic differentiation, as are differences in workplace gender differentiation, housing, and food. Such distinctions may become manifest in conventions and become "symbols of ethnic membership."

These forces are constituent elements in the formation of ethnic groups, Weber contends; racial qualities are only marginally effective. Moreover, wherever new groups move into regions previously sharply demarcated by grouping, the apparent sharp contrast in customs is often explained by "the idea of blood disaffinity." However, this understandable conclusion must not be readily accepted, he argues, even though "ethnically determined action" or action "determined by the belief in a blood relationship" may become widespread.

History demonstrates that political action was often the source of group-forming action that later became understood as rooted in ethnicity. Although understood today as rooted in blood relationships and common descent, even tribes often came into being as "artifacts" of political associations. Common customs, which "have diverse origins," may have originated out of adaptation to environmental conditions and the "imitation of neighbors" rather than ethnicity.

If "'ethnically' determined social action" is to be explained, he concludes, a broad array of social factors must be distinguished. Indeed, because it conceals various forces and is far from uniform, the term "ethnic" would have to be abandoned. Once terms are precisely defined, he contends, the notion of "'ethnic' group...dissolves."

Weber confronted Alfred Ploetz (ca. 1860–1940), a prominent representative of the "race biology" school. This exchange took place at a meeting of the German Sociological Association in Frankfurt in 1910. Ploetz's lecture, "The Concepts Race and Society and Some Problems Associated with Them," had summarized his position. On the basis of a sweeping overview of Western history that combined Darwin and Nietzsche, he sought to legitimize "the necessity" for a "racial hygiene" turn, that is, for the social sciences to follow a eugenics agenda.[2]

The most modern advances in biology and genetics legitimized such a paradigm change, he argued. In its grandeur, the large collectivity – or "vital race" (*Vitalrasse*), as he prefers[3] – must take precedent over the ephemeral, miniscule, and imperfect existence of individuals, for the race represents the organic unity of life. Moreover, society contains the blood of its members, according to Ploetz, and hence its health depends upon the purity of the "blood of the race." The weak and infirm, who lower the quality of the gene pool, must be prohibited from reproducing.

To him, the social welfare policies of the German state, which had developed in a manner diametrically opposed to the Darwinian "survival of the fittest" axiom, threatened the vigor of the Germans. Along with his mentor Ernst Haeckel (1834–1919), Ploetz, as "the apostle of a new race theory,"[4] would become a major early proponent of the priority given to das Volk by National Socialism and of the eugenics policies it adopted.[5]

Weber, who was the last commentator on Ploetz's lecture, states his opposition to all attempts to explain social occurrences and developments by reference to biological forces or "inheritable traits" in extremely forceful terms. He offers several explanations anchored in economic and political factors that, he proposes, better explain "societal circumstances" than the "blood of a race." In respect to the fall of ancient Rome, for example, reference to economic forces provides an entirely convincing explanation, Weber holds, and any use of a hypothetical "racial theory," as Ploetz had offered, is speculative and methodologically unwarranted.

And no proof exists that relationships between blacks and whites in the United States are "rooted in inherited instincts," as Ploetz had argued.[6] Similarly, social causes, rather than instinct, explain the diverging social esteem accorded to blacks and Indians by whites in North America. And what, in the end, is a "race"? Weber then calls attention to his own "situation of personal embarrassment, [as] I ... am a cross-section of many races."

To him, the concept "race" possesses "a completely mystical character" and implies "subjective evaluations." At present, he contends, "innate and inherited qualities" fail to explain a "single fact relevant for Sociology." Perhaps, when research tools and methodologies have been significantly refined at some distant point in the future, an "exact proof" of the impact of inheritable qualities for social life can be acquired, he holds. For now, however, "theories of race allow one to prove and disprove whatever one wishes."[7]

Moreover, Weber contends that science, given its limits for purely methodological reasons, can never determine the ultimate superiority or inferiority, as Ploetz had claimed, of races, let alone the superiority of one culture over another (*RCM*, p. 331). Weber opposes vehemently all pushing to the side today of "known and accessible causes in favor of hypotheses that are speculative."

Finally, his comments include a succinct criticism of all approaches that view society as an organism and all schools that ground their conclusions upon analogies across human and animal species.

The final reading is from Weber's "Prefatory Remarks" to his Collected Essays in the Sociology of Religion. Here, he argues against the idea that, because specific types of rationalization can be discovered only in the West, heredity must be seen as playing the decisive causal role. In sum, Weber's views on ethnicity, race, and heredity conform to those held widely by social scientists today.

13.2   Selections from Weber's Texts

From "Race" Membership, Common Ethnicity, the "Ethnic Group," and Heredity. 1968. Pp. 385–87, in *Economy and Society*, translation by Guenther Roth and Claus Wittich; slightly revised by Stephen Kalberg.

A much more problematic source of social action than the sources analyzed above is "race membership": common inherited and inheritable traits that actually derive from common descent. Of course, race creates a "group" only when it is subjectively perceived as a common trait: this happens only when a neighborhood or the mere proximity of racially different persons is the basis of joint (mostly political) action, or conversely, when some common experiences of members of the same race are linked to some antagonism against members of an obviously different group.

The resulting social action is usually merely negative: those who are obviously different are avoided and despised or, conversely, viewed with superstitious awe. Persons who have a different external habitus are simply despised irrespective of what they "accomplish" or what they "are," or they are venerated superstitiously if they are too powerful in the long run. In this case, antipathy is the primary and normal reaction. However, this antipathy is shared not just by persons with anthropological similarities, and its extent is by no means determined by the degree of anthropological relatedness. Furthermore, this antipathy is linked not only to inherited features but just as much to other visible differences.

If the degree of objective racial difference can be determined, among other things, purely physiologically by establishing whether hybrids reproduce themselves at approximately normal rates, the subjective aspects, the reciprocal racial attraction and repulsion, might be measured by finding out whether sexual relations are preferred or rare between two groups and whether they are carried on permanently or temporarily and irregularly. In all groups with a developed "ethnic" consciousness, the existence or absence of intermarriage (connubium) would then be a normal consequence of racial attraction or segregation. Serious research on the sexual attraction and repulsion between different ethnic groups is only incipient, but there is not the slightest doubt that racial factors – that means common descent – influence the incidence of sexual relations and of marriage, sometimes decisively.

However, the existence of several million mulattoes in the United States speaks clearly against the assumption of a "natural" racial antipathy, even among quite different races. Apart from the laws against biracial marriages in the Southern states, sexual relations between the two races are now abhorred by both sides, but this development began only with the Emancipation and resulted from the Negroes' demand for equal civil rights. Hence, this abhorrence on the part of the whites is socially determined by the tendency toward the monopolization of social power and honor, a tendency which in this case happens to be linked to race.

The connubium itself, which means the fact that the offspring from a permanent sexual relationship can share in the activities and advantages of the father's political, economic, or status group, depends on many circumstances. Under undiminished patriarchal rulership, the father was free to grant equal rights to his children from slaves. Moreover, the glorification of abduction by the hero made racial mixing a normal event within the ruling strata.

However, patriarchal discretion was progressively curtailed with the monopolistic closure – by now familiar to us – of political, status, or other groups and with the monopolization of marriage opportunities; these tendencies restricted the connubium to the offspring from a permanent sexual union within the given political, religious, economic, and status group. This also produced a high incidence of inbreeding. The "endogamy" of a group is probably everywhere a secondary product of such tendencies. "Pure" anthropological types are often a secondary consequence of such closure; examples are sects (as in India) as well as pariah peoples, which means groups that are socially despised yet wanted as neighbors because they have monopolized indispensable skills.

Reasons other than actual racial kinship influence the degree to which the blood relationship is taken into account. In the United States the smallest admixture of Negro blood disqualifies a person unconditionally, whereas very considerable admixtures of Indian blood do not. Doubtlessly, it is important that Negroes appear esthetically even more alien than Indians, but it remains very significant that Negroes were slaves and hence disqualified in the status hierarchy. The conventional connubium is far less impeded by anthropological differences than by status differences, which means differences due to socialization and "upbringing" (*Bildung* in the widest sense of the word). Mere anthropological differences account for little, except in cases of extreme esthetic antipathy.

All in all, the notion of "ethnically" determined social action subsumes phenomena that a rigorous sociological analysis – as we do not attempt it here – would have to distinguish carefully: the actual subjective effect of those "customs" conditioned by heredity and those determined by tradition; the differential impact of the varying content of "custom"; the influence of common language, religion, and political action, past and present, upon the formation of customs; the extent to which such factors create attraction and repulsion, and especially the belief in affinity or disaffinity of blood; the consequences of this belief for social action in general, and specifically for action on the basis of shared custom or blood relationship, for diverse sexual relations, etc. – all of this would have to be studied separately and in detail. It is certain that in this process, the global term "ethnic" would be abandoned, for it is unsuitable for a really rigorous analysis.

However, we do not pursue sociology for its own sake and therefore limit ourselves to showing briefly the diverse factors that are hidden behind this seemingly uniform phenomenon. The concept of "ethnic" group dissolves if we define our terms exactly.

Comment on the Lecture by Alfred Ploetz on "The Concepts Race and Society."

From "Business Report and Discussion Contributions." 1924. German Sociological Association Convention (1910), in *Gesammelte Aufsätze zur Soziologie und Sozialpolitik* [Collected Essays on Sociology and Social Policy], edited by Marianne Weber and translated by Stephen Kalberg (Tübingen: Mohr Verlag), pp. 456–62.

Professor Max Weber: Dr. Ploetz began his lecture by noting that the principle of brotherly love has dominated our ethics for millennia. I would ask: when? With what consequences? And is its domination today strengthened over the view of race of the past, which was "more favorable" to a racial hygiene position?[8] Of course, the ethic of brotherly love exists in the official catechism just as in the Middle Ages.

But the real problem concerns how the praxis of life related in the past relates today to this official postulate and influences selection. That is, whether the routine of life does so in such a way that the racial hygiene position is less tenable today than earlier. Certainly, the population of the Middle Ages was subject to a sharp selection process in respect to reproduction chances. From the point of view of racial hygiene, two points surely should not be dismissed. First, childhood mortality had a particularly strong effect on the lower strata of society, as did the increasing factual – and even legal – restrictions regarding marriage for all people without a livelihood.

On the other hand, in the Middle Ages, the principle of brotherly love drove many into cloisters, knight orders, and the celibacy of the priesthood. All these people were then weeded out of that population propagating the species, and none were inferior in terms of physical capacities or intelligence. The same principle of brotherly love is also manifest in the systematic support for mendicancy.

If we look at the path of development from the Middle Ages to the modern period, it appears to me that a reversal of this principle has made headway even on Christianity's own ground, which one never would have presumed possible in the case of a religion that once possessed certain Biblical foundations. I am reminded that Calvinism viewed poverty and unemployment as a misfortune caused by one's own failings or as a consequence of God's unknowable decree. It then acted accordingly, that is, to a great degree excluding the "weak" from reproduction. Hence, in the case of this religion a place for brotherly love cannot be found, and I further doubt whether the modern development by and large has taken a pathway that has allowed precisely an excess spread of brotherly love in our society to become an urgent danger.

Moreover, that which one commonly calls social policy (as advocated by Dr. Ploetz) can have a very varying and a very desired significance, also in terms of racial hygiene, in keeping with the spirit of Dr. Ploetz. That is, social policy can give to the physically and intellectually stronger (although weaker in regard to the pocket book), namely, stronger when viewed from the standpoint of racial hygiene – the possibility, hand in hand with the possibility of upward mobility, of a healthy propagation of the species. Yet even such a development is in no way necessarily a consequence of an indiscriminating brotherly love (as the argument of Dr. Ploetz would imply).

Dr. Ploetz also noted that societal circumstances rooted in blood are perpetually dependent upon the blood of the race. This or something similar! Gentlemen! This is, regardless of which concept of "society" and "race" one applies, a completely unproven assertion – one which I believe cannot in the least be demonstrated in light of the present state of our science and research methods.

I'm quite aware of present theories that, by reference to the development of Antiquity, contend support can be found for this frequently argued theory. Excellent historians occasionally assert that the fall of ancient civilization was caused by the weeding out from the general population, as a consequence of the wars and conscription by the military, of the strongest and most capable – who then ruled the globe. In fact, it is now demonstrable that the development proceeded in exactly the opposite direction: the Roman army became increasingly composed of foreigners and entirely so in the end. The longer this development proceeded, furthermore, ever less were demands placed upon the population of the Roman Empire for the purposes of conscription and the more defense was put in the hands of barbarians.[9] There can be no question that not the slightest bit of this theory remains valid.

In addition, we know enough today of the reasons for the great transformation of ancient civilization in order to be able to say that, in so far as issues related to ethnicity played a role here at all, not the selective weeding out of the Roman clans from the officer corps and administration was relevant but their conscious exclusion. And this development did not have any "racial" or "biological" significance recognizable to us. On the contrary, in so far as it was relevant for the destiny of the Roman Empire, the exclusion of the Roman clans involved much more an attempt to banish groups rooted in traditional values and to favor peoples without traditions and culture, who could then be appointed officers and administrative functionaries.

Moreover, the disappearance of the ancient tastes, the old educated stratum, the Roman army's old traditions, and consequently the disappearance of the ancient administrative procedures – all these changes are so convincingly explained by changes in the administration rooted in economic forces that reference, as a complementary cause, to even a trace of this or that racial theory proves unnecessary.

This having been said, perhaps racial considerations nonetheless did play a role, I freely admit, in a manner no longer knowable to us today. Yet we do not know this and never will know it. And any pushing aside of known and accessible causes in favor of hypotheses that are speculative today and will remain so in the future opposes scientific methodology.

Now, however, in general: "The blood of societal circumstances is dependent upon the blood of the race." If one understands here "race," gentlemen, in the manner commonly understood by the lay person – inheritable traits bred through reproductive communities – then I would be put in a personally embarrassing situation, namely, I feel I am a cross-section of many races or at least of several particular ethnic heritages. Many in this circle would be in similar circumstances, I believe. I am part French, part German, and certainly on the French side somewhat infused with Celtic blood. Which of these races, for the Celts have been here referred to as a "race," blooms then in me or must bloom whenever the societal circumstances bloom in Germany or ought to bloom?

Dr. Ploetz (interrupting): You are here referring to a race system (*Systemrasse*). That involves the variety within races! I have discussed races as large populations as "vital races," which has nothing to do with this variety. All of these variations at least belong to a vital race.

Professor Max Weber (proceeding ahead): I must go through the different possibilities implied by the concept of race. In other words, I am now placing myself on your ground and establishing that even from this perspective a number of your statements have a completely mystical character. What does it actually mean to say: "the race blooms?" Or "The race reacts in a specific way?" What does it mean to say that a race "is a unity," if not a unity rooted in blood? Should not, in respect to the existence of this "unity," the simple fact of a physically normal reproductive capacity (which is then, of course, viewed in the case of illegitimacy as diminished) be decisive? And does the capacity to develop certain elements of culture belong to the race's "capacity to preserve itself" – or to what else?

The concept "vital race" takes us ultimately into the unbounded realm of subjective evaluations. And this realm is everywhere entered into by Dr. Ploetz whenever he decrees that connections exist between race and society.

If, of course, one assumes that certain races, identifiable in some purely empirical manner through characteristic traits, exist in proximity, and if one substitutes societal relationships and societal institutions for the purely conventional concept "society," then one can say that the unique features of institutions are in a certain way the rules of the game. With reference to the factual validity of these rules, specific human inheritable qualities acquire a likelihood of "winning" in the selection process, that is, of increasing their chances of survival or (and this is naturally not the same), on the other hand, of reproducing themselves (which in part proceeds according to entirely different laws).

That differences exist in respect to survival chances is not only the case today; it would not be otherwise in an eventual, however constituted, future socialist state. Of course, different inherited qualities would attain power, fortune, and reproductive capacities in this future state. Nonetheless, some qualities would exist more than others even in this socialist state and, regardless of how one constitutes a society, selection processes do not lie dormant. Rather, the question can be asked only of which inherited qualities are offered a chance in an ordering X of society as opposed to an ordering Y of society.

This appears to me a purely empirical question acceptable to us (as social scientists). And it is not otherwise if this question is reversed: which inherited qualities are the *preconditions* for the possibility now or in the future for an ordering of society in a certain way? This is also a meaningful question and one that can be used to study presently existing races.

However, if one takes these ways of formulating the issues, then it becomes immediately evident that nothing can come of the concept of race, as articulated by Dr. Ploetz (at least, this is my belief for now; I am willing to be persuaded otherwise). His concept of race seems to me not at all to be differentiated to the necessary extent. This will be confirmed if we ask ourselves what has crystallized until now as empirical sociological research from the application of this particular concept of race. Gentlemen, extremely stimulating and interesting theories have come out of it.

The journal edited by Dr. Ploetz is clearly an arsenal of boundless hypotheses, some of which have been formulated with an enviable abundance of intelligence in respect to the socializing effect of all possible institutions and processes. No one can be more thankful than I for this intellectual stimulation. However, I oppose with all forcefulness the notion that today there exists even one single fact relevant for Sociology – indeed, even one exact concrete fact related to a specific category of sociological processes – that actually, clearly and definitively, precisely and incontestably, leads back to innate and inherited qualities that one race possesses and another definitely – note well: definitely – does not possess. And I will continue to oppose this position categorically until this fact is precisely identified to me.

For example, and although it is today often believed, it is not correct to say that the respective social situations of whites and Negroes in North America can be traced back incontestably to racial qualities.

It is possible that, and to me to a high degree likely, such inherited qualities are here present and perhaps even considerably so. To what extent and above all in what way, however, is not firmly clarified.

Gentlemen, it has been asserted, for example, and it is still being asserted, also in Dr. Ploetz's journal and by very prominent men, that "race instincts" are at the basis of the opposition between whites and Negroes in the United States. Please prove to me the existence of these instincts and their content. They apparently are, among other ways, revealed in the way Negroes smell.

My own nose can here be called upon; I perceived, in closest contact, nothing of the sort. It is my impression that the Negro, when unwashed, smells exactly as does the white person – and the reverse. I further note that a scene can be daily observed in the southern states in which a lady – sitting in a horse-drawn coach and holding the reins in her hands – is nestled closely shoulder to shoulder with a Negro. And apparently her nose is not suffering from this proximity.

As far as I can ascertain now, the smell of the Negro is an invention of the Northern states to clarify their recent (1910) turning away from the Negro cause.[10] If we today, gentlemen, had the possibility to inject black skin into babies at birth, then even these people would be continuously in a rather precarious and peculiar situation in white society. However, any proof that the specific type of racial relationships in America is rooted in innate and inherited instincts has not yet been reliably demonstrated, even though I will always admit that the evidence might perhaps exist someday.

Before moving in this direction, it must be noted how striking it is that these "instincts" function in an entirely different manner in respect to different races. Yet this occurs for reasons that have absolutely nothing to do with the requirements for the preservation of the race. The reason for the highly divergent evaluation by whites in America of Negroes and Indians is repeatedly articulated by whites thus: "They didn't submit to slavery."

However, to the extent that their specific qualities played a part, the Indians were not slaves because they were not able (while the Negroes were) to endure the degree of work demanded by plantation capitalism – and it is uncertain whether this was purely on account of inherited qualities or also as a consequence of their traditions. Yet this circumstance clearly did not form, either consciously or unconsciously, the basis for a specific and varying "instinct" among whites that causes a different reaction to blacks and Indians. On the contrary, it was more so the case that the old feudal scorn for work (among upper-class Southerners) – that is, a social factor – here played a role. This being said, I will grant immediately to Dr. Ploetz.

Dr. Ploetz (interrupting): Not in the Northern states. The scorn for work did not there play this role.

Professor Max Weber (continuing): First, that is for the present no longer entirely correct. And the scorn for the Negro appears in the northern states only in the present. Second, if you investigate the position of Negroes in unions, then you will note that they, as workers who – as a consequence of traditions – lived simply and did not expect high wages, were increasingly despised and feared.

Finally, one can easily convince oneself that the middle-class American today, as everyone else, has read his Darwin, his Nietzsche, and, under certain circumstances, his Dr. Ploetz, and comes on this basis to a certain conclusion: a man – and I'm speaking here without any hint of a mocking tone – who wishes to be an aristocrat in the modern sense of the word must possess something that he can despise, and we Americans wish to be aristocrats in the European sense. At issue here is simply a Europeanization process, one that by chance in America carries with it this residual effect.

Now, honored gentlemen, I must come to a very few concluding remarks. Dr. Ploetz has characterized "society" as an organism. He has done so by reference to the well-known argument, which he has also presented here in a compelling lecture, regarding the relationship of society to cellular organizations in particular. It may be the case that, in terms of Dr. Ploetz's aims, something fruitful has crystallized (which he himself naturally knows best); however, for the sociological approach, the unification of many precise concepts into an imprecise concept never yields anything useful. And that is the case here.

We have the possibility to understand the rational action of the single human individual by intellectually reliving it. If we wish to comprehend a human association (regardless of the type) only according to the manner in which one investigates an animal society, then we would have to abandon those modes of knowing found among human beings and not found among animals. This – and no other – is the reason why, for our aims, no utility in general can be discovered from placing, as the foundation of any investigation, the entirely unquestionable analogy between a beehive and any human state-oriented society.

Finally, gentlemen, Dr. Ploetz has said that the study of society is a branch in the field that studies the biological influence upon races (*Rassenbiologie*).

Dr. Ploetz: The biology of society (*Gesellschaftsbiologie*), not the study of society in general!

Professor Max Weber: Yes, then I admit that perhaps I have misunderstood. However, it is not entirely clear to me how and where societal biology distinguishes itself from race biology, unless precisely the relationships between societal institutions and the selection of specific human qualities, as I earlier discussed them, ought to be the subject matter of societal-biological research. I would like to add on this topic only a general comment. It does not appear to me useful to exclude arenas and domains of knowledge a priori, that is, before this knowledge has congealed, and to say: this belongs to our science and this other does not. Only the most unproductive conflicts will be multiplied by doing so.

Of course, we can say that all societal processes ultimately play out on Earth and that the planet Earth belongs to the solar system. We can then come to the conclusion that everything occurring on Earth must actually be an object of study for astronomy. We can further conclude that it is only an accident – namely, it makes no sense to observe events on Earth with a telescope – that heuristic tools other than the telescope are used. However, would anything come out of this?

It is undoubtedly the case that the processes with which Biology is concerned – the processes of selection – are influenced by societal institutions. In turn, it is also not to be doubted that inherited racial qualities in a great many cases influence the imprint of societal institutions.

However, on the basis of these observations, I would ask whether it makes sense to appropriate any object or problem and to make it a component of a science which will be created ad hoc just to study these influences.

We expect from the race biologists exact proof that completely definable inheritable qualities are of decisive importance for practical, single occurrences of societal life. On the basis of the impression I have acquired from the research of Dr. Ploetz and his friends, I do not doubt that we can expect this achievement at some point from them. However, gentlemen, up until now, this proof has been lacking.

This is not a reproach against a science still so young. Nonetheless, it must be stated as a fact. And doing so will perhaps serve to prevent the utopian enthusiasm which characterizes the embarkation upon such a new field from degenerating into a situation in which the practitioners of this new endeavor fail to recognize the objective limits of its own way of framing questions. We experience just this today in all fields. Some believed that, as we have seen, the entire world, including, for example, art and all that otherwise exists, could be explained by reference alone to economic forces.

We have observed how modern geographers address all cultural phenomena "from the point of view of geography." They do so even though they fail to demonstrate that which we would like to know from them, namely, which specific and practical components of cultural production are conditioned, in the specific case, by climatic or similar purely geographical forces. Rather, they include something like the following in their "geographical" presentations: "the Russian church is intolerant." We then ask, to what extent does this conclusion belong within the realm of geography? The answer: "Russia is a region with a clear location, the Russian church expands across a defined location, and hence it constitutes an object of study in Geography."

Wherever each separate science fails to achieve that which it alone can and should achieve, it misses, I believe, its goal. I would like to express the hope that adherents of the study of societal events from the point of view of Biology will not wish to follow this route.

"Prefatory Remarks" ("PR") to Collected Essays on the Sociology of Religion (2011 [1920]). P. 250, in *The Protestant Ethic and the Spirit of Capitalism*. Translation by Stephen Kalberg; emphasis original (New York: Oxford University Press).

"... [T]he anthropological side of the problem should also be considered. If we again and again discover in the West, and only in the West, specific types of rationalizations (and also in arenas of life [such as religion, the economy, and law] that seemingly developed independently from one another), then naturally a certain assumption appears plausible: heredity is playing a decisive role." The author confesses that he is inclined, personally and subjectively, to estimate highly the importance of biological heredity.

However, despite the significant achievements of anthropological research at this time, I do not see any manner of exactly comprehending, or even hinting at in terms of probabilities, the share of heredity, namely, according to its extent and, above all, type and points of impact – in the development investigated *here*.

As one of its major tasks, sociological and historical research will have to reveal as many as possible of those influences and causal chains that are satisfactorily explainable as reactions to the effect of (biological) fate on the one hand and that of social milieu on the other. Only then, and only when, in addition, the comparative study of racial neurology and psychology moves beyond its rudimentary beginnings of today (1920) (which are promising in many ways, if one examines the discrete studies), can one *perhaps* hope for satisfactory results, even for the problem studied here. However, any development in this direction appears to me for the time being not to exist and any referral to "heredity" would be, it seems to me, tantamount to both a premature abandonment of the extent of knowledge perhaps possible today and a displacement of the problem onto (at this time still) unknown factors.

Notes

1 Weber arrived at this conclusion somewhere around 1900. His study of the East Elbian (Poland) farmworkers in the 1890s uses the notion of race as a causal force that explained some qualitative differences between Germans and Poles, largely to the detriment of the Poles (see Ernst Moritz Manasse, "Max Weber on Race," *Social Research* 14 (1947), pp. 191–221). That Weber no longer held this position by the time of his visit to the United States is clear from Marianne Weber's biography (1975, pp. 295–96). See also "Max Weber, Dr. Alfred Ploetz, and W. E. B. Du Bois," edited and translated by Benjamin Nelson and Jerome Gittleman (*Sociological Analysis* 34, 4 [1973], pp. 308–12).

2 Ploetz was the main founder and editor of an influential eugenics journal, *Archiv für Rassen- und Gesellschafts-Biologie* (1904–1944). See Detlev J. K. Peukert, *Max Webers Diagnose der Moderne* (Göttingen: Vendenhoeck u. Ruprecht, 1989), pp. 92–101.

3 This is Ploetz's term. It refers to the entire population of a race as opposed to variations and sub-variations within a larger race population. The latter are to him "race systems" (*Systemrasse*; see below). See "Max Weber, Dr. Alfred Ploetz, and W. E. B. Du Bois" (n. 1), pp. 309–10.

4 Manasse, p. 199 (see note 1).
5 The historian George Mosse summarizes Ploetz's views thusly:

> According to him, it was the Aryan race alone that represented the apex in racial development. He suggested that during a war it would only be fitting to send inferior members of the race to the front line as cannon fodder. Furthermore, as an added measure to insure physical fitness, Ploetz suggested that at a child's birth a consultation of doctors should judge its fitness to live or die. (See George L. Mosse, *The Crisis of German Ideology* [New York: Grosset & Dunlap, 1964], p. 99.)

See also Daniel Gasman, *The Scientific Origins of National Socialism* (New York: American Elsevier Inc., 1971), pp. 149–50. For an examination of the important influence of Ploetz and his journal, see Hedwig Conrad-Martius, *Utopien der Menschenzüchtung* (Munich: Kösel Verlag, 1955), chapter 3. See generally Hans-Günter Zmarzlik, "Der Sozialdarwinismus in Deutschland als geschichtliches Problem," *Vierteljahreshefte für Zeitgeschichte* XI (1963), pp. 246–73.

6 See Marianne Weber (1975, pp. 295–96 [note 1]). Weber refers to W. E. B. Du Bois, who had attended his lectures as a student in the 1890s in Germany, as "the most important sociological scholar anywhere in the Southern States" (see "Max Weber, Dr. Alfred Ploetz, and W. E. B. Du Bois"; *op. cit.*, p. 312). Upon meeting him in St Louis in 1904, Weber sencouraged Du Bois to write an article for the journal he edited (see "Die Negerfrage in den Vereinigten Staaten" [The Negro Question in the United States], *Archiv für Sozialwissenschaft und Sozialpolitik* 22 [1906], pp. 31–79). Weber's attempt to secure the translation into German and publication of Du Bois's "splendid work," *The Souls of Black Folk*, failed despite Weber's plan "to write a short introduction about [the] Negro question and literature." Weber also intended to write an article on "the recent publications [on] the race problem in America." See Weber's letter in English to Du Bois in Herbert Aptheker (ed.), *The Correspondence of W. E. B. Du Bois*, vol. 1, 1877–1934 (Amherst: University of Massachusetts Press, 1973), p. 106.

7 "Zum Vortrag von F. Oppenheimer über 'Die rassen-theoretische Geschichtsphilosophie.'" 1988. P. 489 in Weber, *Gesammelte Aufsaetze zur Soziologie und Sozialpolitik* (Tübingen: Mohr). Weber continues, addressing here the question of whether racial factors played a role in the decline of ancient civilizations: "It is a scientific crime to attempt the circumvention, by the uncritical use of completely unclarified racial hypotheses, of the sociological study of Antiquity, which of course is much more difficult, but by no means without hope of success; after all, we can no longer find out to what extent the qualities of the Hellenes and Romans rested on inherited dispositions. The problem of such relationships has not yet been solved by the most careful and toilsome investigations of living subjects, even if undertaken in the laboratory and with the means of exact experimentation" (*E&S*, p. 398, note 1; translation by Guenther Roth).

8 The "racial hygiene" position advocated a complete separation, on behalf of a maintenance of purity, of the races. Weber is noting that this view stands in opposition to the ethos of universal brotherly love.

9 See Weber, "The Social Causes of the Decay of Ancient Civilization." 1971. Pp. 254–74 in *Max Weber*, ed. by J.E.T. Eldridge (London: Thomas Nelson and Sons).

10 Weber is referring to the rise of Jim Crow laws in the post-Reconstruction era.

14

MAX WEBER'S SOCIOLOGY OF EMOTIONS

A Preliminary Analysis

Max Weber's mode of sociological analysis is distinguished from all structuralist theories, whether those more indebted to Emile Durkheim, Karl Marx, or Georg Simmel, above all by its orientation to subjective meaning and interpretive understanding (*verstehen*). This approach takes cognizance of a variety of motives for action, including the emotions.

The main source for the exploration here of *affectual action's* firm rooting in Weber's sociology is *Economy and Society*, Weber's major systematic treatise.[1] In this regard, this three-volume opus defines several central concepts. However, *The Protestant Ethic and the Spirit of Capitalism* (PE) also proves pivotal for this brief investigation. In the process of examining the religious sources of a "spirit of capitalism," this study analyzes the ways in which emotions vary in intensity across a variety of religious groups. Affectual action was severely constricted, Weber maintains, among adherents of a major carrier group along modern capitalism's early pathway of development: Puritanism. This "ascetic Protestantism" was influential over the longer term. Its contours remain visible in secularized manifestations even in the industrial epoch, Weber holds.

Albeit in different ways, *E&S* and *PE* offer analyses that assist demarcation of the intensity and location of emotions in varying social milieux. The widespread view that Weber's sociology attends exclusively to rational action and neglects affectual action must be revised.

DOI: 10.4324/9781032631813-19

14.1 Economy and Society: The Four types of Social Action, Social Relationships, and Charismatic Rulership

The importance of the emotions to Weber is apparent in *E&S*. He attends to affectual action in this study primarily in three separate discussions: in his typology of the "four types of social action," in his examination of social relationships, and in his typology of rulership.

The Four Types of Action. Weber's foundational definition of sociology must be noted at the outset:

> Sociology...is a science that seeks interpretively to understand social action. By doing so it wishes to explain the causes behind its course and its effects. "Action" should imply human behavior (regardless of whether it is external or internal, neglected or permitted) whenever, and insofar as, the acting person attaches a subjective *meaning* to this behavior. However, "social" action should imply that type of action in which the intended meaning of the actor or other actors relates to the behavior *of others*. Furthermore, social action implies that this meaning remains oriented to the behavior of others across the course of its development. (*E&S*, p. 4; emphasis original; translation altered)

This definition leads Weber to the formation of his foundational "four types of social action." For him, social action can be best conceptualized by reference to one of four types of meaningful action: as means-end rational (*zweckrational*), value-rational (*wertrational*), traditional (*traditional*), or affectual (*affektuell*) (see *E&S*, pp. 24–26). All types of action are found in every epoch and every civilization (*E&S*, pp. 399–400, 422–23; see Kalberg, 1994, pp. 44–45).

As noted, affect-based action is "determined by the actor's specific affectual and feeling states." It may involve "an uncontrolled reaction to some exceptional stimulus." Moreover, "Action is affectual if it *satisfies* a need for revenge, sensual pleasure, devotion, contemplative bliss, or for a working off of emotional tensions" (*E&S*, p. 25; emphasis original).

With this definition, Weber establishes the unconditional importance of affectual action for his sociological research. However, he does so in two further ways.

Social Relationships. To Weber, a social relationship "denotes the behavior of a plurality of actors insofar as, in its meaningful content, the action of each *takes account of* that of the others and is thereby oriented" (*E&S*, p. 6). The content of this relationship may vary across a wide spectrum, Weber emphasizes:

The content may [vary greatly]: conflict, hostility, sexual attraction, friendship, loyalty, or market exchange. It may involve the fulfillment, the evasion, or the violation of an agreement; or economic, erotic, or other forms of "competition." It may also involve common membership in status, national, or class groups (provided it leads to social action). (*E&S*, p. 27; translation altered)

Hence, in addition to the four types of action, social relationships also provide a firm grounding for affectual action, according to Weber. Moreover, a certain type of social relationship – the *vergemeinschaftete* – does so in a particularly firm manner, he contends. This relationship is based "on a subjective *feeling* of the participants (whether affectual or traditional) that they *belong* together" (*E&S*, p. 40; emphasis in original; translation altered).

Weber's examples include "a religious brotherhood, an erotic relationship, a relationship of personal loyalty, a national community, and the *esprit de corps* of a military unit" (*E&S*, p. 41). The family in particular represents this type of relationship. According to him, "the great majority of social relationships have this characteristic *to some degree*, while being at the same time to some degree determined by associative (*vergesellschaftete*) features" (*E&S*, p. 41; emphasis in original). Even in the purely calculating business relationship, such as that between retailers and customers, over time emotions may enter in:

Every social relationship between the same persons over a longer period that goes beyond actual means-end rational action and is not from the outset exclusively confined to the restricted associations related to the technical achievements of each person -- namely such cases as association in the same military unit, in the same school class, or in the same workshop or office – tends in this direction, although the degree, to be sure, varies enormously. (*E&S*, p. 41; translation altered)

Once again, Weber firmly anchors affectual action in his *verstehende* sociology. Finally, he does so when he turns to his typology of rulership (*Herrschaftstypologie*).

Charismatic Rulership. A typology of rulership is central to *E&S* and to Weber's sociology generally. Looking far into the past and broadly across civilizations, he identifies three types of rulership as appearing on a regular basis. The foundation for their legitimacy can rest upon:

> A "rational character" (on the belief in the legality of enacted pre-scriptions, rules, or laws (*Ordnungen*), or a "*traditional* character" (rooted in a belief in daily-life routines and their anchoring in the sanctity of forever valid traditions), or a *charismatic* character (resting in the legitimacy of those called, on the basis of these traditions, to exercise authority. (*E&S*, p. 215; translation altered; emphasis original)

Of direct concern here, charismatic rulership varies dramatically from both traditional and "rational-legal" rulership. It is characterized by a *belief* widespread among a group of people in respect to particular persons, namely, that they are endowed with extraordinary features, exceptional powers, and unusual personalities. Obedience to their pronouncements and commandments takes place on the basis of this belief.

Examples of this *attribution* of charisma can be found in both the religious (Jesus Christ, the Buddha, the Old Testament prophets, and Mohammad) and secular realms (Lenin, Hitler, and Martin Luther King). Moreover, an *emotional* connection between the leader and followers stands at the foundation of this type of rulership. Indeed, this affectual bond renders this relationship unusually intense and constitutes the basis for a "charismatic community" (*E&S*, pp. 215, 242–46, 1112–48).

In sum, fundamental concepts in Weber's major analytic treatise ground emotions in his sociology firmly and systematically: affectual action, social relationships, and charismatic rulership. However, our attention thus far to the *conceptual* location of the emotions in his sociology foreshortens their full significance to him; they play a large role as well in his comparative-historical studies. Both *E&S* and *PE* chart their diminution and marginalization in respect to a major theme in Weber's sociology: the uniqueness of the modern urban, industrial, and capitalist West, and its singular pathway of development. This theme must be briefly examined.[2]

We turn first to Weber's general depiction of the industrial West and then to a prominent causal force in his analysis of the Western economy's development to modern capitalism: the spirit of capitalism. *E&S* serves as the central source in regard to the first theme; *PE* does so in respect to the second theme.

14.2   Modern Capitalism: The Urban and Industrial West – The Marginalization of the Emotions

Several major life spheres acquire an independent causal capacity – or *Eigengesetzlichkeit* – to a significant extent with the rise of modern industrial societies, Weber contends. Rather than intertwined to the degree that generally occurred in agrarian and feudal societies, the economy, rulership, and law domains develop in industrializing and industrial societies to a greater extent in reference to "their own" questions and dilemmas.

To Weber, relationships in these arenas[3] in preindustrial epochs in-corporated a *personal* element. For example, under feudal rulership, the peasant knew the lord of the manor.

Moreover, rights and duties on both sides were specified by a feudal *contract* that should remain inviolable despite a clearly asymmetrical distribution of power. If the ruler exercised his domination in ways beyond the boundaries of accepted custom and convention, the peas-ant could protest – referring to age-old ways – directly to the master. Indeed, owing to the personal character of this relationship, an *emo-tional* bond between the ruler and the ruled *could* develop and *could* serve to regulate this relationship (see *E&S*, pp. 346, 584–85, 1186–87). Similarly, although also asymmetrical, economic relationships in feudal economies *could* significantly include a personal element. Pre-industrial legal relationships can be characterized in a parallel manner.

Scrutiny of highly urban and industrial societies reveals distinct transformations: in the economy, rulership, and law spheres, *imper-sonal* relationships have come to predominate, Weber holds. The laws of the market determine the production and exchange of products in the economy arena as well as hiring and firing. Whether in regard to the acquisition of a home mortgage by an individual or the applica-tion by a business for a bank loan, decision-making occurs by refer-ence to "objective" (*sachlich*) criteria. Credit reports, past repayment histories, budgets, and income levels are salient rather than personal relationships or personality features (*E&S*, pp. 346, 584–85, 635–40, 1186–87).

Similarly, in the domain of law, judges render decisions by reference to legal precedent and (in some states) a Constitution. Cases must "fit into" and become strictly "aligned with" the juridical statute. *Formal-rational* procedures "without regard for the person" must prevail (see *E&S*, pp. 852–55).

The bureaucratic organization also conducts operations in an extremely impersonal manner. Responsibilities and tasks are fixed by a firm hierarchy and chain of command, superordination and subordination lines, and demarcated "positions" and "offices." Performance occurs according to specified job descriptions and evaluation takes place on the basis of impartial criteria. Similarly, hiring and promotion occur on the basis of certificates, examination scores, and prescribed procedures. The civil servant, "the specialist," and "the manager" are all placed within this social milieu saturated by rules, prescriptions, and statutes. An evaluation *of persons* – their unique qualities, personalities, and emotions – has diminished in importance:

> Bureaucracy develops the more perfectly, the more it is "dehuman-ized" (*entmenschlicht*), the more completely it succeeds in eliminating from official business love, hatred, and all purely personal, irrational, and emotional elements that escape calculation. This is appraised as its special virtue by capitalism. (*E&S*, p. 975)[4]

Weber argues that the rulership, economy, and law spheres experienced a massive transformation along these lines with the rise of industrialism in the late nineteenth and early twentieth centuries. *Functional and associative* (*vergesellschaftete*) relationships and modes of decision-making came to the forefront. Among other consequences, this shift implied a marginalization of the emotions in these arenas generally, he emphasizes. In the workplace dominated by huge bureaucracies, in the courtroom, and in the offices of factory owners, financiers, and bankers, affectual relationships are pushed to the side by impersonal evaluative criteria and a "get the job done" ethos.

The consequence is apparent to Weber: defined as dysfunctional in the rulership, economy, and law spheres, compassion and deep feeling more and more pulsate intensely only in the private realms of intimate friendship and family. Threatened severely, the emotions have fled to this refuge: "It is not accidental that...today only in the smallest intimate circles, from person to person,...something is pulsating corresponding to the prophetic frenzy which, in former times, swept through large communities like a firebrand and welded them together" (*RCM*, p. 339).

Weber's full *causal* discussion of this far-reaching transformation refers to a broad array of patterned action-orientations and their dynamic interactions. It avoids the linear explanations of Durkheim (increasing "moral density") and Parsons (expanding differentiation) as well as the emphasis by Marx upon the sheer power of the bourgeoisie and its capacity to utilize new technologies and to exploit the proletariat.

Although Weber's multi-causal and multidimensional analysis must await a more extended discussion, the major role he attributes to "deep cultural" orientations can be noted. They crystallized in a pure form with Puritanism in England and New England. His analysis of the manner in which this *ascetic Protestantism* severely constricted the emotions now captures our attention.

14.3 The Protestant Ethic and the Spirit of Capitalism: The Puritan Flight from the Emotions

Puritanism appeared in the seventeenth century as a consequence largely of revisions to John Calvin's (1509–1564) doctrine of Predestination by a group of ministers and theologians in England known as Puritan Divines (*PE*, pp. 158–79). An inscrutable Old Testament God, omniscient and omnipotent, has decided unequivocally for all time that only a chosen few will be saved, according to this doctrine (see *PE*, pp. 115–17).

However, despite its seeming finality, devout believers in this intensely religious epoch continued to seek a clear answer to *the* overriding and burning question: "Am I among the saved?" Now, on the basis of the revisions formulated by the Puritan Divines, the faithful were given hope. What modes of activity proved crucial and how did they intensify or restrict the emotions? Labor and the search for profit and wealth moved to the center of the Puritan's life.

The faithful knew that God "commanded all" to work methodically. In addition, in order to glorify His majesty and honor, this short life must be one of engagement in the construction of God's earthly kingdom of justice and abundance. Surely this task could be accomplished only through systematic work. Moreover, consistent labor effectively constrained base impulses, creaturely appetites, and raw emotions, the Puritan Divines argued, as well as the believer's overpowering anxiety regarding the salvation question. Thus, it facilitated the focus of thought and energy upon Him and His commandments.

Nonetheless, a taming of desires and continuous work proved difficult to sustain. In this religious era, the few who succeeded in doing so comprehended their capacity to organize their lives around work as a consequence exclusively of God's energy *within* – and this majestic Deity, the devout also knew, would bestow His assistance *only* upon the "elect" chosen for salvation.

Finally, those who acquired the wealth that rendered God's kingdom one of abundance were aware that their achievements had not occurred by chance: their capacity to extoll God's glory in this manner itself constituted *evidence* (*Beweis*) of intervention on their behalf by this omnipotent and omniscient Divinity. And, they were convinced, only the chosen would be favored in this way; a *sign* (*Merkmal*) had been sent to them. Wealth and profit became further sanctified in this way, Weber maintains; a "psychological premium" was bestowed upon them (see *PE*, pp. 158–79; *E&S*, pp. 1198–1200).

This social-psychological dynamic led to a relocation of work, profit, and wealth: Puritanism placed all at the center of life. Furthermore, daily activities acquired a rigorous and disciplined – a methodical – form. By organizing their entire lives systematically, as Weber notes citing the sixteenth-century German mystic Sebastian Franck, believers "became monks" – yet they now lived *in* the world rather than secluded in monasteries as *other*worldly ascetics (*PE*, p. 132).

This all-consuming quest for redemption, focused intensely upon labor, profit, wealth, and the attainment of certainty of salvation (*certitudo salutis*), deemed the emotions worthless. Indeed, they proved disruptive and constituted obstacles to all consistent striving for salvation.[5] The devout were convinced that on behalf of this all-important aim, a disciplined effort to constrict affectual action comprehensively must be undertaken.[6]

Because oriented in an extremely rigorous manner to tasks, goals, sustained work, and wealth, this "Protestant ethic" created an entirely new person, Weber held (*RCM*, p. 270). It contributed significantly also to Puritanism's secular offspring: the "spirit of capitalism."

Carried by sects,[7] this frame of mind (*Gesinnung*) in the eighteenth and nineteenth centuries became especially widespread in many New England regions. It facilitated the rise of modern capitalism and the modern bureaucracy, he insisted (*PE*, pp. 158–79; *E&S*, pp. 1200, 1209–10). Indeed, this "spirit" called forth a human being (*Menschentyp*) that fit perfectly into the rhythms of the modern workplace: "The cool *matter-of-factness* characteristic of association promotes the precise ordering of the individual into the instrumental task pursued by the group" (*RCM*, p. 232).

14.4   Internal and External Modes of Constricting the Emotions

Both the industrial epoch's *external* aspects (its bureaucratic organizations, formal-rational legal procedures, and modern capitalist economy) and *internal* features (its frequently Puritanism-based values) stand in a relationship of antagonism to the emotions, according to Weber. And all highly bureaucratized societies not only constrict and marginalize the influence of charismatic leaders, he contends, but also severely curtail the competition of values indispensable for the nourishment of societal pluralism and group-oriented allegiances. When firm, these loyalties awaken *emotional* commitments to a "cause."

Wherever societies lack this dynamism, strictly utilitarian orientations to interests will expand across various societal spheres, Weber argues. A "practical rationalism" that takes the individual's interests and pragmatic calculations as pivotal then congeals and expands. Devoid of values and emotions, it then becomes widespread (see Kalberg, 2012, pp. 13–72).

Despite this analysis Weber cannot be categorized, as has often occurred, as a romantic thinker yearning for a pristine past of person-oriented and emotion-rooted relationships putatively more humane and just. Rather, his ambivalence toward a modern industrial, urban, and capitalist epoch characterized by impersonal and functional relationships is well documented. Weber was acutely aware that bureaucratic organizations alone attained the high levels of efficiency at the foundation of heretofore unimaginable standards of living. Moreover, his defense of the rule of law, however formal and impersonal its execution, remained unwavering. And in spite of its "mechanical foundation" (*PE*, p. 177), a market-oriented capitalism would call forth societal pluralism and group-oriented allegiances with a greater likelihood than would socialism, he maintained (*E&S*, pp. 1399–403). Weber argued indefatigably on behalf of this openness in innumerable speeches given during his last ten years (see *E&S*, pp. 1385–469).

In order to confront – and even postpone – the development of a highly bureaucratized society antagonistic to societal pluralism and emotions-anchored relationships, Weber saw the necessity for an institution capable of fostering powerful *leaders* on a sustained basis. Strong parliaments could offer a training ground for charismatic figures, he was convinced. Unlike civil servants and managers, all would take positions *rooted in values*; leadership skills would be further cultivated in the process.

In addition, the articulation of values-based ethics by leaders would awaken a "passion for a cause," Weber held, thereby endowing values with the capacity to confront directly the manager's formal rationality and the practical-rational organization of life generally prominent in this "modern impersonal cosmos." In the process, the broad tendency for cautious functionaries and civil servants oriented to formal procedures and statutes to extend their influence over policy questions would be contained.

Finally, wherever leaders stood up in public life on behalf of values-anchored positions, individual responsibility – an "ethic of responsibility" (*Verantwortungsethik*) – would be awakened. In turn, causes would be further defended, allegiances formed, and emotional commitments intensified. Rather than interest-based and rooted in a calculating *Realpolitik*, politics must involve this passionate "struggle over values," Weber asserted ("PV"; *E&S*, pp. 1381–462). Confrontations between the practical-rational mode of organizing life and the orientation of action toward values and affectual action must become long-lasting, moderate-level conflicts, he insisted. In this way, an *active* citizenry directed toward value constellations would arise gradually. In due course, citizens would then become insulated against all passive tendencies "to be led like a flock of sheep" (1978, p. 282).

Rare among sociologists, Weber provides an analysis that acknowledges on a regular basis the importance of macro developments for the fate of the emotions. Their diminution and marginalization occurs as a consequence of certain "internal *and* external" constellations, he maintains, and their invigoration and expansion takes place as a result of other "internal *and* external" configurations.

Notes

1 Affectual action must constitute the focus of any discussion of Weber's sociological analysis of emotions. First, only this type of action acquires a systematic location in his sociology (see below) and, second, a tight overlapping with emotion-based action is apparent from his foundational definition: "social action [can also] be determined *affectually*, especially by the *emotions*, that is, through actual affect and feeling situations" (*E&S*, p. 25; translation altered; emphasis original). Aside from the passages noted below, neither Weber's methodological nor empirical writings discuss this type of action systematically, nor do they yield consistent distinctions. Because emotions are infused deeply, according to Weber, with affect, this term can be utilized synonymously (as below). Passions (*Leidenschaften*), which are also infused with affect, relate more to Weber's political writings than to his sociological texts, our main concern here (see below; see also Schützeichel, pp. 104–06, 111–16.

2 This investigation does not seek to offer a complete overview of the role of emotions in Weber's sociology. Its focus on the developing and developed West omits his analysis of the emotions in respect to, for example, otherworldly mysticism (Buddhist monks), inner-worldly mysticism (the classical Hindu Brahmins), and the Confucian literati in particular (see *E&S*, pp. 502–04, 855–56, 902–03, 905–06, 908–10; *RofC*, pp. 226–49; *RofI*, pp. 329–43). It has also been necessary to omit examination of his discussions of the emotions in Catholicism and Lutheranism, as well as in a number of ascetic Protestant denominations, especially Pietism, Methodism, and Quakerism (see *PERW*; *E&S*, pp. 567–76). Finally, this contribution omits a discussion of the ways in which, according to Weber, a sublimation and restriction of the emotions must occur if an ethos of *Wertfreiheit* is to prevail among social scientists ("SV"; "Obj").

3 As noted above, arenas (*Lebenssphäre*), realms (*Lebensbereiche)*, and domains (*Lebensdomäne)* are used synonymously.

4 It must be kept in mind that Weber is here forming *concepts* (ideal types).

5 On the extreme inner loneliness and the devaluation of personal relations that followed from this doctrine, see *PE*, pp. 119, 121–22.

6 To the Puritans, it must also be noted, all cultivation of the emotions implied a "self-glorification" (*Kreaturvergoetterung*) – and this must be avoided at all costs for it placed the needs and wants of believers above their primary obligation: an unequivocal commitment to God and His grand design. His majesty could be served only in this manner, for "any excess of emotional feeling for one's fellow man is prohibited as being a deification of the creaturely, which denies the unique value of the divine gift of grace" (*E&S*, p. 542). For Richard Baxter, the author of the most

complete compendium of Puritan ethics, *Christian Directory* (1673), all of man's passions and emotions were not only antagonistic to God-given "reason" and destroyed the "countenance" of believers, but also – because they belonged among the purely creaturely endowments – tended to distract the faithful from a rational direction of their action and sensitivities to God (*PE*, p. 131; note 95). A constant and active disciplining of all emotions and their subjection to a purposeful will remained the practical ideal of Puritanism, as it had been of Catholic monasticism (*PE*, pp. 130–31).

7 On the manner in which the Protestant sects in America powerfully constricted the emotions, see *PE*, pp. 209–32 and Chapter 2 above.

15

ROUTINIZATION AND RULERSHIP

"Routinization" is an important concept in Max Weber's sociology of civilizations. Its origin can be found in the discussions of rulership (*Herrschaft*) in his massive analytical treatise, *Economy and Society*. Weber's definition of rulership, and its *three types*, must be briefly noted before examining his routinization construct.

Rulership implies for him the probability that a definable group of persons (as a result of various motives) will orient their social action to giving commands, that another definable group of persons will direct their social action toward obedience (as a result of various motives), and that commands are, in fact – to a sociologically relevant degree – carried out. Furthermore, Weber's major concern is not rulership as such, but *legitimate* rulership. A degree of legitimacy is here attributed to the rulership relationship and, for this reason, obedience acquires a voluntary element; it involves a necessary minimum of compliance. Rather than based upon sheer power, a "subjectively meaningful" (*verstehende*) relationship exists.

In daily life, a mixture of custom with means-end rational calculation of one's material interests generally provides the "motive for compliance," according to Weber. However, these motives in his analysis seldom form a reliable foundation for rulership. A further element – a *belief* in the legitimacy of the rulership – is also necessary.

The character of the typical belief, or claim to legitimacy, provides Weber with the criterium he utilizes to classify the major types

DOI: 10.4324/9781032631813-20

of legitimate rulership. For him, ruling groups can be understood as appealing to *rational-legal, traditional,* or *charismatic* principles of legitimation. What typical beliefs establish the validity of these three "pure types?" They are based on rational-legal grounds, which rest on a belief in the legality of enacted rules; on traditional grounds, which rest on an established belief in the sanctity of immemorial traditions; or, finally, Weber holds, on charismatic grounds, which rest on devotion to the exceptional sanctity, heroism, or character of an individual person.

Charismatic rulership arises in "emergency situations." These extraordinary leaders may be prophets, war heroes, politicians, or demagogues, for example. Anchored in an emotional bond and the charismatic personality's values-based message, the activity of followers becomes "value-rationalized." They feel duty bound to devote themselves completely to the charismatic figure (*E&S*, pp. 241–46, 1111–21).

The highly personal character of charismatic rulership as well as its lack of concern for everyday matters, leads to a rejection of all "external order." Under the motto "it is written, but I say unto you," the mission of a charismatic leader opposes all existing values, customs, laws, rules, and traditions as well as the "practical-rational" flow of interests and daily life in general. This innovative and even revolutionary message, as well as the location of this rulership exclusively in a single person, focuses the activity of followers upon the leader alone.

This situation, in addition to the fact that these mighty heroes can easily lose the acknowledgment of their powers as extraordinary if their "miracles" cease, makes for a permanent instability. A *routinization* – or weakening of charisma and its influence – ensues. Indeed, this manner of organizing activity around a single person and a constellation of values is fragile and fleeting, according to Weber. Even the continuation of the leader's teachings cannot be insured (*E&S*, pp. 246–54, 1121–26).

Nonetheless, in his analysis, "pure" charismatic rulership never implies an amorphous situation. Instead, an organization compatible with the leader's task and mission eventually arises, one in which disciples selected according to their charismatic endowment acquire dominant positions distinguished from the wider group of followers. A "charismatic community" then crystallizes, Weber maintains, namely, an organized group capable of preserving the charismatic figure's original aura and message. The appointment as leader of a blood relative of the bearer of charisma – "inherited charisma" – invigorates this development (*E&S*, pp. 1121–26).

15.1   Inherited Charisma and Office Charisma

Another trajectory involves concerted attempts by members to bind the new community to the primary community. Here, the original charismatic halo and message are cultivated to such an extent that they become attached to a successor community. Members of this group, as they become more formally organized into "offices" and "positions," proclaim their special status. Although in less intense, routinized manifestations, charisma then endures as "office charisma."

Weber views the acknowledgment by followers of office incumbents as possessing charisma on the basis of the halo surrounding *their offices* as of great significance: this recognition implies to him a further cultivation *of values* – and hence their endurance. They confront traditions and oppose the flux and flow of everyday interests. Thus, *neither* this "practical rationality" nor the grip of ancient conventions take full hold of the activities of either office incumbents or followers. Hence, values remain viable as the new organization expands its offices. Indeed, the values-based message of the founder may even become "institutionalized." On the basis of its office charisma, this organization now "carries" values.

In this manner, given powerful carrier groups, charisma's enduring halo provides a legitimation for values-based action. Although the heroism, inspiration, and intense brotherhood ethos of the original charismatic community has faded, its successor organization expands on the basis of constellations of amenable values and in-group solidarity. Thus, charisma retains a capacity to articulate values in all its routinized forms and thus to confront age-old, rigid traditions and daily life's pragmatic calculations, Weber insists. Far from merely a functional group serving utilitarian goals, this organization manifests a charismatic aura and its anchorage in values, he maintains.

Precisely its routinized charisma bestows great influence: group members in search of an improved future share an adhesive glue constituted *from beliefs* and a sense of community rooted in values.

On this foundation all associate *as equals* in their organization, united by legacies of the charismatic figure's message, inspiration, and values. Communities quite distinct from those anchored in ethnic identity and kinship bonds now pull persons together. Religious congregations in particular are empowered to ground a *confraternization* that overcomes insider--outsider dualisms. Charisma, Weber stresses, develops away from a "transitory gift" and loses its revolutionary thrust and radical community-building capacity. In doing so, it becomes embedded in the patterns of daily life (*E&S*, pp. 1119–26).

Weber is quite specific as concerns the routinization of charisma in religious groups. The "empirical fact" of differing "religious qualifications," he argues, serves repeatedly to set routinization processes into motion. Salvation paths must be demarcated and not least, "adjusted" to meet the laity's qualifications. How has this occurred?

15.2 The Routinization of Charisma in Religious Groups

The "virtuosi" devout have repeatedly found it necessary to compromise their ideal demands and to relate their message to the realities of everyday life. Because, for example, the mystic virtuoso's contemplative meditation is a fully "individual charisma" oriented to a silencing of the self and an escape from worldly activity, it proves unable to uproot the lay faithful from magic and ritual. Mysticism also lacks "salvation premiums" to do so, Weber contends. Thus, as religions that uphold this salvation path expand beyond an aristocratic elite of charismatically endowed figures, the contemplative search for salvation very quickly becomes routinized back to sacramental ritualism and magic (*E&S*, pp. 241–46, 1145–47).

For example, both the Hindu and Buddhist classical doctrines of world devaluation and emancipation from the wheel of *karma* rebirth followed, in response to the "religious needs" of most believers, a parallel pattern of accommodation: folk magic and orgiasticism came to permeate their intellectual soteriologies, the classical impersonal god and ethical cosmic order became personalized, and great heroes as well as the charismatic founders of sects became deified. Gurus then arose as indispensable spiritual counselors; eventually, they became worshipped themselves. And wherever a powerful priesthood of "professional practitioners" arose, the charismatic prophet's "ethical unity" and "meaningful total relationship of life to the goal of religious salvation" became routinized into worship and sanctification techniques.

Characteristic of religions carried by lower and disprivileged strata, Weber argues, are promises of compensation for disprivilege and a search for personal redeemers and saviors. Indeed, he sees a shift into savior-based practices as a "typical form of adaptation." Further accommodations occurred wherever salvation doctrines failed to meet the "religious needs" of lay groups (*E&S*, pp. 1145–48).

The charismatic founders and reformers of religions stood against this "contamination," with popularization, of doctrines, the "religious mood," and ethical action. However, beliefs, practices, and doctrines became routinized despite their efforts. Concessions to the laity disrupted the general pursuit undertaken by theologians and religion-oriented intellectuals to rationalize – or systematize – doctrines and salvation paths on behalf of internal consistency and values-based action.

The interests of groups oriented to the economy and to politics, owing to frequent competition with religious groups and sheer survival issues, were also salient to routinization. As religious groups and organizations become cohesive, charisma becomes more and more cultivated not only in order to rejuvenate and sustain the founder's message but also to strengthen the capacity of organizations and groups to "institutionalize" charisma. Status groups, each defending their own prestige, as well as economy-oriented and political groups with clear agendas and values-based aims crystallize.

Indeed, those in possession of economic power, political power, and social prestige seek, with the aim of legitimating positions of privilege, to "capture" charismatic movements and to utilize their ideas, energy, values, and aura for their own ends, Weber contends. Concomitantly, now impersonal and transformed into routinized forms, firm hierarchies appear within the religious organizations. He maintains that religious groups wish to insure a livelihood in *this life as well as* salvation in the next. This conflict-ridden process is also designated as a "routinization of charisma." Charisma's "creative aspect" again becomes absorbed – to varying degrees – into the permanent institutions of everyday life.

APPENDIX I

Civilizations East and West – An Interview

(This Interview appeared in April 2017 in the American Sociological Association's "Religion Section Newsletter"; it was conducted by David Eagle, this Section's Chairperson.)

David Eagle (DE): *The Protestant Ethic* has been on the reading list of nearly every sociologist of religion course for decades. Does it still belong? Have we exhausted the theoretical potential of Weber's thesis? Does it still have contemporary relevance?

Stephen Kalberg (SK): If instructors wish to convey the notion that civilizations are constituted not alone from rational choices, economic interests, technological tools, and the exercise of power, then assignment of *The Protestant Ethic* (PE) is appropriate. Weber's "Protestant ethic thesis" offers on this score a powerful argument: civilizations possess "a deeper level" comprised of configurations of values. Although often "invisible," these values frequently underpin the basic presuppositions in reference to which people act in daily life. Indeed, they *may* possess an independent causal capacity.

PE contends that culture – in this case religion – is relevant if economic development (or lack thereof) is to be adequately explained. This "cultural argument" is too often ignored by macrosociologists today. Weber's position captures the interest of students and sets off lively in-class debates.

PE teaches further lessons of importance to us. First, it maintains that an understanding of the present will not occur without comprehension of the various ways in which it is permeated by the past. This historical "case study", in connecting John Calvin's reforms to the "Protestant ethic" formulated by seventeenth-century "Puritan Divines", offers a vivid example of how this takes place. Second, this volume links the micro (the devout believer's remarkable attribution of *subjective meaning* to systematic work and the methodical pursuit of profit and wealth) to the macro (the capacity of a "spirit of capitalism" to assist the transformation of capitalism to *modern* capitalism). Third, *PESC* stresses that explanations of structural change (the rise of modern capitalism) require reference to the varying strength of traditions ("traditional action") as well as to sets of values ("value-rational action"). Finally, this case study offers an analysis of the ways in which *varying intensities* of values make for different outcomes.

DE: What might Weber make of the trends toward secularization we are witnessing in the West? How does religion fit within his thought about the direction of civilizations?

SK: Weber lived in a Europe that was, among its intellectual classes, mostly secularized – and had been for 100 years. Catholicism and Lutheranism seemed not to possess the staying power of American "ascetic Protestantism." Thus, Western secularization was not surprising to him. However, his posture was one of trepidation.

He perceived the Judaeo – Christian configuration of values – as having provided, through the expansion of its values of charity, universal compassion, and brotherhood, the directing "tracks" for 2,000 years. However, amid the rapid spread of modern capitalism's impersonal market forces, bureaucratization and specialization of tasks across a variety of societal arenas, and states lacking a viable civic sphere, he sought – but could not find in the West – new and influential social carriers for these values.

Religion has heretofore played a central role in defining and carrying pivotal sets of values and singular pathways of development in all the great civilizations, he maintained. Albeit weakened in the West, it will continue – given its pluralistic branches – to produce revivals on a regular basis and into the long-term future, he argues. Nonetheless, to him, the major influence of religions in the past does not alone imply their mainstream endurance.

DE: Durkheim contends that religion is an intrinsic and essential part of society. Would Weber agree? Is religion an intrinsic part of human societies or can non-religion be an option?

SK: A distinction between utilitarian action and values-based action constitutes an underlying theme in the *PE* case study, as well as throughout Weber's writings. He is convinced that the spirit of capitalism could not have arisen alone from a utilitarian striving for wealth. The "desire for riches" has been visible in all epochs and all civilizations, yet *modern* (industrial and highly organized) capitalism appeared first in Europe and northern America in the eighteenth and nineteenth centuries. Weber forcefully argues that significant economic developments do not occur simply as a consequence of an intensification of material interests or a broader appearance of "adventure capitalists" (although they continue to exist amid modern capitalism [e.g., D. Trump]).

Weber agrees in this regard completely with Durkheim: a focus upon material forces omits too much. However, Durkheim's view – religion or secular ideologies are essential to the very coherence and existence of civilizations (for him, for "social order") – is not shared by Weber. Civilizations *can* exist, he holds, on the foundation of mixtures of economic interests and concentrated political power. And if elements of charisma (or its longer-lasting variant: "office charisma") and age-old traditions (customs and conventions) are mixed in, then a longer duration can be expected.

Weber's preferences are clear. He wants civilizations that broadly cultivate an ethos of brotherhood and individual responsibility. However, his fear is evident: Western civilizations will endure but drift toward utilitarian action. Lacking will be universal ethical values adequately embedded to cultivate compassion and to spread widely an ethos of brotherhood into public spheres, whether into the market economy, the workplace, the political arena, or the civic realm. Despite the enduring influence of values-based ethics of action (the "ethic of responsibility" and the "ethic of conviction"), this vacuum will be filled, he fears, by a "pragmatic approach to life" incapable of bestowing broadly, in the end a values-based sense of dignity upon persons.

DE: There has been much ado about "the clash of civilizations" – the notion that following the Cold War, religion and cultural orientation form the primary axis of conflict in the world. Does Weber's thinking about civilizations feed into this idea or does it take us in a different direction.

SK: Weber's sociology of civilizations constitutes a major theme in my *Social Thought of Max Weber* (1917; Sage) and in my volume *Max Weber's Sociology of Civilizations* (Routledge, 2021). The distinct "rationalisms" of India, China, and the West are reconstructed in detail. Civilizations today, even in an epoch of intense globalization, retain their own contours and trajectories to a significant degree, Weber insists. Homogenization developments, rooted in an all-pervasive social media, advanced and interdependent economies, and expansive technologies, are in motion, yet each civilization's indigenous cultural values, conventions, customs, and stratification arrangements are not swept away by external "levelling" movements. Boundaries are still retained. Nonetheless, Weber does not see enmity across civilizations as inevitable. Overt conflict may be avoided even if hostilities simmer for centuries at high levels of intensity. Arrays of on-the-ground, contingent antagonisms must first become manifest.

To him, civilizations are multi-dimensional and generally dynamic. Rather than to be comprehended through an organic holism lens, they are better conceptualized as constituted from various "spheres of life" (the law, religion, economy, domination, family, clan, and status group domains) in constant motion, at times falling into coalitions and at other times into antagonistic relationships. Furthermore, Weber opposes the notion that a "primary" cause exists and remains committed to multi-causal and conjunctural modes of analysis. Hence, he discusses repeatedly the many ways in which the spheres of life, in interaction with empirical developments, call forth paradoxical outcomes and unforeseen consequences. All linear views of historical development and all "inevitable" scenarios are strongly rejected, above all in his opus *Economy and Society*. Cultural and religious differences across civilizations *may* lead to a "clash," but do not invariably do so.

APPENDIX II

Critical Remarks on the Translation of *The Protestant Ethic* by Talcott Parsons

Students of Max Weber have long agreed that the single available translation into English of his most accessible work, *The Protestant Ethic and the Spirit of Capitalism*, is profoundly flawed. I will note here a few of the problems with the translation by Talcott Parsons and summarize several new features of my translation.

It should first be emphasized that the translation by Parsons is now almost 100 years old. As translations age, they become less accessible to younger audiences. The English language changes quickly, and many of Parsons's terms and formulations, while appropriate earlier, today ring hollow and even odd. Some are barely decipherable, especially to *PE*'s major audience today: American undergraduates in social sciences courses.

Moreover, Parsons translated for an audience steeped in classical, liberal arts texts and well versed in the European scholarship of the nineteenth century. Whereas he could assume readers would have some knowledge of persons Weber refers to repeatedly (e.g., Melanchthon, Fox, Alberti, Baxter, Fugger, Zinzendorf), familiarity with his Latin phrases, and a general acquaintance with the history of Western religions, today's reader requires assistance.

For these reasons alone, a new translation that includes a glossary of key terms, endnotes that identify names, places, and religious documents, and a translation into English of Latin expressions is long overdue. Although the remarks to follow are critical of Parsons, there can be no doubt that Weber scholars, as well as sociologists generally, owe to him a tremendous debt for recognizing *PE* as a classic study.

A.1   Problems with the Translation by Parsons

Translation Errors: The weakness of Parsons's understanding of German, and core aspects of Weber's sociology, is apparent to the specialist on every page of his translation. A loss of nuance is evident in every complex sentence and in every paragraph. On a number of occasions, words and passages are left untranslated. Simple errors of translation occur in nearly every paragraph. The following is a partial listing of important terms incorrectly translated[1] that appear on several occasions or frequently.[2]

German	Appropriate translation	Parsons translation	
Adäquateste	Most adequate (in the sense of "causal adequacy")	Most suitable	
Berufsakese	Vocational asceticism	Worldly calling/ vocational tasks	
Berufsethik	Vocational ethic	Rational ethics	
Eigenart	Characteristic quality	Peculiar	
	Particular feature	Peculiar	
Einzelne	A person	Individual	
Lebensgebieten	Separate realms of life	Various departments of life	
Einzigartig	Unique, singular		Peculiar
Entwicklung	Development	Evolution	
Gewinnstreben	Search for profit	Acquisition	
Spezifisch typische	Specific, unique	Peculiar	
Eigenart	Typical quality/ typical uniqueness	Special peculiarity	

Egregious errors, where Parsons loses track of Weber's argument and moves in directions fully contradictory to Weber's text and intentions, are found on nearly every page. Only two examples can be offered:

Translation by Parsons (p. 54/36)*: And in truth, this peculiar idea, so familiar to us today, but in reality so little a matter, of course, of one's duty in a calling, is what is most characteristic of the social ethic of capitalistic culture, and is in a sense the fundamental basis of it. It is an obligation which the individual is supposed to feel and does feel toward the content of his professional activity, no matter in what it consists, in particular no matter whether it appears on the surface as a utilization of his personal powers or only of his material possessions (as capital).

*The second number refers to Weber's *Gesammelte Aufsätze zur Religionssoziologie I* (Collected Essays in the Sociology of Religion, vol. 1; Tübingen: Mohr Verlag, 1920), hereafter GARS.

My translation (p. 18/36): In fact, this peculiar idea of a *duty to have a vocational calling*, so familiar to us today but *actually not* at all self-evident, is the idea that is characteristic of the "social ethic" of modern capitalist culture. In a certain sense, it is even of constitutive significance for it. It implies a notion of duty that individuals ought to experience, and do vis-à-vis the content of their "vocational" activity. This notion appears regardless of the particular nature of the activity and regardless especially of whether this activity seems to involve (as it does for people with a spontaneous, fun-loving disposition) nothing more than a simple utilization of their capacity for labor or their treatment of it as only a material possession (as "capital") (emphasis and inverted commas in original).

Translation by Parsons (pp. 64–65/49; here, Parsons replaces Weber's technical term "adequacy" with the value-laden term "suitable"): To be sure, the capitalistic form of an enterprise and the spirit in which it is run generally stand in some sort of adequate relationship to each other, but not in one of necessary interdependence. Nevertheless, we provisionally use the expression spirit of (modern) capitalism to describe that attitude which seeks profit rationally and systematically in the manner which we have illustrated by the example of Benjamin Franklin. This, however, is justified by the historical fact that that attitude of mind has on the one hand found its most suitable expression in capitalistic enterprise, while on the other the enterprise has derived its most suitable motive force from the spirit of capitalism.

My translation (pp. 26–27/49): Rather than being in "lawful" dependency, the "capitalist" form of an economy and the spirit in which it is operated, in fact, exist generally in a less determinant relationship, namely, one of "adequacy" to each other. Nonetheless, if we provisionally employ the phrase *"spirit of* (modern) *capitalism"* to refer to the *particular frame* of mind that, as in our example of Benjamin Franklin, strives systematically and rationally *in a calling* for legitimate profit, then we are doing so for historical reasons. We do so on the one hand because this frame of mind finds its most adequate form in the modern capitalist company and, on the other, because the capitalist company discovers in this frame of mind the motivating force most adequate to it.

A.2   The Lack of a Standardized Terminology

Parsons translates key terms variously, even randomly. For example:

Arbeit – work, labor, job

Antrieb – motive, pressure, incentive, sanction

Bedeutung – significance, importance

Beruf – calling, professional, worldly affairs

Berufsarbeit – work at a calling, worldly activity, daily work

Berufsleben – occupation, routine of life in a worldly calling, worldly activity

bürgerlich – bourgeois, middle class

Diesseitigkeit – worldliness, worldly activity, workaday world

Entzauberung – elimination of magic, rationalization

Gefühl – emotion, feeling, affect

Gesinnung – attitude, mentality, temperament, outlook, attitude of mind

Lebensführung – way of life, sort of life, manner of life, conduct, actual conduct, practical conduct, elementary forms of conduct, life, ordered life, manner of living, ethical conduct

Lebensstil – way of life, style of life, standard of life, uniformity of life, manner of living

Methodisch – rational, methodical

Nüchtern – sober, moderate, carefully, shrewd, normally, temperate, caution

Unternehmer – managers, entrepreneurs, businessmen

Verhalten – behavior, conduct, action, attitude

Parsons fails to note that *PE*'s major arguments are organized around a set of central terms and dichotomies. Hence, adherence to a standardized vocabulary is indispensable if Weber's analysis is to be clearly rendered. On many occasions, a single English term stands as the translation for several German terms. For example:

"Attitude" for Gesinnung, Gebarung, Verhalten, Lebenstimmung, Lebensanschauung, and Lebensauffassung

"Conception" for Gedanke, Auffassung, Begriff, and Begriffskonzept

"Conduct" for Lebensführung, Wandel, Gebarung, Alltagspraxis, Lebenspraxis, Praxis, and Verhalten

"Worldly" for diesseitig, weltlich, and innerweltliche

Weber's deep concern for terminological precision is lost. Moreover, an entire set of dichotomies emphasized by Weber, owing to non-standardized translations by Parsons, remains scarcely visible. For example: "world" versus "religion," "inner interests" (spiritual) versus "external interests" (political, economic), and "striving for salvation" versus "salvation through a feeling."

The Appearance of the Text: Weber guides his reader to major concepts and themes through the use of italics. Ninety-five percent of his italics do not appear in the English translation (e.g., *modern* capitalism). Moreover, Weber's frequent placing of terms in inverted commas, in order to indicate his awareness of their controversial nature (e.g., "national character," "rational," "irrational," "productivity" under capitalism, "achievements" of the Reformation, the "spirit" of capitalism, "ideas," the "calling"), is omitted from the Parsons translation.

The Failure to Identify Noun Referents: Because German nouns and pronouns are gendered, a pronoun can be traced back easily to the last same-gendered noun. Parsons's routine translation of the gendered pronoun into the non-gendered "it," rather than repeating the noun referent, causes perpetual confusion. Innumerable passages are rendered unclear owing to this practice. For example: "With the breakdown of tradition and the more or less complete extension of free economic enterprise,...the new thing has not generally been ethically justified and encouraged..." (*PE*, pp. 58/43). What is the reference for "new thing?"

Punctuation and Syntax: Parsons generally commands only one mode of punctuation – the comma. Weber's colons, semi-colons, and hyphens, all of which are utilized in a careful manner in order to convey nuance, are uniformly omitted in the translation by Parsons. His syntax itself often prevents understanding. For example:

1 "With that, on the;:other hand, it combined the certainty which, though incidental for Calvin, came to be of great importance for Puritanism, that God would bless His own in this life..." (p. 164/180).
2 "In addition to the relationships already pointed out, it is important for the general inner attitude of the Puritans, above all, that the belief that they were God's chosen people saw in them a great renaissance" (p. 166/182).
3 "In the Netherlands (Pieter de la Court and others), that had been secularized to the effect that the mass of men only labour when necessity forces them to do so" (p. 177/199).
4 "It remained for Puritan Asceticism to take part in the severe English Poor Relief Legislation which fundamentally changed the situation" (p. 178/199).
5 "In this respect Protestant Asceticism added in itself nothing new. But it not only deepened this idea most powerfully, it also created the force which was alone decisive for its effectiveness: the psychological sanction of it through the conception of this labour as a calling, as the best, often in the last analysis the only means of attaining certainty of grace" (p. 178/200).
6 "Like war and piracy, trade has often been unrestrained in its relations with foreigners and those outside the group" (p. 57/42).

The Substitution of a "Parsonian" Vocabulary: Repeatedly, Parsons employs terms that cannot serve as adequate translations of the German original; for example, "norms," "attitude," "fact," "system," "opinion," and "sanction."[3] The effect is to level out nuance, to transform Weber into a structuralist thinker, and to diminish *PE*'s powerful interpretive understanding (*verstehen*) analysis of subjective meaning. Parsons also tones down Weber's vocabulary of conflict and replaces Weber's gender-neutral language with a gendered terminology (e.g., *Mensch* [person] and *Man* [one] are translated as "man"; *Menschengruppe* as "group of men"; *Kaufleute* as "businessmen"; and *Durchschnittsmenschen* as "average man").

The Social Psychology of Belief: Weber's focus upon the motives for action in the different religions (Catholicism, Lutheranism,

Calvinism, Pietism, Methodism, and the baptizing sects) and his subtle and differentiated analysis of *how* they vary depending upon the nature of salvation doctrines and their transformation into pastoral care practices (and, at this level, "psychological rewards") is never apparent in the translation by Parsons. This analysis unveils Weber as a powerful microsociologist concerned with how diverse motivations for action are formulated on the one hand with the reconstruction, through interpretive understanding, of believers' subjective meaning on the other hand. *PE* offers the best illustration of Weber's *verstehende* sociology.

The Pluralism of Weber's Dialogues: The Parsons translation exaggerates, in various ways, the role of Marx in this study (not least by often translating *bürgerlich* as "bourgeoisie" rather than as "middle class" (see *PE*, p. 420) and *Schichten* as "classes" rather than "strata." Weber locks horns as well with Hegel's Idealism, Werner Sombart's evolutionism, Adam Smith's acontextual understanding of the "laws of the market," race-based explanations for behavior and the "superiority of the West," Hegelian schools of theology that drew a direct line from a religion's salvation doctrine to the behavior of believers, and numerous nineteenth-century thinkers who failed to distinguish between ethical action based in values and means-end rational action. To Weber, all of these schools omitted a social psychology of belief. They were also insufficiently attentive to the ways in which religion-based motivations influence action.

The Intertwining of Past and Present: Weber's multiple illustrations of how behavior originating out of belief may slowly lose its religious dimension and become "routinized" into utilitarian action (and how persons then incorrectly understand the causes of this utilitarian action by reference alone to structural forces and means-end rational pursuits in the present) are occluded in the Parsons translation. Yet this "deep cultural" mode of analysis is quintessentially Weberian, as is his intertwining in this manner of past and present.

The Logic of Ideas: While Parsons's translation conveys the importance Weber attributes to ideas and values, it fails to articulate a related central point: theologians, and even the lay faithful, have struggled to render ideas internally *consistent* (particularly in order to decipher appropriate routes to salvation), and these confrontations with ideas follow rational rules of logic. Moreover, the cognitive resolution of dilemmas anchored in ideas may eventually influence the action of believers, indeed even their economic activity (see Kalberg, 2012, pp. 43–72).

The Levelling Out of Causal Analyses: Weber's incessant focus upon issues of causality, as concerns both "internal" (religious) and "external" (political and economic) forces, is seldom apparent in the translation by Parsons. In this regard, the translation of *Wahl-verwandtschaft* (elective affinity) as "correlation" is unfortunate. In particular, the manner in which external forces provide facilitating (though not determining) contexts for the unfolding of internal forces remains scarcely visible (see Kalberg, 1994, pp. 151–86), as is true of Weber's micro level causal analyses of how the lives of the devout become organized around ethical values and "directed" (*methodische Lebensführung*).

A.3   Does It Matter? A Few Passages Compared

The translation by Parsons *does* convey the notion that Weber is, in this volume, a sociologist looking at values and ideas and document-ing their independence from political and economic causes, indeed even their "autonomy" as causal forces. The "spirit" of capitalism, according to Weber, arose in part out of the domain of religion. While this is the book's central message, Weber's complex causal argument is impossible to follow in the translation by Parsons. The crucial Chap-ter 4 on Calvinism, Pietism, Methodism, and the "baptizing sects" (the Quakers, Baptists, and Mennonites) repeatedly loses the thread and thrust of Weber's analysis.[4] Seven examples must be noted from this pivotal chapter.

Translation by Parsons (pp. 120–21/119): But the most important thing was the fact that the man who, par excellence, lived a rational life in the religious sense was, and remained, alone the monk. Thus asceticism, the more strongly it gripped an individual, simply served to drive him farther away from everyday life, because the holiest task was definitely to surpass all worldly morality. Luther, who was not in any sense fulfilling any law of development but acting upon his quite personal experience, which was, though at first somewhat uncertain in its practical consequences, later pushed farther by the political situ-ation, had repudiated that tendency, and Calvinism simply took this over from him.

My translation (pp. 73–74/119): The decisive difference involved another issue, however. In medieval Catholicism, the person who lived methodically in the religious sense par excellence was *actually only the monk*. And he remained the only figure to do so. Hence, the more intensively asceticism took hold of the individual, the *more* it drove him *out of* everyday life and into the monastery, precisely because the uniquely holy life was to be found only in a *surpassing* of everyday morality. Luther first abolished this mode of leading the religious life, and Calvinism here simply followed Luther. It must be emphasized that Luther abolished the monasteries not as an actor fulfilling some "developmental historical trend" (*Entwicklungstendenz)*, but entirely because of his personal experiences (which were, by the way, at the beginning quite unclear in regard to the direction in which they would lead; later, however, they were driven further by the *political* situation).

Translation by Parsons (p. 126/125): The combination of faith in absolutely valid norms with absolute determinism and the complete transcendentality of God was in its way a product of great genius. At the same time, it was, in principle, very much more modern than the milder doctrine, making greater concessions to the feelings which subjected God to the moral law. Above all, we shall see again and again how fundamental is the idea of proof for our problem. Since its practical significance as a psychological basis for rational morality could be studied in such purity in the doctrine of predestination, it was best to start there with the doctrine in its most consistent form. But it forms a recurring framework for the connection between faith and conduct in the denominations to be studied below.

Within the Protestant movement, the consequences which it inevitably had for the ascetic tendencies of the conduct of its first adherents form in principle the strongest antithesis to the relative moral helplessness of Lutheranism. The Lutheran *gratia amissibilis* [loss of grace], which could always be regained through penitent contrition evidently, in itself, contained no sanction for what is for us the most important result of ascetic Protestantism, a systematic rational ordering of the moral life as a whole. The Lutheran faith thus left the spontaneous vitality of impulsive action and naive emotion more nearly unchanged. The motive to constant self-control and thus to a deliberate regulation of one's own life, which the gloomy doctrine of Calvinism gave, was lacking.

My translation (pp. 78–79/125): Moreover, in an ingenious manner, the doctrine of predestination linked absolute determinism, the complete transcendence of the supernatural realm, and the belief in unconditionally valid norms. Simultaneously, this linkage was in principle much more *modern* than the milder doctrines that addressed more the feelings of the devout and subjected even God to moral laws. Above all, as will be repeatedly apparent in the sections below, fundamental for our discussion is the investigation of the idea of a *testifying* to one's belief as the psychological point of origin for methodical ethics.

We proceeded above by examining the doctrine of predestination and its significance for everyday life. In addition, because the idea of testifying through action to belief recurs on a regular basis among the denominations still to be considered, it proved feasible to study this idea first, with Calvinism, in its "pure form." In other words, we constructed a model of the way in which belief and ethics are connected; this model can now be "applied" to the further denominations. In this exercise, because the consequences of the doctrine of predestination were the most broad-ranging, it was necessary to begin with this doctrine.

Within Protestantism, the *doctrine of predestination* had great consequences among its earliest followers, in particular with respect to an ascetic formation of an organized life. Lutheranism, however, most thoroughly blocked its impact. Indeed, Lutheranism formed the *most principled* antithesis to Calvinism. A (relative) lack of moral awareness arose from Lutheranism rather than an ascetic organization of life. Apparently, the Lutheran *gratia amissibilis*, which could always be won back again through penitent contrition, contained *as such* no motivational push toward a systematic, rational formation of the believer's ethical life (which is important for us as a product of ascetic Protestantism). Rather, Lutheran piety left largely unaltered the spontaneous vitality of instinctive action and the untempered life based on feelings. It lacked a motivational push toward an uninterrupted self-control and hence toward a *planned* regulation of one's own life in any sense. Here, Lutheranism stood in contrast to the motivational impulse contained in the melancholy teachings of Calvinism.

Translation by Parsons (p. 149/158): But in so far as Baptism affected the normal workaday world, the idea that God only speaks when the flesh is silent evidently meant an incentive to the deliberate weighing of courses of action and their careful justification in terms of the individual conscience. The later Baptist communities, most particularly the Quakers, adopted this quiet, moderate, eminently conscientious character of conduct.

My translation (p. 97/158): "Waiting" was somewhat altered, however, as members of the baptizing congregations began to stream into this-worldly vocational callings. The original idea – God speaks only when wants and desires are silent – was changed. The devout were now apparently taught to *deliberate* calmly before acting and to orient their action only after a careful investigation of the individual *conscience*. This calm, dispassionate, and supremely conscience-bound disposition of character then became manifest in the practical life of the later baptizing communities (as occurred also, and to an unusual degree, in the case of the Quakers).

Translation by_Parsons (pp. 152–53/161–62): We have preferred rather to take the results which subjective adoption of an ascetic faith might have had in the conduct of the individual. This was not only because this side of the thing has previously received far less attention than the other, but also because the effect of Church discipline was by no means always a similar one. On the contrary, the ecclesiastical supervision of the life of the individual, which, as it was practised in the Calvinistic State Churches, almost amounted to an inquisition, might even retard that liberation of individual powers which was conditioned by the rational ascetic pursuit of salvation, and in some cases actually did so.

The mercantelistic regulations of the State might develop industries, but not, or certainly not alone, the spirit of capitalism; where they assumed a despotic, authoritarian character, they to a large extent directly hindered it. Thus a similar effect might well have resulted from ecclesiastical regimentation when it became excessively despotic. It enforced a particular type of external conformity, but in some cases weakened the subjective motives of rational conduct. Any discussion of this point must take account of the great difference between the results of the authoritarian moral discipline of the Established Churches and the corresponding discipline in the sects which rested on voluntary submission. That the Baptist movement everywhere and in principle founded sects and not Churches was certainly as favorable to the intensity of their asceticism as was the case, to differing degrees, with those Calvinistic, Methodist, and Pietist communities which were driven by their situations into the formation of voluntary groups.

My translation (pp. 99–100/161–62): Instead, we will first examine the effects on *each believer's* organization of life that are possible when individuals convert to a religious devoutness anchored in asceticism. We will proceed in this manner for two reasons: this side of our theme has until now received far less attention, and the effect of church discipline cannot be viewed as always leading in the same direction.

In those regions where a Calvinist state church held sway, the authoritarian supervision *(kirchenpolizeiliche Kontrolle)* of the believer's life was practiced to a degree that rivaled an inquisition. This supervision *could* work even *against* that emancipation of individual energies originating out of the believer's ascetic striving to methodically acquire a sense of certainty as belonging among the saved. It did so under certain circumstances. Just as mercantilist regimentation by the state could indeed give birth to industries but not (at least not alone) to the capitalist "spirit" (which this regimentation crippled in various ways, wherever it assumed a despotic-authoritarian character), the church's regimentation of asceticism could have the same effect. Wherever the church developed too far in a harshly authoritarian direction, it coerced believers into adhering to specific forms of external behavior. In doing so, however, under certain circumstances, the church then crippled the individual's motivation to organize life in a methodical manner.

Every explanation of this point must note the great difference between the effects of the despotic-authoritarianism of state *churches* and the effects of the despotism of *sects*. The latter rests upon voluntary subjection. The creation by the baptizing movement, in all its denominations, of "sects" rather than "churches" contributed to the intensity of its asceticism. Such intensity occurred as well, to varying degrees, in the Calvinist, Pietist, and Methodist communities. In *practice*, all were pushed in the direction of forming voluntary communities.

Translation by Parsons (pp. 132–33/136–37): As a dogmatic basis of systematic religious conduct, Spener combines Lutheran ideas with the specifically Calvinistic doctrine of good works as such which are undertaken with the intention of doing honor to God. He also has a faith, suggestive of Calvinism, in the possibility of the elect attaining a relative degree of Christian perfection. But the theory lacked consistency. Spener, who was strongly influenced by the Mystics, attempted in a rather uncertain but essentially Lutheran manner to describe the systematic type of Christian conduct which was essential to even his form of Pietism than to justify it. He did not derive the *certitudo salutis* from sanctification; instead of the idea of proof, he adopted Luther's somewhat loose connection between faith and works, which has been discussed above.

But again and again, in so far as the rational and ascetic element of Pietism outweighed the emotional, the ideas essential to our thesis maintained their place. These were: (1) that the methodical development of one's own state of grace to a higher and higher degree of certainty and perfection in terms of the law was a sign of grace; and (2) that God's Providence works through those in such a state of perfection, that is, He gives them His signs if they wait patiently and deliberate methodically. Labor in a calling was also the ascetic activity par excellence for A. H. Francke: that God Himself blessed His chosen ones through the success of their labors was as undeniable to him as we shall find it to have been to the Puritans.

And as a substitute for the double decree Pietism worked out ideas which, in a way essentially similar to Calvinism, though milder, established an aristocracy of the elect resting on God's especial grace, with all the psychological results pointed out above.

My translation (pp. 83–84/136–37): In order to ground dogmatically the systematic-religious organization of life, Spener combines Lutheran trains of thought with distinctly Reformist elements: the notion that good works as such are undertaken with a view to the *honor* of God and the Lutheran belief (which also resonated with the Reformist Church) in the possibility for the elect to arrive at a relative degree of Christian perfection.

Yet, precisely the element of logical consistency is lacking in Spener's theorizing. Although the organized Christian life was also essential for the Pietism of Spener (who was strongly influenced by mysticism), he weakened its systematic character. In a somewhat unclear, but essentially Lutheran, way of describing more than grounding, Spener never attempted to derive the *certitudo salutis* from a striving by the believer toward elect status. Instead of the idea of a testifying through conduct to one's belief, he selected the less strict Lutheran notion of faith (as discussed earlier) as the mechanism through which the believer could feel certain of his salvation.

As long, however, as the rational-ascetic component in Pietism retained the upper hand over the element of feeling, the ideas decisive for our vantage point again and again came forcefully to the fore. First, the methodical development of the believer's own holiness in the direction of ever higher degrees of consolidation and perfection, as monitored by conformity to *God's laws*, constitutes in Pietism a *sign* of one's state of grace. Second, it is God's providence *at work* in just this improvement by the faithful; after patient waiting and *methodical reflection*, He is giving a sign to believers. Work in a calling was also for Francke the ascetic means *par excellence*. He was firmly convinced (as were the Puritans, as we shall see) that God himself, through the success of the believer's work, was blessing His chosen.

Moreover, as surrogates for the "double decree" [according to which a few were saved and most were condemned], Pietism created ideas that were essentially the same, although less vibrant, than those following from the idea of predestination (e.g., the idea that God's special grace had established an aristocracy of the elect). The same psychological consequences of this idea followed for both Pietists and Calvinists (as described above) (see *GARS*, pp. 136–37).

Translation by Parsons (pp. 135–36/140–41; on Zinzendorf's Pietism): Also under the influence of the repudiation of conventicles and the retention of the confession, there developed an essentially Lutheran dependence on the sacraments. Moreover, Zinzendorf's peculiar principle that the childlikeness of religious feeling was a sign of its genuineness, as well as the use of the lot as a means of revealing God's will, strongly counteracted the influence of rationality in conduct. On the whole, within the sphere of influence of the Count, the anti-rational, emotional elements predominated much more in the religion of the Herrnhuters than elsewhere in Pietism. The connection between morality and the forgiveness of sins in Spangenberg's *Idea fides fratrum* is as loose as in Lutheranism generally. Zinzendorf's repudiation of the Methodist pursuit of perfection is part, here as everywhere, of his fundamentally eudaemonistic ideal of having men experience eternal bliss (he calls it happiness) emotionally in the present, instead of encouraging them by rational labor to make sure of it in the next world.

Nevertheless, the idea that the most important value of the Brotherhood as contrasted with other Churches lay in an active Christian life, in missionary, and, which was brought into connection with it, in professional work in a calling, remained a vital force with them.

My translation (p. 86/140–41): Moreover, there developed in Zinzendorf's Pietism, influenced by those who rejected the conventicles and wished to maintain Confession, an essentially Lutheran-influenced tendency to bind the mediation of salvation to the sacraments. Finally, certain aspects of Zinzendorf's own positions had the effect of strongly counteracting the rationalism of the organized and directed life; for example, his view that the *childlike nature* of the religious experience is best understood as a sign of its genuineness (a basic principle particular to him) and that the drawing of *lots* constitutes a device to reveal God's will.

Indeed, such views standing against the rational organization of the believer's life became so prominent that, as far as Zinzendorf's impact is concerned, on the whole anti-rational, *feeling*-based elements played the greater role (as apparent in the piety of the Herrnhuter much more than in other branches of Pietism). The connection between moral conduct and the forgiveness of sins in [the Pietist Bishop August Gottlieb] Spangenberg's [1704–1792] volume, *Idea Fidei_Fratrum* [Idea of Brotherly Trust"], is likewise weak, as in Lutheranism in general. Zinzendorf's rejection of the Methodist striving for perfection corresponds, here as well as elsewhere, to his basically eudemonistical ideal. He wished, namely, to allow believers even in the *present* to experience salvation (or "blessedness") through *feelings*. Moreover, Zinzendorf opposed advising the faithful to follow the Calvinist route; that is, he opposed the effort to acquire certainty of salvation for the *next life* through rational work and an organization of their present lives.

Nonetheless, other elements in Zinzendorf's teachings had the effect of introducing the organized and directed life among believers. An idea unique to the Brethren Congregation remained viable in Zinzendorf's theology: the idea that the decisive value in the activity of the Christian life lies in missionary work and (as thereby brought into association with it) in work in a calling [bridging material in brackets is mine].

Translation by Parsons (p. 137/143): But compared to Calvinism, the rationalization of life was necessarily less intense because the pressure of occupation with a state of grace which had continually to be proved, and which was concerned for the future in eternity, was diverted to the present emotional state.

My translation (pp. 87–88/143): In any event, however, in comparison to *Calvinism*, the intensity of the rationalization of life in Pietism must necessarily be less. The reason is that the inner motive deriving from the thought of having to testify, over and over again from the beginning, to a state of grace that gives security for an eternal *future* has in Pietism, owing to its orientation to the believer's feelings, been redirected onto the *present*.

Critical themes developed at length by Weber in Chapter 4, such as the varying extent to which believers in the different ascetic Protestant denominations are motivated to organize life methodically around a set of ethical values and hence to overcome the *status naturae*, and the diverging ways in which the ascetic Protestant faithful testify, through their conduct generally and work specifically, to their sincere belief and otherwise pursue courses of action that provide a psychological certainty of "elect salvation status," are obscured. It is nearly impossible to follow (a) the manifestations of Weber's crucial concept (translated usually by Parsons as "prove") in the different denominations or (b) the manner in which some emphasized more so a "striving toward salvation through this-worldly conduct" (*Heiligung*) and others stressed more a *feeling* (*Gefühl*) relationship with God.

Finally, two familiar passages from my translation should be noted. Readers may compare them to Parsons' translation.

Prefatory Remarks (*Vorbemerkung*; "PR," p. 233 / *GARS*, p. 1):

Any heir of modern European civilization (*Kulturwelt*) will, unavoidably and justifiably, address universal-historical problems with a particular question in mind: What concatenation of circumstances led in the West, and only in the West, to the appearance of cultural phenomena that stood – at least as we like to imagine – in a historical line of development that possessed *universal* significance and validity.

Last pages of PE: pp. 177–79/*GARS*, pp. 203–04; all endnotes omitted:

The Puritan *wanted* to be a persona with a vocational calling; we *must* be. For to the extent that asceticism moved out of the monastic cell and was carried over into the life of work in a vocational calling and then commenced to rule over this-worldly morality, it helped to do its part to build the might cosmos of the modern economic order. This economy is bound to the technical and economic conditions of mechanized, machine-based production.

This cosmos today determines the style of life *not* only of those directly engaged in economically productive activity but of all born into this grinding mechanism (*Triebwerk*). It does so with overwhelming force, and perhaps it will continue to do so until the last ton of fossil fuel has burnt to ashes. The concern of material goods, according to Baxter, should lie on the shoulders of his saints like "a lightweight coat that one can throw off at any time." Yet, fate allowed this coat to become a steel-hard casing (*stahlhartes Gehaeuse*). To the extent that asceticism undertook to transform and influence the world, the world's material goods acquired an increasing and, in the end, inescapable power over people as never before in history.

Today asceticism's spirit has fled from this casing – whether with finality who knows? Victorious capitalism, in any case, ever since it came to rest on a mechanical foundation, no longer needs asceticism as a supporting pillar. Even the optimistic temperament of the Enlightenment, asceticism's joyful heir, appears finally to be fading. And the idea of an "obligation to search for and then accept a vocational calling" now wanders around in our lives as the ghost of past religious beliefs. Persons today [1905] usually reject entirely all attempts to make sense of a "fulfillment of one's calling" wherever this notion cannot be directly aligned with the highest spiritual and cultural values, or wherever, conversely, it is not experienced subjectively simply as economic coercion. The pursuit of gain in the region where it has become most completely unchained and stripped of its religious-ethical meaning, the United States, tends to be associated with purely competitive passions. Not infrequently, these passions directly imprint this pursuit with the character of a sports event.

No one any longer knows who will live in this casing and whether entirely new prophets or a mighty rebirth of ancient ideas and ideals will stand at the end of this prodigious development. *Or*, however, if neither, whether a mechanized ossification, embellished with a sort of rigidly compelled sense of self-importance, will arise. Then, indeed, if ossification appears, the saying might be true for the "last humans" in this long civilizational development: "…narrow specialists without minds, pleasure-seekers without heart; in its conceit this nothingness imagines it has climbed to a level of humanity never before attempted."

Here, however, we have fallen into the realm of value-judgments, with which this purely historical analysis should not be burdened.

Nor should it be burdened by judgments rooted in faith. The further task is a different one: to chart the significance of ascetic rationalism. The above sketch has only hinted at its importance.

Its significance for the content of a community-building, ethical *social policy* must now be outlined, that is, for the type of organization of social groups, ranging from the conventicle to the state, and their functions.

A.4 Features of This New Translation

I have undertaken a number of changes in order to offer *PE* in a highly accessible format. Persons, places, and obscure documents and groups have been identified, either within brackets in the text or in new endnotes. Latin, Italian, Dutch, and French phrases have been translated. Weber's italicization and inverted commas, as helpful red threads of orientation, have been restored. Wherever theme changes occur without a subheading, additional spaces have been inserted between paragraphs. The translation of key terms has been standardized and a glossary of approximately 40 terms has been added (e.g., middle class, testify, organization of life, frame of mind, elective affinity, calling, economic form, economic ethic, ideal type, rationalization, *status naturae*, subjective meaning, and utilitarian adaptation to the world). These terms have been set in bold type upon first usage in each chapter. Innumerable partial bibliographical entries have been adjusted and completed. All paragraphs and endnotes that Weber added in 1920 revision have been marked.

Furthermore, I have undertaken a far more radical shortening of Weber's sentences and paragraphs than undertaken by Parsons. In addition, because Weber's text occasionally lapses into a shorthand format, bridging and transitional phrases have been added into the text, in brackets, on behalf of clarity. Finally, I have written an extensive introduction that summarizes major aspects of Weber's argument regarding the origins of the "spirit" of capitalism, examines an array of *PE*'s major themes, discusses the intellectual debates in Germany on the rise of modern capitalism at the time of the writing of *PE*, and investigates *PE* in reference to Weber's sociology generally.

Through these innovations, I'm hopeful that this new translation will present this classic text in a more clear, accurate, and readable manner. The Oxford University Press edition (2011) also includes Weber's two essays on the Protestant sects in the United States (see pp. 209–32). This edition also includes my translation of the "Prefatory Remarks" (*Vorbemerkung*) to his three-volume comparative series published as the *Economic Ethics of the World Religions*.[5] While the former essays complement *PE*, the latter essay conveys, in preliminary form, the contours of the non-idealist macrosociology that Weber believed to be indispensable for comprehension of modern capitalism's rise and expansion in a particular region and in a particular epoch (see Kalberg, 2014, 2021; see chapters 5 and 6).

Notes

1 This phrase is used with caution. Translators can, of course, have honest disagreements and the interpretation of terms is inevitable in the translation of all complex texts. Even Weber scholars in command of both English and German will disagree on the appropriate translation of a number of terms. This (partial) list is comprised only of blatant errors of translation. Furthermore, many of Weber's terms can be translated *only* by reference to the context within which they appear. Such terms are excluded from this list.
2 Hence, this is a list quite different from one that would include *all* translation errors. Such a list, in my view, would comprise approximately 200 terms.
3 Weber himself uses *System* and *Norm* very rarely. (The German is unchanged.)
4 Parsons incorrectly understands "the Baptist Sects" as referring alone to the Baptist denomination.
5 This classic essay was placed in the Parsons edition before *PE* and given the misleading title of "Author's Introduction." Generations of students have incorrectly understood it to be an introduction to *PE*.

REFERENCES

Abbott, Andrew. 1983. "Professional Ethics." *American Journal of Sociology*, 8: 8.

Abel, Richard I. 1985. "Comparative Sociology of Legal Progression: An Exploratory Essay." *American Bar Foundation Research Journal*, 10: 1–79.

Abel, Richard I. and Philip S.C. Lewis (eds.). 1989. *Lawyers in Society: Comparartive Theories*. Berkeley: University of California Press.

Albrow, Martin. 1990. *Max Weber's Construction of Social Theory*. London: Palgrave Macmillan.

Alexander, Jeffrey (ed.). 1985. *Neo-Functionalism*. Los Angeles: Sage.

———. 1990. "Neofunctionalism Today: A Theoretical Tradition." Pp. 33–67 in George Ritzer (ed.) *Frontiers of Social Theory*. New York: Columbia University Press.

Barber, Bernad. 1978–1979. "Control and Responsibility in the Powerful Professions." *Political Science Quarterly*, 93: 599–615.

Bell, Daniel. 1996. *The Cultural Contradictions of Capitalism*. New York: Doubleday.

Bellah, Robert. 1957. *Tokugawa Religion*. Boston, MA: Beacon Press.

Bellah, Robert N., Richard Madsen, William M. Sullivan, Ann Swidler, and Steven M. Tipton. 1985. *Habits of the Heart*. Berkeley: University of California Press.

Bendix, Reinhard. 1956. *Work and Authority in Industry*. New York: John Wiley.

———. 1962. *Max Weber: An Intellectual Portrait*. New York: Doubleday Anchor.

————. 1965. "Max Weber's Sociology Today." *International Social Science Journal*, 17: 9–22.

————. 1978. *Kings or People*. Berkeley: University of California Press.

Bendix, Reinhard, and Guenther Roth. 1971. *Scholarship and Partisanship: Essays on Max Weber*. Berkeley: University of California Press.

Besnard, Philippe (ed.). 1970. *Protestantisme et capitalisme: La controverse post-Weberienne*. Paris: Presses Universitaire.

Brocke, Berhard vom (ed.). 1987. *Sombart's 'Moderner Kapitalismus.'* Munich: Beck Verlag.

Burger, Thomas. 1976. *Max Weber's Theory of Concept Formation*. Durham, NC: Duke University Press.

Buxton, William. 1985. *Talcott Parsons and the Capitalist Nation-State*. Toronto: University of Toronto Press.

Coleman, James. 1990. *Foundations of Social Theory*. Cambridge, MA: Harvard University Press.

Collins, Randall. 1975. *Conflict Sociology*. New York: Academic Press.

Cook, Karen (ed.). 1990. *The Limits of Rationality*. Chicago, IL: University of Chicago Press.

Dahrendorf, Ralf. 1959. *Class and Class Conflict in Industrial Society*. Stanford, CA: Stanford University Press.

————. 1968. *Homo Sociologicus*. London: Routledge and Kegan Paul.

Dülmen, Richard van. 1989. "Protestantism and Capitalism: Weber's Thesis in Light of Recent Social History." *Telos*, 78: 71–80.

Eisenstadt, Schmu. N. (ed.). 1968. *The Protestant Ethic and Modernization*. New York: Basic Books.

Etzioni, Amitai. 1997. *The New Golden Rule*. New York: Basic Books.

Etzioni, Amitai. 1998. *The Essential Communitarian Reader*. New York: Rowman & Littlefield.

Fischoff, Ephraim. 1944. "The Protestant Ethic and the Spirit of Capitalism: The History of the Controversy." *Social Research*, 2: 53–77.

Friedman, Debra, and Michael Hechter. 1988. "The Contribution of Rational Choice Theory to Macrosociological Research." *Sociological Theory*, 6: 201–18.

Friedson, Elliot. 1984. "The Changing Nature of Professional Control." *Annual Review of Sociology*, 10: 1–20.

————. 1990. "The Comparative Advantages of Rational Choice Theory." Pp. 214–29 in George Ritzer (ed.) *Frontiers of Social Theory*. New York: Columbia University Press.

Gerth, H. H. 1946. "Introduction". Pp. 3–74 in H. H. Gerth and C. Wright Mills (eds.) *From Max Weber*. New York: Oxford University Press.

Goody, Jack. 2007. "Weber, Braudel, and Objectivity in Comparative Research." Pp. 225–40 in L. McFalls (ed.) *Max Weber's "Objectivity" Reconsidered*. Toronto: The University of Toronto Press.

Gorski, Philip. 2003. *The Disciplinary Revolution*. Chicago, IL: The University of Chicago Press.

Gouldner, Alvin. 1970. *The Coming Crisis in American Sociology*. New York: Basic Books.

Green, Robert W. (ed.). 1973. *Protestantism, Capitalism, and Social Science: The Weber Thesis Controversy*. Lexington, MA: D.C. Heath.

Hall, John, and Charles Lindholm. 1999. *Is America Breaking Apart?* Princeton, NJ: Princeton University Press.

Hartz, Louia. 1959. *The Liberal Tradition in America*. New York: Harvest Hill HBJ.

Hechter, Michael. 1987. *Principles of Group Solidarity*. Berkeley: University of California Press.

Hofstadter, Richard. 1955. *Social Darwinism in American Thought*. Boston: Beacon.

Jellinek, Georg. 1979 [1895]. *The Declaration of the Rights of Man and Citizens*. Translated by Max Ferrand. Westport, CT: Hyperion.

Kaelber, Lutz. 1998. *Schools of Asceticism*. Philadelphia: The University of Pennsylvania Press.

Kalberg, Stephen. 1979. "The Search for Thematic Orientations in a Fragmented Oeuvre: The Discussion of Max Weber in Recent German Sociological Literature." *Sociology*, 13: 127–39.

———. 1990. "The Rationalization of Action in Max Weber's Sociology of Religion." *Sociological Theory*, 8: 58–84.

———. 1993. "Albert Salomon's Interpretation of Max Weber." *International Journal of Politics, Culture and Society*, 6: 585–94.

———. 1994. *Max Weber's Comparative-Historical Sociology*. Chicago, IL: University of Chicago Press.

———. 2007. "A Cross-National Consensus on a Unified Sociological Theory? Some Intercultural Obstacles." *European Journal of Social Theory*, 10: 206–19.

———. 2011. "Introduction to The Protestant Ethic." Pp. 8–63 in Max Weber (ed.) *The Protestant Ethic and the Spirit of Capitalism*. London: Oxford University Press.

———. 2012. *Max Weber's Comparative-Historical Sociology Today*. London: Routledge.

———. 2014. *Searching for the Spirit of American Democracy*. London: Routledge.

———. 2017. *The Social Thought of Max Weber*. Los Angeles, CA: Sage.

———. 2021. *Max Weber's Sociology of Civilizations*. London: Routledge.

Kim, S.H. 2004. *Max Weber's Politics of Civil Society*. New York: Cambridge.

Kiser, Edgar, and Michael Hechter. 1991. "The Role of General Theory in Comparative-Historical Sociology." *American Journal of Sociology*, 97: 1–30.

Knight, Frank H. 1928. "Historical and Theoretical Issues in the Problem of Modem Capitalism." *Journal of Economic and Business History*, 1: 119–36.

Konwitz, Milton R. and Gail Kennedy. 1960. *The American Pragmatists.* Cleveland, OH: World Publishing Co.

Lamont, Michèle, and Marcel Fournier (eds.). 1992. *Cultivating Differences.* Chicago, IL: University of Chicago Press.

Lehmann, Hartmut. 1987. "Ascetic Protestantism and Economic Rationalism: Max Weber Revisited After Two Generations." *Harvard Theological Review* 80: 307–20.

Lehmann, Hartmut. 1993. "The Rise of Capitalism." Pp. 195–208 in Lehmann and G. Roth (eds.) *Weber's Protestant Ethic: Origins, Evidence, Context.* New York: Cambridge University Press.

Lehmann, Hartmut, and Guenther Roth (eds.). 1993. *Weber's Protestant Ethic: Origins, Evidence, Contexts.* Cambridge: Cambridge University Press.

Levine, Donald. 1985. *The Flight From Ambiguity.* Chicago: The University of Chicago Press.

Lipset, Seymour Martin. 1963. *The First New Nation.* New York: Norton.

Loader, Colin and Jeffrey Alexander. 1985. "Introduction." Pp. 1–6 in *Sociological Theory* 3 (Spring).

Löwith, Karl. 1970. "Weber's Interpretation of the Bourgeois-Capitalistic World in Terms of the Guiding Principle of 'Rationalization.'" Pp. 101–21 in Dennis Wrong (ed.) *Max Weber.* Englewood Cliffs, NJ: Prentice-Hall.

Lynd, Robert S. 1976. *Knowledge for What?* Princeton, PA: Princeton University Press.

MacKinnon, Malcolm H. 1993. "The Longevity of the Thesis: A Critique of the Critics." Pp. 211–43 in Hartmut Lehmann and Guenther Roth (eds.) *Weber's Protestant Ethic: Origins, Evidence, Contexts.* Cambridge: Cambridge University Press.

Marshall, Gordon. 1982. *In Search of the Spirit of Capitalism.* London: Hutchinson.

Miller, Perry. 1961. *The New England Mind.* Boston: Beacon.

Mommsen, Wolfgang. 1970. "Max Weber's Political Sociology and his Philosophy of World History." Pp. 183–94 in Dennis Wrong (ed.) *Max Weber.* Englewood Cliffs, NJ: Prentice-Hall.

Mommsen, Wolfgang. 1974. *Gesellschaft, Politik und Geschichte.* Frankfurt: Suhrkamp.

———. 1989. *The Political and Social Theory of Max Weber.* Chicago, IL: University of Chicago Press.

Moore, Barrington. 1966. *The Social Origins of Dictatorship and Democracy.* Boston, MA: Beacon Press.

Nelson, Benjamin. 1971. "'Introduction' to Max Weber on Race and Society." *Social Research*, 38, 1: 30–32.

———. 1973. "Weber's Protestant Ethic: Its Origins, Wanderings, and Foreseeable Futures." Pp. 71–130 in Charles Y. Glock and Phillip E. Hammond (eds.) *Beyond the Classics?* New York: Harper and Row.

———. 1981. *On the Roads to Modernity*. Edited by Toby E. Huff. Totowa, NJ: Rowman & Littlefield.

Nipperdey, Thomas. 1993. "Max Weber, Protestantism, and the Debate Around 1900." Pp. 73–82 in Hartmut Lehmann and Guenther Roth (eds.) *Weber's Protestant Ethic*, New York: Cambridge.

Oberschall, Anthony. 1972. *The Establishment of Empirical Sociology*. New York: Harper and Row.

Otsuka, Hisao. 1976. *Max Weber on the Spirit of Capitalism*. Tokyo: Institute of Developing Economies.

Parrington, Vernon L. 1954. *Main Currents in American Thought*. New York: Harcourt Brace & World.

Parsons, Talcott. 1928. "'Capitalism' in Recent German Literature: Sombart and Weber." *The Journal of Political Economy*, 36: 641–61.

———. 1935. "H. M. Robertson on Max Weber and His School." *The Journal of Political Economy*, 43: 688–96.

———. 1951. *The Social System*. New York: Free Press.

———. 1963. "Introduction." Pp. xix–lxvii in Max Weber (ed.) *The Sociology of Religion*. Boston, MA: Beacon.

———. 1966. *Societies: Evolutionary and Comparative Perspectives*. Englewood Cliffs, NJ: Prentice-Hall.

———. 1971. *The Evolution of Societies*. Edited and with an Introduction by Jackson Toby. Englewood Cliffs, NJ: Prentice-Hall.

Parsons, Talcott. 2007. *American Society*. Boulder CO: Paaradigm.

Parsons, Talcott, and Edward A. Shils. 1951. "Values, Motives, and Systems of Action." Pp. 45–275 in Talcott Parsons and Edward Shils (eds.) *Toward a General Theory of Action*. Cambridge, MA: Harvard University Press.

Parsons, Talcott, and Neil J. Smelser. 1956. *Economy and Society*. London: Routledge.

Parsons, Talcott, Robert F. Bales, Edward Shils, et al. 1951. "Some Fundamental Categories of the Theory of Action: A General Statement." Pp. 3–29 in Talcott Parsons and Edward Shils (eds.) *Toward a General Theory of Action*. Cambridge, MA: Harvard University Press.

Poggi, Gianfranco. 1983. *Calvinism and the Capitalist Spirit: Max Weber's Protestant Ethic*. Amherst: University of Massachusetts Press.

Putnam, Robert D. 2000. *Bowling Alone*. New York: Basic.

Riesebrodt, Martin. 2005. "Dimensions of the *Protestant Ethic*." Pp. 23–52 in William H. Swatos and Lutz Kaelber (eds.) *The Protestant Ethic Turns 100*. Boulder, CO: Paradigm Publishers.

Ritzer, George. 1990. "The Current Status of Sociological Theory: The New Syntheses." Pp. 1–32 in George Ritzer (ed.) *Frontiers of Social Theory.* New York: Columbia University Press.

Roth, Guenther. 1968. "Introduction." Pp. xxvii–ciii in Max Weber, *Economy and Society.* Edited and translated by Guenther Roth and Claus Wittich. New York: Bedminster Press.

———. 1971. "Max Weber's Comparative Approach and Historical Typology." Pp. 75–93 in Ivan Vallier (ed.) *Comparative Methods in Sociology.* Berkeley: University of California Press.

———. 1976. "History and Sociology in the Work of Max Weber." *British Journal of Sociology,* 27: 306–18.

———. 1997. "The Young Max Weber: Anglo-American Religious Influences and Protestant Social Reform in Germany." *International Journal of Politics, Culture and Society,* 10: 659–71.

———. 1985. "Marx and Weber on the United States—Today." Pp. 215–33 in Robert J. Antonio and Ronald M. Glassman (eds.) *A Weber-Marx Dialogue.* Lawrence, KS: University Press of Kansas.

———. 2005a. "Europaeisierung, Amerikanisierung und Yakeetum. Zum New Yorker Besuch von Max und Marianne Weber 1904." Pp. 9–32 in Wolfgang Schluchter and Friedrih Wilhelm Graf (eds.) *Asketischer Protestantismus und der 'Geist' des modernen Kapitalismus.* Tuebingen: Mohr.

———. 2005b. "Transatlantic Connections: A Cosmopolitan Context for Max and Marianne Weber's New York Visit." *Max Weber Studies,* 5: 81–112.

Roth, Guenther, and Wolfgang Schluchter. 1979. *Max Weber's Vision of History.* Berkeley: University of California Press.

Rueschemeyer, Dietrich. 1973. *Lawyers and Their Society.* Cambridge, MA: Harvard University Press.

Salomon, Albert. 1934. "Max Weber's Methodology." *Social Research,* I, May: 147–68.

———. 1935a. "Max Weber's Sociology." *Social Research,* II, Febraury: 60–73.

———. 1935b. "Max Weber's Political Ideas." *Social Research,* II, August: 368–84.

———. 1945. "German Sociology." Pp. 586–613 in Georges Gurvitch and Wilbert Moore (eds.) *Twentieth Century Sociology.* New York: Philosophical Library.

Savelsberg, Joachim. 1994. "Knowledge, Domination and Criminal Punishment." *American Journal of Sociology,* 99: 911–13.

Scaff, Lawrence, 1989. *Fleeing the Iron Cage.* Berkeley: The University of California Press.

Scaff, Lawrence. 2011. *Max Weber in America.* Princeton: Princeton University Press.

Schluchter, Wolfgang. 1979. "The Paradox of Rationalization." Pp. 11–64 in *Max Weber's Vision of History*. Edited by Guenther Roth and Wolfgang Schluchter. Berkeley: University of California Press.

———. 1981. *The Rise of Western Rationalism*. Berkeley: University of California Press.

———. 1989. *Rationalism, Religion, and Domination: A Weberian Perspective*. Berkeley: University of California Press.

Selznick, Philip. 1992. *The Moral Commonwealth*. Berkeley: University of California Press.

Simmel, Georg. 1950 [1917]. "Individual and Society in Eighteenth- and Nineteenth-Century Views of Life." Pp. 58–86 in *The Sociology of Georg Simmel*. Translated, edited, and with an introduction by Kurt H. Wolff. New York: Free Press.

———. 1971 [1908]. "Subjective Culture." Pp. 227–34 in *Georg Simmel on Individuality and Social Forms*. Edited and with an introduction by Donald N. Levine. Chicago, IL: University of Chicago Press.

———. 1971 [1913]. "Freedom and the Individual." Pp. 217–26 in *Georg Simmel on Individuality and Social Forms*. Edited and with an introduction by Donald N. Levine. Chicago, IL: University of Chicago Press.

———. 1971 [1918]. "The Conflict in Modern Culture." Pp. 375–93 in *Georg Simmel on Individuality and Social Forms*. Edited and with an introduction by Donald N. Levine. Chicago, IL: University of Chicago Press.

Skocpol, Theda. 1979. *States and Social Revolutions*. Cambridge: Cambridge University Press.

Skocpol, Theda, and Margaret Somers. 1980. "The Uses of Comparative History in Macrosociological Inquiry." *Comparative Studies in Society and History*, 22: 174–97.

Sombart, Werner. 1913. *Der modern Kapitalismus*. Leipzig: Dunker und Humblot.

———. 1967 [1913]. *The Quintessence of Capitalism*. New York: Howard Fertig.

Sprinzak, Edward. 1972. "Weber's Thesis as an Historical Explanation." *History and Theory*, 11: 294–320.

Swidler, Ann. 1986. "Culture in Action." *American Sociological Review*, 51: 273–86.

Tawney, R. H. 1954 (1926). *Religion and the Rise of Capitalism*. New York: New American Library.

Tenbruck, Friedrich. 1980. "The Problem of Thematic Unity in the Works of Max Weber." *The British Journal of Sociology*, 31: 316–51. (Originally published in 1975 in *Kölner Zeitschrift für Soziologie und Sozialpsychologie*, 27: 663–702.)

————. 1987. "On the German Reception of Role Theory." Pp. 410–45 in Volker Meja and Nico Stehr (eds.) *Modern German Sociology*. New York: Columbia University Press.

Tilly, Charles. 1964. *The Vendee*. New York: John Wiley and Sons.

————. 1978. *From Mobilization to Revolution*. Reading, MA: Addison-Wesley.

Tocqueville, Alexis de. 1945. *Democracy in America*, Vols. 1 and 2. New York: Vintage Books.

Wallerstein, Immanuel. 1974. *The Modern World-System*. New York: Academic Press.

————. 1979. *The Capitalist World-Economy*. Cambridge: Cambridge University Press.

————. 1980. *The Modern World System* II. New York: Academic Press.

————. 1984. *The Politics of the World-Economy: The States, the Movements and the Civilizations*. Cambridge: Cambridge University Press.

————. 1989. *The Modern World System* III. New York: Academic Press.

Weber, Marianne. 1975 [1926]. *Max Weber*. Translated by Harry Zohn. New York: Wiley and Sons.

Weber, Max. 1930. *The Protestant Ethic and the Spirit of Capitalism*. Translated by Talcott Parsons. New York: Scribner's.

————. 1972 [1910]. *Max Weber: Die protestantische Ethik 11, Kritiken und Antikritiken*. Edited by Johannes Winckelmann. Hamburg: Siebenstern Verlag.

————. 1978. *Weber: Selections in Translation*. Edited by W.G. Runciman and translated by Eric Matthews. Cambridge: Cambridge University Press.

————. 1978 [1906]. "The Prospects for Liberal Democracy in Tsarist Russia." Pp. 269–84 in W. G. Runciman (ed.) *Weber: Selections in Translation*. Translated by Eric Matthews. New York: Cambridge University Press.

————. 1985 [1906]. Pp. 7–13 in "'Churches' and 'Sects' in North America: An Ecclesiastical Socio-Political Sketch." Translated by Colin Loader. *Sociological Theory* 3 (Spring).

————. 1988 [1924]. "Geschäftsbericht und Diskussionsreden auf den Deutschen soziologischen Tagungen (1910, 1912)." Pp. 431–91 in Marianne Weber (ed.) *Gesammelte Aufsätze zur Soziologie und Sozialpolitik*. Tübingen: Mohr Siebeck.

————. 1994 [1917]. "Suffrage and Democracy in Germany." Pp. 80–129 in Peter Lassman and Ronald Speirs (eds.) *Weber: Political Writings*. Translated by Ronald Speirs. New York: Cambridge.

————. 2012 [1906]. "Critical Studies in the Logic of the Cultural Sciences." Pp. 139–84 in *Max Weber: Collected Methodological Writings*. Translated by Hans Henrik Bruun and edited by Bruun and Sam Whimster. London: Routledge.

White, Morton. 1957. *Social Thought in America*. Boston: Beacon Press.

Wiley, Norbert. 1985. "The Current Interregnum in American Sociology." *Social Research*, 52: 179–207.

———. 1990. "The History and Politics of Recent Sociological Theory." Pp. 392–415 in George Ritzer (ed.) *Frontiers of Social Theory*. New York: Columbia University Press.

Zaret, David. 1980. "From Weber to Parsons and Schutz: The Eclipse of History in Modern Social Theory." *American Journal of Sociology*, 85: 1180–201.

———. 1994. "Max Weber und die Entwicklung der theoretischen Soziologie in den USA." Pp. 332–66 in Gerhard Wagner and Heinz Zipprian (eds.) *Max Webers Wissenschafislehre*. Frankfurt: Suhrkamp.

INDEX

Note: *Italic* page numbers refer to figures and page numbers followed by "n" denote endnotes.

For Product Safety Concerns and Information please contact our EU
representative GPSR@taylorandfrancis.com
Taylor & Francis Verlag GmbH, Kaufingerstraße 24, 80331 München, Germany